Ross Lee Finney

Profile of a Lifetime

23 Bank Street, 1989

ROSS LEE FINNEY

PROFILE OF A LIFETIME

A MUSICAL AUTOBIOGRAPHY

SERIES EDITOR: DON GILLESPIE

✳ EDITION PETERS ✳

C. F. PETERS CORPORATION
NEW YORK · LONDON · FRANKFURT

Copyright © 1992 by C.F. Peters Corporation
373 Park Avenue South, New York, NY 10016
International Copyright Secured. All Rights Reserved.

Library of Congress Cataloging-in-Publication Data
Finney, Ross Lee, 1906-
Profile of a lifetime : a musical autobiography / Ross Lee Finney.
p. cm. — (Composer profiles ; 3)
Includes index.
SBN 0-938856-05-7 :
1. Finney, Ross Lee, 1906- .2. Composers—United States—
Biography.   I. Title. II. Series.
ML410.F455A3   1992
780' .92—dc20
[B] 92-22109 CIP MN

This book is a special publication in the series *Composer
Profiles*. Previous volumes are devoted to the music of
Roger Reynolds and George Crumb.

ACKNOWLEDGMENTS

This memoir would not have been written without the encouragement of my friends at C.F. Peters Corporation: Evelyn Hinrichsen and her "Peters Family." I am, however, especially indebted to Don Gillespie, who meticulously edited the manuscript, tightening its structure and checking each factual detail. Memory, a precarious source for fact, needs the critical eye of such an editor.

Kurt Michaelis read the text carefully and offered the added wisdom of his thirty-five years at Peters and his European background and perspective. With his eagle eye for detail, Cole Gagne made many helpful suggestions, and Lynn Ozer assisted in the arduous task of proof-reading. My wife Gretchen often argued with me about dates and other sundry matters, and with the aid of her diaries, proved to be almost always right. To set these memories on paper I needed the help of all these people, and I thank them for it.

Ross Lee Finney

Ross Lee Finney

Profile of a Lifetime

CHAPTER I

1906 - 1913

My father was the Methodist minister in Wells, Minnesota, when I was born in 1906. I had two older brothers, both named "God-Given": Theodore (Greek) and Nathaniel (Hebrew). My mother and father had both attended Upper Iowa University, a small college in Fayette, Iowa, she earning her degree in music, and he earning his in theology. Later Father went to the University of Chicago and then to Boston University where he earned his Ph.D. My parents had both fallen in love with New England, especially the small town of Bryantville, Massachusetts, where Father preached and Mother organized the music every Sunday. After my father received his degree, he was sent to pastorates in several small Midwestern towns, including Wells.

I don't think either of my parents were happy in Wells. The parishioners felt that "God would provide" and failed to pay the promised salary. If the German-Lutheran grocer had not brought them boxes of food frequently, they would have gone hungry. The ladies of the church expressed to my mother their disapproval of my arrival. Perhaps the added burden made it hard for Mother to organize the church music for which she was never paid, and for which she received little appreciation. She had always had dreams of teaching music to children in rural environments.

The causes of my father's unhappiness were probably more basic. He was sincerely concerned with the problems of human beings and went far beyond the routines of the church to deal with them. Alcoholics were brought to the parsonage to be taken to the local Keely Cure Center. While my father had many friends, he may have antagonized his parishioners. He was, perhaps, disillusioned with the ministry as an outlet for his idealism. At the end of the year, he accepted a position to teach philosophy at Illinois Wesleyan University.

My memory of our life in Illinois is very vague. There are vivid patches that are rich in the sensations of sound and smell, but there is little temporal continuity.

We lived on Fell Avenue in Normal, Illinois, on the edge of Bloomington in a great big, rambling, old house. There was a cannery nearby, and we boys would follow the wagons carrying sweet corn from the farms and pick up those ears that fell off onto the road. Mother would boil the corn and cut it off the cob, mix it with butter and salt in a big wooden tray and place it in the sun to dry. My job was to stir it. Finally, when it was as hard as rice, it was packed in cloth bags and stored in the attic. Apples were also dried this way and I had the job of stringing them in loops to be hung in the attic.

My father would buy a cherry tree each summer for the fruit, and the whole family would join in picking the cherries. It was a festive picnic day. When we got them home, Mother started canning them. For some days our meals were mostly cherry pies. The sweet-sour smell remains with me, as does the more acrid smell of the sauerkraut that Mother made. Only the smell of shelling peas bothered me, but I learned to overcome that dislike.

My memory of sounds is more limited and not connected with work. There was an ice cream wagon that went by every day with its special bell ringing. There was a wagon with a calliope that puffed exploding wheat into a big glass box. But mostly there was Mother's upright Kimball piano. I spent hours improvising at the piano, pretending that I was reading the notes from the Bible placed upside-down on the rack. I was never criticized. Then there was Mother's rocking me and singing folksongs like "Who killed cock robin?"

One of my father's students was connected with a kennel that bred collies for Pierpont Morgan, we were told. We were given a runt of the litter, and we raised him on a bottle and called him Pierp. I remember him as a handsome dog, gentle and very affectionate. We would hitch him to our coaster wagon, and he would pull us like a pony, but never across a street. He must have been a valuable dog because he was stolen from us. A childhood tragedy! I decided to visit my Aunt Bertha who lived in Champaign, and I managed to get all the way to the Bloomington railway station with Pierp before someone had to bring us home.

My Grandmother Finney died on her way home to Fayette, Iowa, after visiting us, and my father went to help. We were left alone in our big house. It was a very cold spell, and Mother had us all sleep in the one downstairs room that had a stove. I slept on the top of the dining room table.

My father had not yet given up the ministry and preached every Sunday at Gridley, a small town a few miles north of Bloomington. On nice summer days he took me with him because I loved to gather wild asparagus along the railway tracks. The prairie was filled with wild flowers. The new short stalks of asparagus were a great treat for us, and the lady with whom we always had lunch loaded me with rock cookies to take home.

I realize now that during those years in Illinois my father was growing more and more away from the ministry. He ran for State Senator on the "Bull Moose" ticket and was soundly defeated, an experience that was much more humiliating for my brothers than for me. I found among his papers the manuscript of a novel that he finished during those years. It was about a young minister struggling to keep his faith in the Bible as infallible truth when he knew that there were fossils of animals that had lived many hundreds of thousands of years ago. From the marginal notations one can see that he realized that it was not a good novel, but it showed his growing interest in writing.

When he accepted the position as head of the Education Department of the Valley City Normal School in North Dakota, he left the ministry permanently.

I was seven years old then, and my most vivid early memories are of this trip. Our train moved up the eastern shore of the Mississippi River at night, and I stared out the window of the lower berth, across the moon-bathed river to the dark western shore. My father had told me about the river and about the western frontier where we were going to live. My parents had grown up on farms in Iowa when it was still very close to the frontier. They told of Indians and of cold winters when the wolves killed their chickens, and now we were moving to another frontier where there were Indians and open prairies. The river seemed to me the boundary of that mysterious world.

On the way we would cross into northeastern Iowa at Dubuque

and live with my grandmother while my mother went to the Mayo Clinic in Rochester, Minnesota, to have a bad goiter removed. Fayette would be filled with memories.

For several generations my family had been moving into new frontiers. The Widow Finney arrived at Plymouth from England in 1630 with a large family of children, and over two centuries the family moved west, ending up in Elizabethtown, New York. From there my Grandfather Finney had moved west with other members of his family, first to Ohio and then to northeastern Iowa. After the death of a first wife, my grandfather married a Pennsylvania Dutch girl by the name of Bike, and they had three children: my father, my Aunt Myra, who now lived on a farm near Sedan, Minnesota, and my Uncle Harry, who lived in Chicago and was a distinguished accountant. My father also lived on an intellectual frontier, bringing to the Middlewest social ideas that he had learned in the East.

My mother's family had migrated from Scotland in the nineteenth century. Her Grandfather Mitchell and his two brothers had worked their way as sailors to distant places. One brother migrated to South Africa. Another moved to Melbourne, Australia, and his daughter Nellie Mitchell became the famous diva, Nellie Melba. My great-grandfather settled in Fond du Lac, Wisconsin. His son married Matilda Dusenbery and moved to a farm in northeastern Iowa. The Finney family and the Mitchell family finally left their farms and settled as next door neighbors in Fayette. En route to North Dakota, we would visit my Grandmother Mitchell in Fayette and my Grandfather Finney and Aunt Myra at their farm in Sedan, Minnesota.

The father-son relationship was pretty much a one-way communication. I certainly respected and admired my father, and I responded immediately to his quick sense of humor, but I seldom talked back.

In going to Fayette, Iowa, I was visiting my mother's childhood home, the scene of so many of the stories she had told me. She was a good storyteller, making her mother and brothers and sister and all the animals and activities of the farm vivid in my mind. I shivered when she told me of Indians visiting the farm. I wept when she related the failure of the neighbors to pick her up and drive her to the circus, but my tears changed to laughter when she told of her mother finding the old setting hen way out in the woods trying to make a nest. She dunked it in cold water, telling it to lay eggs. She made a special chicken dinner to make up for missing the circus.

We were to spend most of the summer with my Grandmother Mitchell. She was a tiny little woman living in a tiny little house in a tiny little village. When my Grandfather Mitchell died, my grandmother, to her children's horror, sold the big house and bought herself the little gingerbread house near the college. It was just right for her. There were two tiny bedrooms, a tiny living room and dining room and a great big summer kitchen in back. There wasn't much yard, but there was a big garden, filled with more flowers than vegetables.

My grandmother sparkled all the time, giving long lectures to every fly before she swatted it, and telling the chicken what she thought of it while she plucked the feathers. She was like a hummingbird — constantly busy, chattering to herself and to every animate or inanimate thing around her, and endlessly concerned with good food.

While my father never told us any stories of his childhood, he did introduce us to all the swimming pools in the Little Volga River that wound through the town, cutting its way through limestone rocks. He showed us where to find fossils of shells and plants that lived in the ocean that covered the area millions of years ago, and he collected for us beautiful agates the size of our fists, colored by layers of silicon.

It was my job to pick black raspberries for my grandmother to use in making a pudding which was called an "old" or a "young" Jonathan, depending on how many berries I had picked. The thick clotted cream made this dish one that I will never forget. (I still make this pudding: one egg, one cup of flour, one teaspoon of baking powder, sugar, one cup of milk, and at least one cup of berries.)

After her surgery — the Mayo Clinic operated without fee for ministers' families — my mother returned to Fayette to recuperate. Then we traveled northwest to Glenwood, Minnesota, to visit my father's sister on their farm in Sedan. My three cousins were boys about our ages, so we joined quickly into all the chores that made their day. My Grandfather Finney was visiting them, and this was the last time I ever saw him. He seemed to me a very dour individual with none of the sparkle that my Grandmother Mitchell had.

The farm was a real farm, with cows, chickens, geese, horses and fields of grain and hay. I learned how you must move your fingers when you milk a cow so that you pushed the milk out rather than in. It was arranged that after we got settled in North Dakota, my father would return to Sedan and drive a horse and wagon back to Valley City for us to use.

When we finally arrived in Valley City, my father rented a house not far from the Normal School. There was an outside privy that made life complicated during the very cold winter. The little town was located in the valley that the Sheyenne River has carved out of the prairie. The bluffs on each side of the valley seemed very high to me, and the prairie winds would blow right over the town. One was trapped in a wind tunnel with the blizzard blowing above and the snow filtering down into the valley. I suspect I didn't venture out of the town that first winter, not yet daring to investigate the outside, upper world of the prairie. Not until spring did I adjust to the new location and all the joys that opened up for me as a boy. But this memory of the closed space of the valley and the open space of the prairie and the outer space of the high western sky became the basis for my orchestral work *Spaces* that I composed in 1972.

It was a very different environment than we had ever known. The trees were fewer and shorter. The view of the prairie from the top of the hills was endless — a sea of foxtails always moving in the wind, and fields of vivid yellow wheat in the fall. The sky had its own life, apart from the land. Great black clouds would sweep in from the west and tower ominously overhead. Sunsets always varied, sometimes a riot of color, sometimes a pale yellow green. At night the stars shone with a clear intensity, and in the winter the northern lights played over the entire sky. Great flocks of ducks and geese flew overhead in spring and fall. One could not ignore either the beauty or the loneliness of the prairie, but it was always a pleasure to return to the protection of the valley. Home and family, especially in the winter, had a different meaning there. People were friendly and depended upon each other to make life civilized and the environment tolerable.

CHAPTER 2

1913 - 1919

My father bought an old house on Euclid Avenue that ran along the bottom of the bluff and past the women's dormitory to the Normal School. He planned to remodel the house himself with some professional help. It was a very simple box which he changed into a bungalow with a porch across the entire front. There was a living room the width of the house with a fireplace in the central chimney; a dining room and a kitchen took up the rest of the space on the first floor; and a back, enclosed winter porch was added. The second floor had three rooms, a toilet, and my father's study. There was an attic divided into two rooms with the chimney between for warmth. Each room had a window and a trap door in the roof which could be opened and held upright by a stick.

We slept in the attic, my mother and father in the first room and we three boys in the second. The rooms on the second floor were not bedrooms. Next to the study was my mother's sewing room, and next to that was a large room shared by Nathaniel and myself. Theodore had the corner room. There was a basement under the entire house with a hot air furnace in the center and a very big vegetable cellar and canning cupboard.

7

The house was painted white and stood on a big lot that went all the way from the street to an alley in back. On the alley was a small barn, a chicken coop and a small shed for housing our pig. The walk from the back porch to the barn divided the garden. The smaller part on the left was Mother's kitchen garden, and the larger part on the right was for corn and potatoes and cabbage.

My mother bought a flock of Rock Island chickens that supplied us immediately with eggs and promised large roasting chickens by fall. My father later bought a runt pig which he named Chrysostom. It was almost starved when we got it, and we nursed it back by feeding it from a bottle, as we had Pierp. We kept it washed and clean so it wouldn't smell, and it grew into an enormous animal.

There was one large tree — at least it seemed large to us — at the side of the house which held my swing and my brothers' tree house at the very top. From the top we could look northeast up the valley and see many of our favorite places. To the north and halfway up the bluff was the Indian mound directly across the river from the haunted farmhouse. To the east was the road that entered the valley passing the junk yard and the slaughterhouse and the Normal School farm.

From the tree house we could survey the part of the valley which became our playground. We could see the river flowing into the small dam where it formed a pool and then turned south to encircle the town park. We could see the footbridge that led to the school farm and nearby the dairy where we could always get a handout of ice cream. After the loop the river ran parallel to our street and along the edge of the campus. A big iron footbridge painted white crossed the river from the entrance to the Normal School and from it a street led to the center of town.

We could see all of the Normal School, from the auditorium where we played in concerts, through the office and classroom building where my father taught, to the model school at the furthest end where I went to school. The studios of the music teachers were on the top floor of the school building, and there I had cello lessons with Knute Froysa and piano lessons with a Miss Wright. In back was the mechanical crafts building, where my brothers spent a great deal of time learning to do beautiful cabinet work, an interest that they carried on all of their lives. We could even catch a glimpse of the water tower on the top of the bluff behind the school, and slightly beyond the first of the long white barns that made up the fairgrounds. To the west of the fairgrounds was the prairie and the farm where I went every summer evening for milk and where later we had a large garden. We could almost see the barn that housed the airplane that never flew.

From the school the river ran farther west to the flour mill and the big dam that made a swimming pool for more venturesome boys who could dive from the tops of boxcars. After the mill the river turned south along the bottom of Sugar Loaf and the biggest bluffs until it came to the Chautauqua grounds.

The most striking view from our tree house was of the High Bridge that spanned the valley and over which the express trains traveled on their way to the West Coast. It was built of iron, and even though it was a long way away, we could see the river on its way south.

My father had told me all about the geological wonders of where we lived. We were only a few miles from what had been the shore of Lake Agassiz that had existed long ago when the great glaciers melted. Because the glaciers had stopped south of Valley City and had left deposits of earth, the Sheyenne river could not flow south and join the Missouri, but had to turn north, flowing into the Red River and finally into the Hudson Bay. There was a continental divide not far from us where we used to go to shoot ducks in the fall when they flew, not very high overhead, on their migration south.

Our new house was a haven in the winter, not only protecting us from the bitter cold and the blinding blizzards, but also providing a place to play. My oldest brother became interested in making crystal wireless sets in his room and learned to read messages sent in Morse code. My father played checkers with us and always won. On the window seat in my room I made a theater and cut out figures from the Montgomery Ward Catalogue for the stage. Twice a month the *Youth's Companion* came in the mail with the next installment of a continued story.

We had organized the fossils we found in Iowa into a collection, carefully labeled from books about paleontology that Father got from the library. Our interest in fossils led to our getting acquainted with Miss Parine, who headed the school museum. Once when we were exploring the fairgrounds which were just above the school at the top of the bluff and beyond the water tower, we found a box full of snakes that looked frozen to us. We took them to Miss Parine. She said they must have been left behind after the fair and instead of leaving the area had collected together to hibernate. They weren't dead. She would start a snake collection.

The McMullens lived next door to us, and we constantly played with their two daughters who were our age. They taught us card games that we could play in the winter when it was too cold to play outdoors. Mr. McMullen had a Model T Ford that we greatly admired and envied.

Music, however, was our major occupation in the winter. We would practice our instruments and play duets with Mother. On especially cold weekends when we couldn't play outside, our family orchestra would learn a new piece to play after supper.

Thanksgiving was a neighborhood event and more often than not celebrated at the women's dormitory across the street. Miss Winstead was a great favorite of ours. It was she who organized Thanksgiving for the students since many could not go home. She must have been an ideal matron for a dormitory in a small town. The girls all came from farms or nearby places and planned to be teachers. I suspect there was very little sophistication. I know there was a lot of good humor.

The girls took over the kitchen and planned the entertainment. Miss Winstead invited many of the families that lived on our street. Roast goose was the main dish rather than turkey. Perhaps turkeys couldn't survive in that climate. My favorite dish was the homemade ice cream and the jello loaded with fruit and whipped cream. The vegetables were always Hubbard squash and mashed potatoes.

Miss Winstead was a large, rather stout, motherly lady, always talking in a loud voice or laughing, but Miss Amadon, who was something like Miss Winstead except that she sang very loud, took the lead for the little skits that the girls gave. The stunts were simple tricks like getting out of a chair with a full glass of water on your forehead without spilling the water, or singing rounds with new words about somebody in the school. After the festivities we often went skating on the river with the girls.

Christmas, however, was a family and a church event. The students had all gone home and very often the first snow had fallen. The departure of the students was big business for us. We boys organized a transfer service to carry suitcases from the dormitory to the railway station. We charged five cents a suitcase. It was my job to line up the suitcases for my brothers to transport in our coaster wagon. In time my brothers got too grown up for such business, and I did it all by myself. Sometimes I might line up more suitcases than I could get to the station before the train arrived. I don't think I ever failed, but I surely came very close to it. I always felt excited when the suitcases were delivered and I heard the whistle of the train as it descended into the valley. After a wild hour of rushing about I had earned enough money for Christmas presents.

Christmas Eve was celebrated in the churches. My father taught Sunday School at the Methodist Church on the other side of town, but we rarely stayed for the service that followed. My father had broken with the church, in spirit, if not in fact. The title of his book written at that time, "Personal Religion and Social Awakening," indicates the direction of his thought. He was becoming a sociologist and an educator, and his writings during our stay in North Dakota were mostly concerned with the consolidated school movement. He taught Sunday School for three reasons: he wanted his sons to have an early experience with the church; he viewed the church as an important social force; and he loved the beauty of the Biblical texts. Christmas Eve at the church was an event he wanted us to share.

Of course we loved the music, though I don't recall that it was very good. The organ wheezed and was poorly played. There was a big Christmas tree loaded with candles that were lighted as a part of the service — extremely dangerous, but very beautiful. Each child was given a candy cane. Walking home from the church, we often saw a display of northern lights that seemed to me a cosmic statement of the Christmas story which my father had read to us many times. We had our supper after we got home, and it was always the same: salt fish from Montgomery Ward's that had been soaked and was covered with a cream sauce, boiled potatoes and fruit jello with lots of whipped cream. Then we got into our flannel nightgowns and raced up to our beds in the attic. Sometimes Mother would put heated soap stones wrapped in newspaper in our beds to help us get warm.

When we came down in the morning, there was a big fireplace fire and our presents were in the living room, not under an evergreen tree, because there were few trees shipped in and they were much too expensive for us to buy. We had to eat our breakfast before we could see our gifts. A big scoop of jellied wheat from the kettle on the cookstove with sugar and cream was eaten in record time.

Most of our presents, but not all, were warm clothes — new moccasins that had no soles except the soft hide, and which were laced up the leg about six inches. They were always plenty large so that we could wear at least two pairs of wool socks. There were always warm sweaters and new stocking caps that came down over our ears. Sometimes we found special corduroy pants with leather patches on the knees, and once there was a Mackinaw coat, made in Canada from a Hudson Bay blanket. My brothers had usually made a piece of furniture such as a bookcase or a table. Father usually gave them books like Jack London's *Call of the Wild,* but sometimes he would give Theodore some electrical equipment he needed for making his wireless set. There was always a new music book and perhaps a new collection for our family orchestra. How well I remember my first piece for cello and piano that Mother and I could play together: "Where Is My Wandering Boy Tonight?"

Our decorations were paper snowflakes, designed and pasted on the windows, and strings of popcorn. We hung stockings from the fireplace mantel and would always find in the morning that greatest of treats, an orange. As the smells of dinner became more insistent, we would put on our outdoors clothes and venture out, even if it was below zero.

Blizzards could often be very bad even in the valley. But on the prairie they were really dangerous. It could be forty below zero with the wind so strong that the snow didn't fall but raced parallel with the ground, making it impossible to see more than a few feet ahead. Any exposed skin would freeze quickly and even with several pairs of wool socks, one could get frostbite.

Coming in after only a short time outside, we would have white spots that had to have snow put on them before we took off our clothes. Once I froze my ears, and they swelled to twice their normal size because I had failed to rub snow on them. Because blizzards could come up quite suddenly, we learned to be careful and not venture too far out.

We got milk during the winter from the dairy nearby across the river, for it was often dark in the late afternoon and there could be storms on the prairie that made the trip dangerous. Also, the dairy always let us clean out the ice cream from the big can in which it had been frozen. Even going that short distance, my new moccasins froze solid and were like boots.

These days, when we can look at weather maps on television, we know that storms may be approaching, but in those days the weather could change unexpectedly. It could be twenty degrees below zero one day and sixty degrees above the next. Only by March would there be a real spring thaw lasting for several days. But that did not mean that the winter was over. I remember one March day when the sun was midsummer hot and melted the snow, making a swimming pool. We undressed and swam in it, sporting in the sun, all against parental warnings, I'm sure. Such warm spells became longer and longer until the snow and ice were gone and the pasqueflowers on the hills and prairie burst into bloom, usually by Mayday.

Knute Froysa not only taught violin and cello, but he also taught us how to ski, or at least what passed for skiing in Valley City. We had no binders. All we did was to slip our moccasin-covered feet through the strap, which meant that we had no control of the skis and went where they did, or quickly got out of them. We did learn how to fall gracefully and how to find our skis at the bottom of the hill.

John Bull was our favorite hill for skiing; it was near and had a few trees at the bottom for excitement. The Fairgrounds hill was the best for

12

sliding since it was paved and got quite icy. As my brothers grew older they built a bobsled and joined other boys in what was a hair-raising experience. (There were no cars and few pedestrians on that street.) Shoe skates were unheard of. We clamped the skates onto our boots and hoped for the best. The object was to skate forward as fast as possible using rather short strokes, all in preparation for playing hockey. Turning rapidly or skating backwards were tricks to be learned. It was more important to avoid the airholes that sometimes formed near the bank, or sticks that had gotten embedded in the ice. The dams were a particular hazard because the ice got thinner and thinner as the speed of the water increased. In most places the ice got very thick, and if it was very cold we could build a big bonfire on the ice and put on our skates, roasting on one side and freezing on the other.

Looking back on those years, I realize that our family was changing. As we boys grew into our teens we were less cohesive as a group. I always tagged along, usually tolerated by my brothers. I was always the timid one in the group. Than, as I insisted on calling Nathaniel, was always the leader in any deviltry. If we got into trouble, it was his doing. We broke into the fair barn to get squabs in the cupola where the pigeons nested. We built a fire on the ground in the middle of the barn and cooked our lunch, but unfortunately, Than left his knife with his name on it, so the police called on us.

My oldest brother Theodore — at his request we called him Gus, but outsiders knew him as Ted — showed the greatest change over those years before we left for Minneapolis in 1919. Those were his adolescent years when he found the environment limiting, as I never did. He had remarkable handskills that showed up not only in his violin performance but also in all sorts of mechanical interests. Gus was on good terms with all the teachers who allowed him to work in all the shops.

That was all mysterious to me. I had shown no aptitude in that direction. Than was also very good at woodworking and learned skills that he practiced all his life. When my father bought a Model T Ford in 1916, Than helped Gus take it all apart in our side yard and put it together again with only a few nuts and bolts left over. Than went along with Gus, but he also tolerated me in a way that my older brother at that time did not.

Once there was a cloudburst, and water stood five feet deep in our street. We all went swimming. In 1915 my father and Gus returned to Sedan to pick up the horse named "Lygia" (Lydia) that we had been promised, and drove in a wagon back to Valley City. We all shared Lygia's care in the barn and learned how to put on the saddle and ride.

13

She was no race horse, but in her old age she was very patient with me, for I often didn't get the strap tight enough and the saddle turned and dumped me between her legs. She never went fast enough for my brothers, but she took us places in the wagon and helped with many of the chores.

In about 1918 my Aunt Myra moved from their farm in Minnesota to California. Father went to visit her before she left and drove back Daisy, Lygia's colt. We couldn't have two horses, and since Daisy was peppy and younger, my father sold Lygia to the junk dealer in town. It broke our heart to see old Lygia poorly cared for, dragging junk out to the town dump.

At this time a new faculty member was appointed in the field of Education, and she was a great friend of my parents and very nice to me. She was a rather large, middle-aged woman, something like Miss Winstead but more soft-spoken. Since I was born on December 23rd and had never had any birthday parties, she always invited me to her home for my birthday and told me about concerts and operas she had seen in Chicago, showing me books and pictures about music. I remember one party where she told me about Wagner's *Ring of the Nibelungs* and described what the operas were like and how the orchestra worked.

After my father was defeated in his bid for the Illinois State Senate, he took no part in politics. He probably was interested in the formation of co-operatives in North Dakota because of his interest in consolidated schools. We were interested in the presidential election of 1916 because my brother Gus followed it on his crystal radio set, which he had constantly improved. Nobody in Valley City wanted to be involved in the war, but with the sinking of the Lusitania and the declaration of war, the spirit changed fundamentally. Boys of high-school age wanted to enlist in the army (nobody seemed interested in the navy) and most wanted to fly airplanes. We became increasingly interested in the man at the top of the bluff who had for so long been trying to build an airplane.

Our gardens suddenly became "victory gardens," though I can't recall any difference. Food prices went up and father bought another runt pig which we called Chrysostom 2. It was our job to keep the barn clean and to feed the pig from a bottle. Naturally, we were fond of the animals, but my parents didn't believe in making pets out of barnyard animals. We had no ducks or geese, probably because we had so many wild ducks in the fall. We gathered wheat and hay out on the farms and grew much of the food we ate, as we always had. Now we felt we were helping the war effort.

We always joined in the big pageant that was performed on the bluff across the river — "Custer's Last Stand" — or a pioneer scene with covered wagons and lots of horses and cows. We were often dressed as Indians and had to make our headdress from chicken feathers. We would run around a campfire or die dramatically in the middle of a battle.

It was during one of these pageants that we discovered the Holy Roller camp up under the High Bridge. We viewed the revival meeting from a distance behind bushes. We made up our minds to walk across the High Bridge and got caught in the middle with a freight train coming onto the bridge from the west. We ran to a small platform where we could get off of the tracks and lie down while the train passed. The bridge swayed and rumbled under the train that never seemed to end. My father told us that we should not spy on revival meetings.

Father had rented a large garden from the farmer who supplied our milk. He plowed and got it ready for us to plant. I was eleven and able to work longer hours, and I loved the prairie — its openness and sudden storms and bird songs. We grew potatoes, sweet corn, cabbages, beans for drying, carrots and a few rutabagas, and Mother planted a bed of zinnias and marigolds there to gain a little more room in her kitchen garden at home.

One day we heard the sound of motors in the sky and saw a group of army airplanes flying over the town. We boys climbed onto the roof through the trap door and sat on the ridgepole watching the maneuvers until the planes left. We had never seen an airplane fly, and the experience brought the war a little closer to us. Gus became restless. He had friends who had enlisted and returned home dressed in uniform. They told of driving and repairing army vehicles. He got a job in a machine shop running a metal lathe, but he cut off the end of his first finger on his left hand, and we all feared his days of playing the violin were over. He didn't think so, nor did Knute Froysa, since that finger was a little too long anyway. The trick was to develop a callus over what was left of the fingernail. The medication for that was skunk oil, which gave Gus a pungent and unpleasant odor. For several weeks we called him "skunky Gussy." Once the finger had a callus on the end, he went back to practicing.

My brother and I didn't want to share Gus' cut-off finger, but when he got the pinkeye and could stay home from school, we were jealous and decided to give ourselves the disease. The doctor said we'd have to stay home for two weeks in complete darkness. We soon regretted our action.

About this time my father brought home Martha from the Salvation Army. Her father had died of tuberculosis some years back, and her mother was in the hospital dying of cancer. There were three children: Martha, about my age, and her two brothers. Somehow my father heard of their problem and set out to find homes for them. He found farm homes for the two boys but couldn't find a home for the little girl. So Martha appeared one day as an addition to our family. She slept downstairs in Mother's sewing room.

Martha and her two brothers came out to visit us, and we got along beautifully playing on the roof of the pig house where Chrysostom 3 was growing into an enormous white pig. Over the years we all became as devoted to Martha as though she were our natural sister. She and I are now the only living members of our family. (If she were to tell the story of her coming to our house, it would surely be different from mine.) I had no interest in girls as such and always played with the next-door-neighbor girls as though they were boys. My brothers and I ran around the house naked without any self-consciousness at all.

That all had to stop. I suddenly became aware of myself physically, an event that was mysterious and a little frightening, like finding a wart or a growth that shouldn't be there. I have no idea how my brothers reacted to the change in the family. They had never talked to me about sex, nor had my father or mother. It was just one of those things you had to get used to as best you could.

It seemed to me that Martha would only eat bread dunked in coffee. Our family ate lots of vegetables, but she thought they were fed only to cattle. We were ravenous eaters and she must have been as puzzled as we were. (When she reads this, she'll have a good laugh, because she married a wonderful man who was one of the leaders in the Department of Agriculture in Washington, D.C., and for years they had the most beautiful garden that it would be possible to imagine.)

Meals were always a great social occasion. We talked about books, about music, about what was happening in the war, and we argued about everything. Father was a great talker and loved it when we talked back in disagreement. I think Martha thought we were all mad at each other. Probably she was a little frightened. Surely she grieved about her mother's death, and we boys didn't sympathize or understand her feelings.

After our Model T was put together again, we were much more mobile and planned a trip through the Minnesota lakes. We planned to meet Uncle Harry, my father's brother, in Perham, but there was a downpour of rain that turned the roads into gumbo, making driving impossible. But how to let him know? There was a strike, and only death messages could be sent by telegraph. My father went down to the railroad station with a long, sad face and gave this message to the operator: "Elizabeth dies of aqueous precipitation. Meet the remains in Perham July 6th." The message was sent with sad looks all around.

I can't imagine how we all got into the Model T with all our camping equipment. We had to climb in over the packing along the sides, and we had to stick our feet out of the car. On our way to Itasca Park, which was our first stop, we had a blowout. We all piled out and waited while Gus patched the inner tube.

We did arrive, later than we had planned, and set up our camp on Lake Bemidji. The trees seemed twice as big as those in Valley City, and the lake water was blue, not a pale tan. The next day we all went fishing, and even I caught several big croppies. We boys cleaned them and over a big fire that smelled of pine cones, made a wonderful fish-fry. That was the first of many on our trip. We followed the Mississippi River and then circled back through the lakes.

I still can hear Than playing his cornet in the evening and its echo over the lake, the loons sounding their quivering reply, and always the smell of resin and campfire smoke. We fell in love with the lakes and made several trips there. As soon as we got back to Valley City, Gus got the car in shape so that he could visit his girl in the southern part of the state.

My father was getting to be known as a sociologist which caused us a certain amount of trouble because people thought that meant he was a socialist. Once we got a stone thrown through our window with a note explaining what should be done to all socialists. I was very puzzled, and my father sat down and explained to me the confusion that was in people's minds.

There were several events towards the end of the war that must have greatly troubled my parents. Gus took care of the furnace in the armory on Main Street, and one night heavy rains flooded into the basement, causing a gas that exploded and started a fire. My brother was never blamed for the fire, but it may have been partly the reason why he ran away from home as a teenager. For days we didn't know where he was, until he finally wrote that he was in Minneapolis and had a job. He had been restless for some time. The girl he had been going with was much older than he, and we didn't like her. He felt that he couldn't get any further on the violin studying with Knute Froysa. Mostly he was just growing up.

There was also the flu epidemic which was very serious in our area. The students were not permitted to go downtown. Because I went to the model school, I couldn't go downtown either, but Than could, since he went to the high school. So we started a business. I ran a stand in our front yard which the students could visit on their way to the dormitory, and Than bought candy bars from the wholesale grocery house for me to sell. The result was that we had quite a nice income for several weeks. I put what I earned in the bank, and it became the nest egg that we used to buy a lake cottage after we moved to Minneapolis.

My father had spent part of the year teaching at Columbia Teachers College in New York City. On his return he accepted an appointment as Professor of Educational Sociology at the University of Minnesota in Minneapolis. We left for the city in the summer of 1919.

CHAPTER III

1919 - 1925

IN Minneapolis we lived in Florence Court at the corner of University Avenue and Tenth Street. It was a string of connected houses built, I should imagine, in the late-19th century and backing onto the railway tracks that connected the Twin Cities. We called it the "Rookery." There was a first floor with living room, dining room and kitchen, a basement that opened onto a long back terrace that all the houses shared, a second floor with bedrooms, and an attic with a nook that became my private space. It was very near the University and handy for my father's work and also close to my grade school and Than's high school. Gus, who was again living at home, entered the University Music Department, which at that time was housed in an old building only a few blocks away.

We boys were almost eliminated early in the game in our process of learning to live in the city. We sat down in a row on the railroad tracks just back of our house viewing the mills across the river, when suddenly we got off the tracks a minute before a passenger train raced over where we had been. I have no idea why we suddenly got off the tracks; perhaps we felt the vibration of the approaching train.

21

The jobs that had fallen to me in North Dakota didn't exist in the city, so I got a job carrying water to construction workmen. I had a hard time adjusting to city life, but my brothers immediately enjoyed the city and were able to find interesting jobs. While I didn't mind my school, I didn't find it as interesting or challenging as I had the Model School in Valley City. I took cello lessons from Engelbert Roentgen, the first cellist of the Minneapolis Symphony and an excellent musician. He was a sympathetic and a lovely person, but I had to almost relearn the cello. I was given a full scholarship covering my lessons, so somebody must have thought I had talent. For me, it was a year of pure agony. I had been taught to flatten the fingers of my left hand, and now I had to learn to round them in a more natural position so I could play thumb positions. The way I had held the bow was wrong — with wrist caved in and fingers unnaturally bent, which resulted in stiffness. I tried hard, but ended in tears. I suppose it was that year that I decided I could never be a cellist.

There was no music in our house any more — no family orchestra. And there was no music at my school. Gus played in the University Orchestra and for some reason Abe Pepinski, the conductor, allowed me to play in the cello section. Pepinski was a wonderful person, and our debt to him can never be exaggerated. It was he who introduced me and my brother to great orchestral and chamber music. From the standpoint of my learning to play the cello properly, playing Beethoven's *Symphony No. 1* may have been bad, but from the standpoint of my musical growth, it opened up a whole new world.

I had never been very close to my older brother until then, but we began to feel a musical companionship that lasted throughout our lives. His best friend was Gerald Greeley who was studying piano in the music department. The two of them organized a piano trio with the idea that we might get jobs playing at Chautauqua during the summer. We learned some of the Haydn Trios which were certainly a step above anything I had played in Valley City. I began to think about writing music for us to play and turned out a little trio called "Freaks of Fancy." The *Minneapolis Journal* published a story about me with a picture of my composition (my first published score!).

I entered the University High School the second year that we were in Minneapolis. It was a very good school, nearer our home and close to the University Music Department, then housed in a new building. Donald Ferguson, who became such an important figure in my life, accepted me as a piano student. He was the finest musician in the Twin Cities and at that time was productive as a composer. (He died in 1986 at the age of 103.) Engelbert Roentgen left to become the first cellist of the Metropolitan Opera in New York, and I then studied cello with Chris Erck and worked with him as long as I lived in Minneapolis. He was a good teacher and tried hard to correct my bad habits. My cello wasn't a very good instrument and did little to increase my enthusiasm as a performer. I continued, however, to play in the University Orchestra and joined in all kinds of chamber music.

I think "Fergy" realized that he would never make me into a fine pianist, so he did everything he could to increase my enthusiasm for and my understanding of music. He encouraged me to sit in on his harmony course and later his class in counterpoint. Any class with "Fergy" ranged over a wide territory. He was a great teacher for those who wanted to learn. He was not interested in contemporary music. (As far as I know, no one was.) In the early twenties Ferguson's interest stopped with Brahms and a few English composers. But his own music was much more chromatic. He had no interest in being an "American" composer and no sympathy for a composer who just wrote notes with no idea of their overall relationship and meaning.

The musical experience in Minneapolis at that time was fairly conservative. The Symphony under Emil Oberhoffer played the standard literature with now and then a contemporary work like Max Schelling's *A Victory Ball*. There was a concert course at the University, held in the old Armory, where artists like Paderewski appeared. I went to many concerts using tickets given to me. I was impressed when Rachmaninoff played his own music and when Eva Gautier sang Canadian Indian songs. Probably my concern for contemporary "American" music dates from that time. It seemed to me almost impossible to master all there was to know about music. I was thankful for the new opportunities, not critical of them.

It was during these high school years that I became a part of Harlow Gale's chamber music "Stube" which was held in his rooms. "Papa" Gale was an elderly member of a distinguished Minneapolis family. He had studied in Germany and fallen in love with such informal musical gatherings. On certain days my brother and I, with other string players, would meet and play or listen to string quartets. Usually Mr. Gale played the cello, but now and then he would let me do a Mozart Quartet. The "Stube" was, I realize now, a kind of romantic German idea, and my parents didn't much approve of it, nor were they sure that I should aspire to a professional life in music. In retrospect I have a good deal of sympathy for their fears. A professional life for a composer is a gamble even today, but in the twenties it wasn't really considered a normal ambition for a boy.

Minneapolis was an interesting city and the University was an integral part of it, located as it was on the bluff that formed the north bank of the Mississippi River. From the University High School, which I attended, one could look across the river to the panorama of the flour mills next to St. Anthony Falls and the tall buildings of the city. High bridges spanned the river, and University Avenue, on which we lived, could be seen all the way to the main bridge that led into the town. That walk down University Avenue was one of our favorites, leading as it did to the theaters and the restaurants and stores of the business center.

In 1921 my father bought an old house further from the University and away from the river. Gus and Than shared a large bedroom, and Martha and I had small rooms. We especially enjoyed the parlor where our trio could practice. The area was residential, with nice old houses, and on one of the main streetcar lines.

We had become familiar with the public transportation system and often went swimming at one of the lovely lakes located within the city or played golf at one of the many public golf links. We discovered the Public Library that had an unusually fine music collection and the secondhand book stores where we could buy cheap sets of the complete works of authors like Dickens. We were all great readers and spent many hours in our rooms reading. As we learned of the interesting things we could do, we became adjusted to the city and loved the special qualities of Minneapolis. We were often given tickets to the Symphony Orchestra concerts or to performances of plays given by traveling companies. It became a special treat to have chow mein at "John's Place" and then see a Shakespeare play.

Nevertheless, we boys had always wanted a summer place on a lake. We wanted it near enough to Minneapolis so that we could spend shorter holidays there. Gus felt we should buy the land and then build our cabin whenever we could afford it. So we started out in the Model T in search of a lot on a lake. Mille Lacs was big and quite near and not yet a popular resort. We turned north at Sauk Centre and arrived at the lake by early evening. We passed a swamp filled with wild rice before we came to the south shore of the big lake. As we drove around the west side of the lake, we fell in love with the big pines and the beautiful sandy shore.

Beyond a little town where the main highway turns north to Brainerd we came to a two-mile section where the highway ran inland a little, cutting out a beautiful wooded shore along the lake. We immediately decided that this was exactly what we wanted, and on inquiring found it was divided into lots that were for sale at a very low price. We chose a lot that had twin pines on the highway and where the slope was such that we could drive up to the shore, where there was a beautiful view southeast across the lake. There was a perfect place for a cabin on the top of a knoll and a beautiful sandy beach below. The lake was shallow for several yards before one came to the drop-off and deep water. We bought the lot partly, at least, with the money I had saved selling candy during the flu epidemic.

That summer we spent camping on the knoll while Gus and Than built our cabin. Mr. Enger, the farmer down the road, let us use his horse to snake out long spruce trunks to use as the foundation. Posts were set in the ground with the tree trunks on top, connecting them. On this platform my brothers built the house.

It was very simple indeed. There was a long front porch which didn't get screened that summer, and then a long room where we had a cookstove with a chimney for a kitchen. A third of the room was taken up by a balcony where we boys slept. We didn't drive a well that summer but carried water from the lake. Before we left for school we proudly moved in.

In 1921 or '22, Than entered the University. Gus was in his last year and was courting Gerald Greeley's sister, Myrle, who was a Home Economics student at the Agriculture Campus located between the two cities. Pepinski was head of music at the "Ag School" and Gus and I and Gerald often played trios there. We were in such demand that my brother felt I should have a dress suit instead of the Little Lord Fauntleroy suit that I had been forced to wear and hated.

"Papa" Gale had a dress suit he had used when he was a student at Yale, and it just fit me. I had grown tall and thin and everybody called me "Slats," a nickname that stuck with me for a long time. (My brother Than gave out the nicknames in the family. Ted was always Gus to us. Than insisted that he be called Nat. I became Slats.) Fortunately I was not cursed with that dress suit very long, because at a concert where we performed the Beethoven Piano Quartet and were taking a bow, my pants split with a resounding rip, leaving a kind of "Doctor Denton" flap that revealed my underpants. I held my cello as we left the stage so that nobody could see my exposed rear.

In March, Nat (Than) was fired from the University. He had written something in the *Minnesota Daily* that offended the administration. The University would let him return in the fall if he could decide what he wanted to study. He wanted to go to Mille Lacs and help Mr. Enger build boats. My parents felt building boats might be a good idea. Mr. and Mrs. Enger were the salt of the earth. They had no children and were glad to have Nat stay with them. So off he went for the rest of the spring.

He not only helped Enger build boats, but Enger helped him to build a flat-bottomed boat for us. It was during that time that Nat decided he wanted to be a newspaper man and return to the University to study journalism. He was especially fond of a Professor Casey in the Journalism Department, which was one of the best in the country. So what had seemed like a catastrophe turned out to be all for the best.

Mille Lacs was a great attraction for us. Gus loved to build and he loved to fish. There was lots of work to do clearing out the brush and giving our beautiful pines more space. We needed to drive a well so we could pump water into a sink in our kitchen, and we needed to build stairs down the hill to the beach. So we left for the lake as soon as we could.

I think Gus knew that our Ford wasn't working right and needed repair, but if we didn't set out soon our parents might not let us go. By the time we got to Anoka we knew we had to stop. Gus drove off the road and up a hill and parked next to a little river. He told Mother that the gears were stripped and would have to be replaced. He'd bought the needed parts in town, so we camped and he went right to work under the car. In several hours he had the new parts in and started the car only to find he had put the gears in backwards so that we had two speeds in reverse and one forward. So after we cooked dinner he went at it again. Before dark he had it right, and the next morning we drove up to Mille Lacs.

Gus loved to fish for bass. There was a small pond not far from our cottage where he could fish from the shore and catch big ones. Once when he was fishing he discovered a still where some young fellows were making moonshine. They invited him to lunch and were very friendly. It turned out they were students working their way through a theological seminary by making and selling moonshine.

I remember one trip we made to Mille Lacs in the late fall when it was freezing. We slept warm in our balcony bunks and woke up in the morning to hear the eggs popping as they froze. Gus had built a big fireplace from the stones we had gathered along the shore, and we looked forward to wonderful fires from the ample supply of dead spruce that we found back in the swamp. Gus had finally made a radio on which we could get KDKA and other broadcasts. He had set it up in our cottage and wanted to see how Mr. Enger would react when he heard it. Mr. Enger thought we were pulling his leg and went all over the cabin trying to figure it out. When Gus showed him the set, he was finally convinced, and Gus had to build him one, too.

Many years later when Gus was married and out of a job (and of course our cottage had been enlarged and winterized), he and his wife

Mollie spent a year there while Gus wrote his *History of Music*. Once again Mille Lacs proved to be of unpredictable value.

The teachers at the University High School were very good, and I was used to having students take over under the supervision of the room teacher. I did well in my courses, studying as little as possible outside of the set study hours. My favorite course was English because the teacher encouraged me to write music instead of essays. I ended up with a bunch of piano pieces and a song or two. I did like debating though, and was on the school team. History was also a favorite course, and then geometry, though I could never add any better than I could spell. My father didn't approve of my taking Latin and suggested German instead. Foreign languages have been hard for me, perhaps because I never worked hard enough to learn the grammar.

Since the school was on the campus, I felt very much a part of the University. We were always being given psychological tests, which I found amusing. My father permitted it only if I were never told any of the results. Mary Ellen Chase, who was my English teacher during my freshman year in the University (and later my colleague at Smith College) told me that she and I baffled the Psychology Department in our answers on some of the tests. I have no idea why. I suspect testing in the early twenties wasn't yet recognized or used as a tool in counseling. I don't think my father believed very much in the whole business.

I was puzzled by a boy who was said to have perfect pitch but had absolutely no musical training. I knew I didn't have perfect pitch (and had no great desire to have it), but the examiner often said I did. That was because I was pretty good at guessing what he would probably play on the piano. If he stood in the middle of the keyboard, the chances were he'd play middle C. Being a string player, I had a good sense of A, and could often figure other pitchs from that, especially if it was on the lower register of the keyboard. High notes were often a different matter. But not for this boy with perfect pitch. He could spot anything, even when the piano was out of tune. I've known plenty of people who claim to have perfect pitch but very few who really did. Does it relate to pitch color? I have no sensation of color with pitches — at least I don't think I have. Then why am I so sure about A?

Nat went into journalism with a vengeance. He had a part-time job with the *Minneapolis Star* and reviewed two or three theaters every week — the Pantages, a movie theater on Hennepin Avenue, and sometimes the Gaiety. He usually saw the shows on Sunday and often took me with him. I loved it. We would walk down University Avenue to the bridge and across the river to the main part of town. Between shows we would go to Alexander's near the West Hotel and have a huge slab of roast beef on a hunk of bread, and root beer. A whole rump of beef would be out on a block, and the man with an enormous butcher knife would slice off a chunk. We got to know him pretty well and, being from the press, could depend on a big slice and even seconds if we wanted, which we usually did since we were always hungry.

I guess I liked the movies best, though I liked the vaudeville too, especially the clowns, who were always looking under the bed or stumbling over the chairs. We would walk home in the evening and enjoy the lights of the city from the other side of the river.

Nat belonged to a literary club that invited celebrities to their meetings, and he often let me tag along. These meetings were held in a yellow brick building that was called the Bible College. It seems to me that F. Scott Fitzgerald met with the group once while he was living in St. Paul. We were all excited to meet him since we had read several of his books. He talked all the time about getting away from the University and going someplace so he would have something to write about.

Gus graduated at about this time and got a job playing viola in the Minneapolis Symphony Orchestra. Gerald had also left, so our trio ceased to exist. We now had a Model A Ford. I learned how to drive and taught my mother. My father tended to spend the summer teaching somewhere else or lecturing at various universities. Once Mother and I went with him when he lectured at the Normal School in Gunnison, Colorado. I took my cello, and Mother and I gave a mini-recital of light pieces like "The Swan" by Saint-Saens for a big school audience. It was a great success. Well, why not? Mother and son were playing schmalz to an audience that probably had never been to a concert of any kind. We had to repeat it so often that I never wanted to hear those pieces again. The whole experience of that trip, however, was wonderful. We got there on the narrow-gauge railway from Salida crossing high mountains into a beautiful valley. From Gunnison we were taken on fishing trips up the river into the snow peaks of the Continental Divide. There were big fish-fries where we ate quantities of freshly caught trout. We visited an old silver-mining ghost town, and I climbed a mountain to the snow line. Everybody was nice to us. We had never seen mountains before, and we were taken on trips by narrow roads to large ranches or to the Black Canyon.

None of the music that I composed as a teenager had any distinction at all. Donald Ferguson, the only teacher who gave thought to my efforts, was certainly not at fault. Nobody took seriously the idea that an American could compose music. Ferguson came to think of himself as a scholar rather than a composer and suffered from the cultural limitations of the environment.

I did know two composers who were both older than I and serious in their efforts to write music. Celius Dougherty was the most talented music student at the University and already gaining distinction as a pianist, especially as an accompanist for touring concert artists. The only works of his that I knew were songs, and I thought they were unusually good. He had never seen my music and had never influenced me. Herbert Elwell, a most distinguished composer, often visited his parents who lived just around the block from us. He was living in Paris and studying with Nadia Boulanger. During his visits I got to know him and he talked to me both about my music and about an American composing music. He was also a friend of "Papa" Gale, and we met at chamber music evenings in the "Stube."

I remember clearly his remarks about the method he used when he found himself stuck in the middle of a composition. He viewed the time-span of the piece as a mathematical equation. The first theme might be 16 measures, the bridge 5, the second theme 21, and the closing theme 7. Perhaps it took 22 measures in the development to reach the climax. That totaled 71 measures and was the first half of the equation to be balanced by the second half. If he cut the duration of the second half, then there would have to be a coda to balance the two sections. I can recall how puzzled I was by all this talk. Two things stuck in my mind. Here was real talk about composing music, not just theory about some music that had already been composed. I realized how rarely a teacher ever got around to dealing with the process of composing music. Here also was a process that was not just intuitive but dealt with durations as an abstraction. I began to suspect that composing was a lot more complicated than I had supposed — that there was a lot to be learned and a new way of going about the process of learning. I began to feel that composing was a more worthwhile activity for a musician than even performing.

I don't know how much I sensed at the time. Probably a good deal, but certainly not all. At this point my interest in analyzing music increased, and I began to rebel against other routines of academic theory. The attitudes of the environment towards living composers seemed to me sterile. (Mrs. Scott, the wife of the head of the music department made the remark about Herbert Elwell that he was an expatriate because America had no need for composers.)

I entered the University in 1924. During my senior year in high school there had been more social life — more school dances and parties, all very much centered in the University environment. So entering the University was no great change. I had already audited several of Ferguson's courses, and I had played in the University Symphony for years.

Joining a fraternity didn't interest me, partly because I couldn't afford it, but mostly because I was so active in musical and theater groups. My career as an actor was short-lived because I realized I had no gift. People laughed when I came on the stage, not because I was a successful comedian but because I was so awkward. I was a success as the corpse of Julius Caesar in Fritz Lieber's performance.

The year was almost too pleasant, so crowded with activities that I didn't have time to compose or to practice. A major in music was my objective, but none of my courses were in the school of music. My English course was taught by Mary Ellen Chase, a remarkable teacher. Marjorie Nicolson gave several lectures required of all students in English. Professor Herzog's course in economic geography had a lot of substance that interested me. And Professor Savage's course in Greek Literature in Translation was a favorite. Even the lectures and laboratory work in biology, though very time consuming, were interesting.

Military drill was required and might have been a bore, but I was selected to be a flag guard on the Twin City Trade Tour that traveled by train for two weeks through Minnesota and the Dakotas. It was fun to sleep in a Pullman and eat in the dining car and parade down the main street in one small town after another. Somebody must have been off their rocker to have chosen me, since I wasn't outstanding in drill. I enjoyed the vacation.

My most vivid memory is of people drinking on the train. I had been aware earlier in my life, before the Volstead Act, of main streets in Minnesota lined with saloons. (North Dakota was dry because of a state law.) On the train, men drank pure alcohol mixed with ginger ale and often became seriously ill. It seemed a curious way to advertise Twin City business. I hadn't the slightest interest in either smoking or drinking, not until years later.

It must have been during this year that we moved to a house in Prospect Park, still within walking distance of the University, but in a much more pleasant wooded area along the river. On one side of us lived Dr. Koos and his wife who was a pianist and had taught at the Hull House in Chicago. On the other side lived a family with a deaf son who was a remarkable artist. He had always been deaf and spoke with difficulty, but in spite of that we became friends. I admired his paintings, and he would "listen" to my music by putting his hand on the piano while I played.

Gus and Mollie were married in the summer of 1925 and went

immediately to a house they had rented in Northfield, Minnesota. Gus had accepted a job to teach violin at Carleton College. The college offered me a full scholarship covering room, board and tuition if I transfered there and taught cello in the music department. They had five students who were enrolled in cello, one of them Betty Cowling, a daughter of the president. My brother very much wanted me to come so that he could start a string quartet.

When I told Chris Erck about my move to Carleton College and my decision to be a composer, he said, "Just another bluebird shot to hell." I realized that I would miss my cello lessons and also my work with Donald Ferguson. When I expressed my doubts at Carleton, they said I could make the trip to Minneapolis every week for my lessons and my work there would be given credit towards my degree. I left for Northfield in 1925 at the age of nineteen for my first college teaching job.

CHAPTER IV

1925 - 1927

COLLEGE openings always seem to start on rainy September days. There was a "bumble-zug" that went from the Twin Cities to Owatonna, stopping at Northfield. Everyone took that, arriving at the train station, which was only a block or so from the bank that the James Brothers robbed in the nineteenth century. From the main street you climbed up a couple of blocks to the college campus which was dominated by the chapel and the clock tower of Willis Hall. Right next to it was a lovely small, greystone, ivy-covered library and down a few steps were the men's dormitories built of brick in what might be called the Academic Tudor style.

I was given a corner room on the first floor all to myself. It hadn't entered my mind that I wanted to get away from home, though I was at the age when that idea does occur. But I did feel a little more grown-up when I began to get my possessions around me.

I had a phonograph and four record albums with scores (Stravinsky's *Firebird Suite* and *Petrouchka*, Holst's *Planets*, and Scriabin's *Poem of Ecstasy*), the most valuable things I owned, except perhaps for my cello. I had very few clothes, but I did have a red wool shirt that I treasured. I had a few books, but the only one I remember was "Loves of the Composers" that had belonged to my mother — a dreadful book that even then I thought was a little funny. I had some scores of quartets and symphonies and some piano music that had been sent to me by a visiting friend from Germany. They were Peters Editions, printed on war-thin paper. I still have them.

Meals were at a set time and if you missed them, you either ate crackers in your room or you went to the snack bar in Willis Hall, under the clock, and got a sandwich.

I walked across the commons to the music building to take possession of my studio. The music building was a nice little structure, again in Tudor style with all the proper sounds coming out of it. (I like the sounds of music buildings — the kind of free-wheeling social improvisation of people practicing hard.)

My studio was on the top floor at the very end and facing the commons, and a little removed from the practice rooms. There was a piano — a real piano for my use alone — and two chairs, a music stand and a small desk. The first thing I did was to put my music paper and pencils on the table and then play the piano a little to see what it sounded like. It was a little out of tune but not a bad piano at all, better than Mother's old Kimball at home. I realized how little I had been able to think about music during my freshman year at the University, and I looked forward to spending as much time as I could practicing and composing. Yes, composing, for I had made up my mind: If I could, I would be a composer. It was a big gamble, and I realized it. I had no idea about my talent, certainly no inflated opinions. I knew I wasn't a very good pianist or cellist, but I knew that I had musical ideas in my head that I had to learn to get out. I remembered the remark my father had made when he saw a piece of music I had written: "Can anyone else read that?" It had made me mad at the time, but he had put his finger right on the problem. You had to learn to write out the music that was in your head so anybody else could read it.

My brother wanted to organize a Carleton String Quartet immediately so that he could plan a concert tour in the state. One of his students, Betty L'Amamour Rice, often played second violin and a senior, Jon Kuypers, played viola. We started by learning several easy pieces such as "Drink to Me Only with Thine Eyes," to lighten programs and to have something we could play at the daily chapel exercises. We started with Schubert's "Death and the Maiden" Quartet, knowing that it would be some time before we would dare play it publicly. We were asked suddenly to play for chapel, and Gus had to locate me and get the group together. I appeared wearing my red wool shirt and never lived down the impression I made at our first performance.

I was considered "Bohemian," which was absurd, and made me think quite a lot about what the term meant. I realized that the academic environment confuses the artist who works hard and produces (though he may be somewhat eccentric as a person) with the Bohemian who lives an affected life style, loafs and talks a lot about "art." I came to have no respect for what I considered a Bohemian.

One of my friends was Gould Stevens, who lived in a room across from mine. He draped black cloth over all the walls, put red wax paper over the windows and dressed in red Chinese pajamas with a black dragon design on the front. He talked all the time about the ballet he would one day design, but as far as I know he never did it. He was bright enough and fun to talk to, though he drew my dander almost immediately by barging into my room and smudging an inked manuscript I was working on. He was a typical Bohemian. (He was running a book store in Minneapolis the last I heard.)

Elmer Peterson, on the other hand, was just the opposite. He was interested in journalism and reminded me a little of my brother Nat. Peterson became nationally known as the broadcaster from Czechoslovakia at the start of the Second World War. As a student he wanted to be a writer of novels, but at the time he did short news stories about college activities for the *Minneapolis Star.*

My closest friend was Jon Kuypers. He was older than I and was working very hard on the viola during his last year at Carleton. He wanted to get a job playing viola in the Minneapolis Symphony Orchestra. It was only towards the end of the year that he told me he had married a philosophy teacher who was teaching at the University of Minnesota. That was why he wanted a job with the orchestra. The marriage didn't last very long, but it seemed very romantic to me at the time. His background was romantic too. He was Dutch and had gone to sea as a young fellow, travelling all over the world in tramp steamers until he finally left ship in New York and settled in Passaic, New Jersey. He worked his way through high school and got a scholarship to Carleton. He was a very bright and gifted student, a little aloof because of his age, and a little overconfident of his abilities. I valued his friendship for many years.

He left the orchestra to be the head of the music department of Hamline College and later of the department at Cornell University. Finally he was made the Dean of the School of Music at the University of Illinois. In the thirties he was very active as a choral conductor in the Minnesota Federal Music Project.

We often walked over to St. Olaf College on the other side of

Northfield to watch F. M. Christiansen rehearse his famous Lutheran Choir. ("Somebody has a buzz in his voice. If he doesn't get rid of it, out he goes.") We talked a lot about music and enjoyed playing in the quartet. I remember once when we were giving a concert in Sioux Falls, South Dakota, a nice young man met us at the train and asked if the violist and cellist would be his guests while we were in town. It turned out that he and his wife played violin and his two daughters were just starting viola and cello. After our concert we played quartets all night with the family, the little girls following the parts as though they were playing them. Then we had a big breakfast and left for the next town.

Perhaps I wasn't too bad as a cello teacher, since I had worked so hard to overcome bad habits. My students weren't very gifted, but one of them, Betty Cowling, did become a cellist and taught at the University of North Carolina at Greensboro. I kept on studying with Chris Erck and struggled that year with the Saint-Saens *Concerto in A Minor,* which I disliked very much as music. I still had to think consciously about keeping my left wrist high so that I could play thumb positions.

I very much valued my piano lessons at Carleton with Marie Sloss. She was a flighty individual, but an excellent musician, and we got along very well. I had come to view the piano as a tool that I could use in composing music. To view it as an instrument with all its subtle differences of tone and touch was foreign to me and surely one of the things that limited my ability to be a performer. Memorizing music didn't interest me as much as reading a lot of music. Marie Sloss understood and to a degree sympathized, but she insisted on my giving a graduation recital and memorizing the entire program. It was a demanding program and included Chopin's *Ballade in G minor* which made a deep musical impression on me. (My *Narrative in Retrospect* for piano, written in 1984, reveals my love of that work.) Miss Sloss took an interest in the piano pieces that I wrote and introduced me to the piano music of Scriabin and contemporary French composers.

Most of my other courses at Carleton compared very poorly with those I had taken at the University. I had a course in psychology from a professor who spent most of his time arguing that acquired characteristics are transmitted, and contending that the soul hovers above the head of the individual. My father almost had apoplexy when I told him what I was being taught! Ian Holburn's course in the history of art was given without pictures or slides and was really not a history of art but of esthetics, and not even contemporary esthetics. An elderly man who came every year for one semester from the Orkney Islands, he was a poet of sorts and reflected the Victorian attitude towards art. I enjoyed him as a person and found his lectures interesting and very well prepared, but I always felt that I was hearing an echo of Walter Pater. My course in acoustics was excellent, but not as demanding as the course in biology I had taken the year before. Certainly no teacher had the power to communicate the importance of artistic honesty which Mary Ellen Chase had done so well, or the clarity of thought that Herzog had revealed in dealing with economic geography.

It is embarrassing to remember my music courses, because Carleton is now one of the fine music departments in the area. I signed up for Analysis, Ear Training, and the History of Music. They were all subjects that I needed badly. James Gillette, the head of the music department, met the Analysis course and told us to buy Mendelssohn's *Songs Without Words*. When we met the next day, he didn't appear, nor did he ever thereafter. All inquiries went unanswered, so we all forgot about the class until the end of the semester, when I received an A in the course. Ear Training was taught by Bert Linnell, who was in charge of the school music courses and was a very nice person. After the first meeting of the class, she decided I had perfect pitch and thought there was no point in my coming to the course. At the end I got both credit and a grade!

The voice instructor taught the music history course and was about as ignorant a musician as I have ever known. He used a terrible text and obviously didn't know what he was talking about. The students gave him a bad time, but I found it hard to blame them. The trouble was with the administrative policy of the college. A teacher had to justify his salary by the income from teaching voice or piano or violin etc., and courses were given to anyone who could be persuaded to take them.

My second year at Carleton was much better, not because of courses, but because of emotional involvement. The department asked me to teach the course in music history as well as cello. Looking back on it, it seems incredible, but I said I would and spent the summer taking Ferguson's course at the University of Minnesota in preparation. The personnel of the string quartet was changed. Jon Kuypers had gotten a job with the symphony, and Bertha Smiley, the wife of the professor of classics, took his place. A young teacher in the English department, Gretchen Ludke, became second violinist. It was a much more congenial group. Bertha Smiley was also a good pianist — she had been a pupil of Josef Lhévinne — and as fine a musician as I had ever met. She was a lovely lady and adored music and played the viola very well. Gretchen Ludke struck me at first as a rather timid person but very intelligent and very good-looking. We all enjoyed each other and began practicing with a vengeance.

In teaching music history, I tried to put into practice my conviction that one should hear as much of the music as possible. In 1926 that was easier said than done. There were very few recordings of even the basic classic literature, and the only contemporary music I could play were the four albums I treasured so much. It is hard for anyone to understand today the problems of teaching a course in music without a record collection. The library had only a few of the basic books that were needed for teaching such a course. I got rid of the book that had been used and required instead, the Waldo Selden Pratt *History of Music* that Ferguson had used, even though it did seem a little encyclopedic. To cover the medieval period was almost impossible, except for singing a few things like "Sumer is icumen in." We sang English madrigals and someone played a few keyboard works. The baroque period was a little easier because the Minneapolis Public Library had the parts for a few instrumental pieces. We went over to hear the St. Olaf Lutheran Choir sing a Bach motet and a student played some organ pieces. My brother had the score and a recording of Bach's *Double Concerto*. I had studied one of the works for cello alone. Beethoven was easier until we got to his late works, so I asked Bertha Smiley to come in and play two of the piano sonatas. It had all taken much more time than I had expected, and so the romantic period got slighted, and my few records had to represent contemporary music. I suspect I learned more from the course than did my eight students. I also learned that I never wanted to teach the history of music again.

I found that I could get my Bachelor of Arts degree in two years at Carleton because of the courses I had taken at the University during my first year and summer sessions, and because of the private lessons in cello that I had had with Chris Erck. I was an honors student in 1927 and composed what I thought was a "Sonata for Cello and Piano," a collection of piano pieces that I called "Attitudes," and three songs. I had worked very hard, but I badly needed good teaching in composition. Nobody looked at what I had composed, and nothing was performed. I realized, even at that early age, that one could teach the composition of music and that the College had an obligation to perform the works that a student composed.

That year I fell in love with Gretchen Ludke. Neither she nor I can remember when it all started. Gretchen had a car and every week drove a group of teacher friends to the St. Paul concert of the Minneapolis Symphony Orchestra. Once in the fall I went along. Mostly we went for long walks together or rented a canoe and paddled down the river that ran through town. Sometimes we went to the Northfield Hotel for dinner. My reaction to this experience was emotionally overpowering. It was like an illness, an endless torment! I had never felt that way before. The experience was probably perfectly normal, but it seemed to me unique. I had never enjoyed so much being with anyone. Many of our friends may have looked upon our involvement as a schoolboy crush, though I never did. I went to Alexandria, Minnesota after Christmas to spend a few days meeting the Ludkes. Gretchen's father owned a wholesale grocery business. He had a wonderful sense of humor; perhaps he needed it to face his daughter's involvement with a musician. Her mother had grown up in Canada, and she outdid herself to serve special meals. We spent our time skating on a lake nearby and going for winter walks. Our relationship was stronger during the spring, and we reached the point of talking seriously about it. Gretchen thought it was a tempest in a teapot. I didn't.

Sometime during the winter of 1925 I went to a lecture that Nadia Boulanger gave at the University of Minnesota. Her subject was "Migot, the Beethoven of the Twentieth Century." I had never heard of Georges Migot (nor have I since) but I was very impressed by the lecture. I discovered that a friend of Albert Parker Fitch, my philosophy professor, had studied with Nadia Boulanger and urged me to go to Paris and work with her. Herbert Elwell had also praised her as a teacher. Little by little I made up my mind that I would do just that, but how could I finance it? I found that there was a Johnson Foundation in Minneapolis that would give me a scholarship of five hundred dollars (quite adequate then) for such a project. So I began to make plans.

My aunt, who had been on a Mediterranean tour the summer before, told me about an orchestra made up of college students who had all their expenses paid in return for playing for dances and helping out when the tour made inland trips. She wrote to the professor at Cornell who supervised the orchestra and urged that I be considered. When he wrote asking whether I would be interested and what instruments I could play, I was perfectly honest and replied that I wasn't very good at jazz and could play piano and cello, but that I had a small scholarship to study in Paris and would have to leave the ship in Southampton. I could hardly believe it when Cook's Tours wrote that I had been chosen to be a member of the student orchestra and should report in New York in June.

I was invited to a St. Paul Music Club concert featuring Bela Bartók as pianist and lecturer. I have no memory of what he said, but I was completely overwhelmed by the performance of his *Sonata for Piano,* which was unlike any music I had ever heard before. It was percussive and very tight with very little rubato, yet beautifully shaped, with a slow movement that evolved like an improvisation around a pedal tone in the upper voice, often foreign to the harmony of the bass. I had a

chance to meet him after the concert and he seemed to know Boulanger and to think highly of her.

When the instructor of the Contemporary European Drama course
for which I was registered became ill, Gretchen Ludke took over the
class in mid-semester. She was a very good teacher and turned what
might have been an embarrassing experience into a very enjoyable one.
I don't suppose I was a very good student, but that was partly her fault!
We spent a great deal of time together that spring and finally came to
the conclusion that we would be engaged. It was just before the
examination period and I asked her to proctor the final exam in my
course so I could go to Minneapolis to buy an engagement ring. She
wanted lapis lazuli because of a Browning poem she admired (so she
said, though I suspected it was to save me money). I must have gone to
every jeweller in the Twin Cities looking for that ring, and finally in
desperation bought one with the smallest diamond possible.

Nadia Boulanger wrote me a note saying that I could study with her
and suggesting that I come to Gargenville where she lived during the
summer months. Several American students would be there, she wrote,
and it would be a good way to start my lessons before the Paris season.

Gretchen decided to spend the summer in London and would plan
to stay for a week or so after I landed at Southampton after the
Mediterranean tour. We planned to travel together to Hardy country.
Mary Ellen Chase had told us about her visit there and of how she
unexpectedly met Thomas Hardy after he helped free her from a fence
on which she was caught. We didn't expect to see Hardy, but we
thought it would be a wonderful chance to visit cathedrals and the old
towns in western England.

It is typical that I have no memory of how I got to New York City. I
must have gone by train since I had my cello and so much baggage to
take along. I do remember meeting with the orchestra and practicing
hard all day so that we could immediately play for a dance.

The new songs we had to play gave me great pleasure. It was my
first experience with dance music parts and learning to know when the
breaks would be interpolated. I can't remember the names of the boys
in the orchestra, but they came from all over the place. We enjoyed
each other. The pianist was from Harvard, and he was very good, only
asking me to play the piano in a few of the most obvious waltzes. The
rest of the time I played the bass parts on the cello, or sometimes a cello
part that was included in the set.

We expected to play during tea as well as for dances, and I was
given the job of organizing the tea music. This was the time of the
"Charleston" which included such pieces as "Sundown" and "Hallelu-

jah." It was explained to us that a big part of our job was to be nice to the tourists and to do everything we could to help out.

The ship was the "California" of the Anchor Line and our rooms were on the lowest deck at the prow where there was the most motion. We were eight in the orchestra, four to a stateroom. We would stay on board except in a few ports such as Cairo, Jerusalem, Constantinople, and Athens, when we would be assigned to help those tourists who stayed at the smaller hotels.

In New York we rehearsed on board ship, so we saw nothing of the city until night. I saw little even then, because I got caught on the shuttle train between Times Square and Grand Central Station. I went back and forth several times before I realized I was going nowhere! We had a nice view of the skyline from the ship and saw other ocean liners entering the Hudson River to dock. There was great activity along the waterfront — passenger trains coming to the piers, taxis with passengers, baggage being unloaded, blasts from the ships that were about to leave. It was an exciting part of New York that has largely vanished.

Most of the crew were Scottish and very friendly. They warned us that we would feel a good deal of motion in our staterooms and suggested a glass of Worcestershire sauce before we started. Then we should eat solid foods like steaks, avoid oranges and lemons, and never, but *never,* miss eating a good solid breakfast of bacon and eggs. It didn't sound to us like a bad preventative, since we were all starved to death all the time.

We thought we should be devilish, so we went to the bar and bought bottles of liquor to drink when we were beyond the ten-mile limit. I bought a bottle of Benedictine and drank it all down. Expecting to be very drunk, I topped it off with a glass of Worcestershire sauce, rushed to the w.c., threw up the whole mess, and then slept like a log all night. I got up early in the morning and walked the decks a little, had a heavy breakfast of bacon and eggs and everything else that was offered, and never had a touch of seasickness during the entire trip. But be careful about advising elderly ladies to follow that regimen. It might kill them if they took your advice (which they won't), but the mere talk of bacon and eggs may keep them in their staterooms for days.

The "California" was a beautiful ship and beautifully run. The food was unusually good and very ample. The orchestra boys were seated at different tables, usually with elderly people. It was good training. We had to be polite. Curiously, we all loved it and became devoted to the people at our table. If anyone got sick, we hustled around to make them comfortable in their deck chairs, tucking blankets over them, getting them books to read, stopping now and then to see how they were. The fact that we all came from colleges, were about the same age, and played together every day in the orchestra made us something of a group. We never had to be told to do anything because everyone was so nice to us, and as far as I know, none of us had to be disciplined.

There was a larger ship's orchestra that played in the salon. We always played for dancing on the deck and were very popular. The younger people liked to dance to our music and the older people liked to watch the younger people. Now and then we would play in the salon for a special party or to give the ship's orchestra a break. Then we used their music and played the kind of thing expected when tea is served. For that my cello proved very useful.

Our first landfall was Madeira. What a sight! The town of Funchal climbing up the slopes of the mountain, white buildings with red roofs and flowers growing over everything. The ship anchored out in the bay and a tender went back and forth to the shore. Boys swam out to the ship to dive for money that was thrown to them. They always got it. The water was so clear we could see the bottom. There were hundreds of little boats that came out loaded with merchandise, mostly Madeira linen. On shore there were shops filled with produce, and every time one entered a shop he was offered a glass of Madeira wine. When the ship sounded its horn announcing its departure, the prices of linen table cloths dropped to a fraction. I bought one for Gretchen.

We stopped at Gibraltar to let off a few passengers who would travel inland and return to the boat at Malaga, where we would be docked for two days. The orchestra learned some new pieces, got a good sun tan and generally relaxed. We were invited to the local dance pavilion on the shore to be their guests and play for a few dances. It was my first experience with foreign dance music and its differences of tempo and rhythm. Our tempos were about twice as fast as the languorous, seductive Spanish tempos, and the local crowd went absolutely wild when one of the boys showed them how to dance the Charleston. The evening was a great success. We let the Spanish orchestra know how much we liked their music, and they let us know they liked ours, even though we could not speak their language.

The next day we arrived in Naples. We visited the city but slept on the ship, which was no great hardship since from the boat we had the famous view of the bay.

We stopped at Alexandria and boarded a train for Cairo. Out of the train window we could see farming that looked very primitive. At one stop we bought little round watermelons that were delicious and cool. Almost everyone went to the Shepherds Hotel when we arrived in

Cairo, but I was assigned to a small group that went to a little hotel on the other side of the river not very far from the Pyramids. It seems to me it was called the Athletic Club.

Two of us decided to walk to the Pyramids at night (romantic!) and see what we could find. We climbed all over the place and talked as much as we could to the camel drivers, most of whom could speak English. We talked about everything — religion, girls, the desert, the Pyramids, camels, cars, America, the ocean — with lots of laughter and excitement. Anything I knew about foreign places I got from reading Thomas Haliburton; we must have gotten the idea of spending the night on the Pyramids from him. I have no doubt that we missed most of the important things to see and that we behaved like the twenty-year-olds we were, but I have never regretted that my introduction to foreign travel was on such an immature level. We visited the dark streets of the bazaar and took off our shoes when we entered the mosques. We joined the conducted tour or went alone at night when there was no tour.

All the elderly ladies knew I wanted to buy presents for my girl and helped me to find what I wanted at a price I could afford. So I got a little bottle of jasmin perfume essence and found a lapis lazuli stone that could be made into a pin.

Our next stop was Jaffa where once again we had to anchor off the coast and go to the shore by tender. At this stop we left the ship and traveled with the tourists to Jerusalem. It was certainly the most exciting part of the whole tour for me. We traveled up through the dry hills by car on a gravel road that twisted and turned through gorges with Biblical names. Finally we came to the city which was surrounded by medieval walls and was perched on a mountain top. We entered through gates that crusaders had built. We were led by guides to the various hotels that had been reserved. Several of us were assigned to the group that would stay in the American Colony on the edge of the city outside the Damascus Gate. To get there we walked down through the narrow streets of the old city, following the "Way of the Cross" and then turned and mounted to the Gate in the old wall.

Outside was the new city. The American Colony was a quadrangle that enclosed a rather large square where Bedouins were camped in their colorful tents, and where they parked their Cadillacs. It was very different from being housed in the King David Hotel, and some of the tourists felt they hadn't been given a fair deal. Our job was to make them feel comfortable and not too separated from the main group, to run messages for them, and to see that they were not neglected on the sight-seeing tours. We were kept busy. It wasn't long before they realized that the American Colony was much more modern and in some ways more interesting than the older hotels, and certainly the food was very much better.

There is not space to describe all the many points of interest that we covered. I found the most interesting right in the Colony compound. The Bedouins drove up from Trans-Jordan to the American Colony to purchase items they needed in their camps. They were handsome men in gorgeous, dusty robes with turbans and eyes that seemed especially white because of the darkening around them.

The American merchant introduced us to them, and it was decided that we would have a concert in the evening just for them. It was interesting to me that they responded equally and similarly to both our classical music and to our jazz. I played the Chopin First Ballade on the old beat-up piano and we made up a combo of piano, drums (which had been borrowed from some place), clarinet and trumpet. The Bedouins wanted us to visit their Trans-Jordan camp and offered to drive us there and back. I thought it might be possible because the tour was staying an extra day in Jerusalem waiting for the group visiting Galilee to return.

Evidently these Bedouins were people of some importance. The merchant had to make special arrangements with the tour director for us to go. We started out in the afternoon in one of the big Cadillacs and drove down to the bridge that crosses the Jordan River at Jericho, and then turned south along the east bank of the Dead Sea until we came to the camp.

Two of the young Bedouins spoke some English and translated for us. The tents were set in a circle and were much more elaborate than I had expected them to be. There were beautiful oriental rugs on the ground, lots of leather cushions and even a few pieces of furniture. A banquet had been prepared. (I wonder how they could have known we were coming?) The merchant in Jerusalem had warned us what to expect and had told us, very carefully, how we should act. We would be served half cups of coffee that would be very thick and sweet and we must drink it all. Dinner would be served on a big brass tray around which all the men would sit, and from time to time the host would pass us morsels that were considered especially choice. We must accept them and eat with pleasure regardless of what we were served. It was polite to smack our lips and even to belch. We must never hurry. The meal was a big event and shouldn't be interrupted by too much talking.

The tray was very large with an edge about six inches high. The mutton or goat was cooked so that there was a very greasy sauce with all kinds of bits floating in it. This had been poured over some kind of cooked cereal. In the middle were pieces of vegetable marrow.

We ate with our fingers, dipping into the tray for anything we wanted. Should we use our right hand or our left? We waited until they started to eat and followed their example. We were passed pieces that were round and looked like eyeballs, but tasted delicious. Everything tasted good and we ate ravenously. I have never since had vegetable marrow that tasted so delicious — a little firm and juicy with just a slight sweet taste. The cereal was like rice but tasted like barley. It too combined well with the meat. There were no women to be seen, and young boys served bowls of water and a towel at the end of the meal.

Everyone was serious, and we talked, through two men who translated, about our trip and where we lived. What was our school like? What were we going to do when we got home? I said I was going to be a composer and was stopping to study for the year in Paris. That puzzled them. Who would I study with? I said with a woman who was a great teacher, Nadia Boulanger. They were amazed. Did women teach in our colleges at home? Yes, I said, and I was going to marry one of my teachers. We didn't talk about politics in any serious way. Who was our President? Where did he live? Actually we didn't know anything about the politics of Palestine, and frankly, little enough about the politics of the United States.

After dinner we were served coffee in little cups, and since they scooped out the dregs into their mouth with their fingers, we did the same thing. Then the preparations were made for the concert.

One of the men played the rebabeh — a one-stringed instrument played with a very simple bow. (The player was told that I played a very big rebabeh that had four strings.) They explained that the song they would play could go on all night and when we had had enough we should stop them.

The song started with a rebabeh solo playing an introduction with lots of slides, ornaments and trills and then settled down to a more steady tune with someone occasionally clapping hands. Towards the end a singer started in a falsetto, again with many ornaments. Finally with what must have been a chorus, everyone would sing.

It was a story-telling ballad, and the young fellow translated for us: The tribe met a beautiful girl and followed her to Damascus (a chorus), and then to Jerusalem (more chorus). And so it went, verse after verse chasing the girl from one place to another. After this had been going on for fifteen minutes, we signaled that we would like to hear another song. It ended this way: the girl, they discovered, belonged to their own tribe, so they were no longer interested.

Their songs seemed pretty much alike to us. Some were serious, like the one I have just described, and some were funny, and everyone laughed a lot and pounded the ground with their hands. Most of the time we had no idea what it was about, though our translator tried to explain. It dawned on me that it was as hard for them to explain their music as it was for me to explain ours, and that everything in our music sounded alike to them. I loved most the sound of the rebabeh and the curious nasal singing. The experience was the most exciting of the whole tour.

After playing they let me look at the rebabeh and try to play it, and then urged me to play a song on it. I did my best, trying to imitate how they had played and sung. They went into gales of laughter and didn't want me to stop.

The other boy had brought his clarinet, and they insisted that he play some American music. He was a fine performer and it was surprising how well he could play jazz on just the clarinet alone. Finally I joined him improvising on the rebabeh, which was pretty weird, but they thought it was wonderful. Since it was getting dark, and we had to return to Jerusalem, the concert had to end. Everyone embraced us and slapped us on the back and laughed a lot, and off we went in the Cadillac.

I came to realize, perhaps for the first time, how much I love to hear the sound of music from below, especially the sound of children singing or of sheep bells ringing below, or of church bells. I realized that in Minnesota I had loved the sound of a French Canadian singing over the lake. Perhaps the two experiences are related in their special resonance. On the way to Bethlehem one could look down the hill and see women washing clothes and singing and children singing and goat bells ringing. There were bells ringing in Jerusalem most of the time.

Constantinople was a city that needed more than the sophistication I had and the few hours that we were there to appreciate it. We weren't included in the tour and wandered around seeing what we could. Santa Sophia was in itself worth the trip, but how much more it would have meant to me if I had known its history then. I bought two rugs at the Covered Bazaar (domestic life must have been much on my mind) and walked the main street, but I was glad to get back to the ship with my loot and look at the skyline from the deck.

Sailing through the Sea of Marmara and the Bosporus to the Black Sea with the villas and castles on the steep shore and the weather soft and cool was more fun than being on land. From the Black Sea we turned back and headed for Greece.

The ship made Piraeus in midday, making our trip through the islands and past Sounion spectacular. Since we were on our own, we went to the Acropolis in the late afternoon and spent the whole night there. One heard the sounds of Athens below and saw the sunset reflected from the temples and from Mount Hymettus in the distance. Perhaps the gates to the Acropolis were locked, but I don't think so. We had no feeling that we were trespassing. Our experience was no substitute for seeing the sights of the city, but it is a nice memory of an experience that cannot be repeated today. We returned to the ship in the early morning and sailed for Naples and a short stop, letting off passengers who planned to travel to London by land. At Southampton I left the ship and took the boat train to London where I met Gretchen.

Gretchen was living with two other girls at a pension on Russell Square and had made arrangements for me to spend the night there. Our meeting, which I had looked forward to all summer, was as exciting as I had hoped it would be. She liked the gifts I had purchased, especially the lapis lazuli stone which I had had set into a brooch in Naples. But they complicated her luggage, which, with her ship sailing from Southampton in about ten days, she had to get into shape before we could leave on our tour of the Hardy country. Our main interest was to be together, which explains why neither of us can recall the exact route that we traveled the next few days.

We went by train to Dorchester where Hardy had lived. (He died in 1928.) We walked along the road that is described in *Tess of the D'Urbervilles*. There were several villages that we connected with the novels, but what they were and where we ended up, I have no idea. Finally we caught a train and spent a wonderful Sunday in Wells. We got rooms in a boardinghouse in the Cathedral Close and had to claim that we were brother and sister. We didn't act like brother and sister, I must say, and we got chased out of the Cathedral grounds for being too affectionate, which has always puzzled me because we saw plenty of young English couples "necking" on the grounds.

Always in my mind was the realization that in a few days Gretchen would catch her boat to return to the States and I would catch mine to go to France for the year. In retrospect it was the right thing to do, but I had no ability to see it that way at the time. I don't know where we went from Wells — perhaps to Shaftesbury (the market town that Hardy wrote about) and then to Salisbury. It was only a short trip from there to Southampton.

On the day the boat sailed we got there early and I spent time with Gretchen on her boat and saw her leave. I had arranged to take a boat from Southampton to Cherbourg, and all my luggage had been checked through to Paris. I felt very low after Gretchen's departure, but still I was eager to get to France and begin my studies.

CHAPTER V

1927 - 1928

THE boat train arrived in Paris in the early evening, and I went to the Palais Hotel which had been recommended to me, obviously by people who had a lot more money than I. It was well located on the river and I had a long walk down the left bank and across to Notre Dame. Crossing to the right bank, I stopped for a ham sandwich, which I discovered was something different and quite special — a long bun cut in two, and well buttered with a large slice of ham in the middle. Then I went mournfully back to the hotel and to bed.

The next day I took the train out to Gargenville, checked my luggage at the hotel and set out to find where Nadia Boulanger lived. Gargenville was a little town on the north bank of the Seine west of Paris. The red-roofed houses bordered the river and ran up to the top of the hill. My French was very bad (it still is!), and when I asked for Boulanger I was sent to every bakery in town. Finally I stopped at a small garage where a man was working and said, "Boulanger." He said, "What the hell do you want, a bakery or the villa of the great teacher Nadia Boulanger?" As it turned out, he was an American veteran of the war who had

47

settled in France. He pointed out the villa down the road, and at last I was ringing the bell at the gate. When the maid announced me, Nadia Boulanger rushed out, gave me a hug, and said I should wash up and have lunch with them immediately. She had reserved a room with a piano in a pension in Juzier, where some other students lived only a short walk away. After lunch I could get settled there and then come back to Gargenville later in the afternoon.

My room — very tiny, with a piano, a chair, a table and a cot — was in a villa up the hill. It was surrounded by vegetable gardens and big beds of dahlias. Roy Harris lived next door but was away for the day. There were several other students, but I remember only a French boy who could speak English and was very nice.

We walked back together in the late afternoon to Mademoiselle's villa and met the other students. Two Americans, David Dushkin, a brother of the violinist Samuel Dushkin, and Dorothy Smith, who had graduated from Smith College, became my closest friends. They were married at the end of the year and organized schools, first in Wilmette, north of Chicago, and later at a famous summer music camp in Weston, Vermont. There was a girl from Scotland and several other students who had come up to Gargenville from Fontainebleau.

The meeting was largely social, but not entirely so. The students were working at harmony and counterpoint, and Mademoiselle said I should buy the Dubois books and do the exercises, which I would show her at my lesson. She asked David Dushkin to show me how to do them, using different clefs and doing six exercises for each example. Afterwards Mlle. Boulanger encouraged our proposal to organize a picnic. By the end of the afternoon I felt that I was accepted as a part of the group.

Soon after I arrived in Gargenville, my father wrote that Mother was coming over to France in September to keep house for me during the year, and that I should find an apartment rather than a room with a French family. I was delighted, since it would make me feel more at home and would be a great help with finances, even if it did make learning French more difficult. I knew that Gus and Mollie would be leaving soon to spend the year in Berlin, but they had not planned to visit Paris en route. There was some chance, too, that Nat would take a short vacation from his new job at the *Minneapolis Star* and visit France and England. All these possibilities meant that I would have to find an apartment large enough for Mother and me and for guests. It was no easy job.

(I realize now, as I didn't at the time, that my mother and father's marriage was in jeopardy. No child knows much about the intimate lives of his parents. I was aware that my father's views had changed fundamentally from his early religious background. He had not become a radical. He had become more pragmatic, and this was probably the reason for their conflict. Mother was intuitive and emotional and held to the moral values of her youth. Leaving the church had not bothered her, but leaving the old concepts of the family relationship did. I suspect that my father was very highly sexed and possibly that my mother didn't respond to his needs. She became bitter in her last years and pleaded not be buried next to my father. He became a lonely, frustrated man with no religious beliefs and yet unable to embrace the "scientific methods" of modern sociology. He developed hypertension that shortened his life.)

I have great admiration for my father's creativity and extremely rational approach to the techniques of writing — his insistence on using the right word in the right place. On the other hand, I loved the warmth and the honesty of my mother. She had never been able to use those qualities to teach music, except to her children.)

Unconsciously, I rebelled a little against spending all my time doing harmony and counterpoint exercises, though every time I went for my lesson with Mlle. Boulanger, I took along a big batch for her to look over. But I also took along something that I had composed during the week. Thinking back on her abilities as a teacher, I realize that she had a great talent for understanding her students and adjusting to their needs. She would whizz through my exercises, making marks above and below, saying very little when she gave them back to me. Then she would play the composition I had written and criticize places that she thought were not right for the overall shape of the piece.

At last I had a teacher who realized I didn't have perfect pitch or always hear what I had written down. I confessed my lack and asked her what I should do. Did it mean that I ought not to be a composer? "No," she said. "A composer's job is to imagine his music. He hears it when it is performed." When she discovered that I always knew A when it was played, she suggested that by singing and reading I would learn to associate other pitches in terms of A. This would increase my sense of relative pitch and the hearing of intervals. I whistled and sang a lot, starting out on A and finding melodies with strange interval progressions.

We students often discussed our lessons and commented on what Mademoiselle had criticized. When she said a spot in our music was bad, we all believed it was bad, but not necessarily for the reason she gave. We realized that her corrections of our counterpoint exercises had meaning far beyond her explanations. The little marks above showed that we returned to the same note too frequently or not at the right time, and the marks below meant that we had not heard the implications of the bass we had written or that could be implied in the *cantus firmus.*

I came to realize more and more that she didn't waste her time talking about things beyond the notes written on the staff. She had the conviction that there was a right way and a wrong way and that the composer's job was to find the right way. Even if we disagreed with what she thought was the right way, we all agreed that there was a right way for each individual composer and that it was up to him to find it.

Perhaps this explains why she could be devastatingly critical in our lessons. Still, we came away buoyed up and ready to try again. She was never negative. I don't mean that she didn't have favorites or prejudices. She did. But she respected our prejudices, too. So, during the year she spent little time at my lessons worrying about harmony or counterpoint or analyzing Fauré, knowing that I didn't respond. I don't know whether she liked my music (why should she have?), but she took it seriously and tried to help me improve.

Our "peekneek" was a great success. We followed all of Nadia Boulanger's mother's instructions, taking a folding table, folding chairs and even a carpet up the hill. We collected "petit pain," ham and cheese and bottles of wine. Madame Boulanger didn't think it was quite proper for us to lie on towels and soak up the sunshine, of which there was an abundant supply that afternoon. At the top of the hill were acres of apple orchards. We were warned not to pick the apples because they had all been sold in advance to England. We were not to pick the blackberries because they were poisonous. Ignoring this last warning, we picked quarts of them and ate them, to the horror of Madame Boulanger. Perhaps I have given a false picture of her. She was a plump, motherly Russian woman, constantly worried about the morals of the students. No one died from eating the blackberries, which I'm sure didn't change for a moment Madame's convictions.

There were other events. Plans were made for visiting Chartres Cathedral where Mademoiselle would play the organ. Aaron Copland drove us there. We could see the spires for miles before we arrived. At lunch, while Mademoiselle practiced, we sat at a café listening to Aaron talk about being an American composer. It was heady talk, full of his ebullience. I had never met him before, nor did I know his music, but his confidence fed my ambitions.

After lunch we listened to Nadia Boulanger's recital. There was always a special quality to her performances — a quality that showed both her knowledge and love of the music she played. After the concert we wandered around the cathedral, very much as tourists, except once, when we stopped in the transept. Mlle. Boulanger held forth on the architect's error in breaking the upward sweep where the nave and the transept met. I remember this especially because it illustrated her belief in the simplicity that highlighted the main objective of a work of art. She frowned on ornaments that confused rather than enhanced.

That summer I got to know Roy Harris very well. It was the beginning of a friendship that endured for many years. I think we were drawn to each other because he talked of Oklahoma and I of North Dakota. We would go for long walks through the hills, viewing the beautiful valley of the Seine. He talked constantly of his ambition to be an American composer and what he thought that meant. I'm not sure that he knew. (Who does?) But his beliefs were so intensely felt that he immediately made a convert of me. We both loved the great open spaces of the prairie, where skies were higher and the winds more persistent. For me, at that moment, it was a counterbalance to Mademoiselle's concern for the symmetry of notes. Time and motion meant a great deal to Roy. I didn't know his music then, except for bits he played for me in his studio. Later, I came to know it very well and remembered what he had been aiming to accomplish as a composer.

The French boy who lived in the house invited me to dinner at his home in Paris. I took my cello along and we played trios. His father was a banker and his brothers were businessmen. They went out of their way to be nice to me, but I felt like a bull in a china shop. For one thing, I wasn't dressed properly. For another, I was not yet able to appreciate the gourmet food which was served at their elegant dinner of many courses and several different kinds of wine. Then, too, my French was poor and I was embarrassed, feeling that I had complicated their evening. It was my first and almost only experience with "high society." I came away determined to improve my French and to learn to be less timid. In time I decided that one had to be what one was.

Knowing that Mother was arriving in a few weeks, I had to go to Paris and find an apartment. Someone had told me that the American Students' Union on Boulevard St.-Germain had a list of apartments available from September to July. I was very lucky and rented an apartment that belonged to an American teacher who was spending the academic year in the States. It was on the fifth floor of an apartment house on Place St.-André-des-Arts. One entered the apartment from the landing into a small dining room with a window that looked out on the chimney pots of the back roofs. Off of the dining room was a small kitchen with a stove and oven, a sink, and all the pans and dishes one would need. The w.c. was around the corner. From the dining room one entered the living room, which was quite large and had French windows opening onto the balcony. A door from the living room led into the bedroom, which was almost as big and also had a balcony.

The furnishings were Spartan but adequate, with beds in the bedroom and couches in the living room. The rent was very low and I could move in immediately. I worried about the walk-up, but Mother was in good health and used to hard work. I immediately rented a piano and collected all my luggage. It seemed homelike, and I thought Mother would like it. Moreover, there was room for my brothers if they wished to visit us.

I left for Cherbourg to meet Mother's boat. The boat train didn't stop between Cherbourg and Paris and I thought it a pity to miss the chance to see some of the Norman cities like Bayeux and Caen. She was delighted when I told her that we would "dribble" to Paris and see a few sights.

Her boat arrived during the night. Early in the morning, after we had checked her baggage through to Paris, we started out for Bayeux. We had two hours there, enough time to visit the cathedral and see the famous Bayeux Tapestry. We had a quick breakfast in an old half-timbered house on our way back to the station and then caught a local train for Caen.

Caen was a bigger city with much more to see. We visited one of the old churches and then had a leisurely lunch. En route to the station we visited the other old Norman church. We stopped at Lisseau but were too tired to do much more than sit at a café and look at the people and the old half-timbered houses. We got to Paris and took a bus to Place St.-Michel. Then we bought milk, eggs, bread and cheese and climbed up the stairs to our apartment.

There was no reason why I should have worried about Mother adapting to life in Paris. There was no refrigeration in the kitchen, which meant that shopping had to be done every day. The limited cooking facilities didn't bother her in the least. She spent the first day cleaning. Her luggage arrived and she took over the bedroom. I had made the living room my studio and slept on one of the studio couches.

The second day she got up early and I heard her leave the apartment. When she returned and made breakfast, I asked her where she had been. First, she had visited Notre Dame, then she had found the bird market nearby and visited that, and then she had walked down rue St.-André-des-Arts and had found a wonderful vegetable and meat market. She was puzzled because they didn't cut the meat the way she was used to. She had gotten everything she wanted except baking powder. I don't think I'd realized until then how ideally we were located and how much this would add to Mother's pleasure during the year.

The next day, early, we walked along the Seine to the cathedral. When we entered, Mother asked if it would be sacrilegious for her to light a candle. "Of course not," I told her. I showed her where to buy the candle and how to light it from another and mount it. The Rose Window was especially lovely with the east sun shining through it.

From the cathedral we walked to the bird market, but that day it was a flower market. We purchased a flowering plant that we could put on our balcony and then headed for the Pont Neuf and the Left Bank. The markets were where rue St.-André-des-Arts ends and meets a short street that leads to Boulevard St.-Germain. Everything was a riot of color. Outside the shops, the vegetables were arranged like bouquets, with great care to contrasting colors and shapes.

Mother had her own way of shopping. She knew her vegetables and always picked the best. Holding up the tomatoes she would shout, "Tomatoes! How much?" And the owner would shout back "Tomat!" and the price. Mother had no idea what the price meant, and so she would hand over her money and receive her change and the tomatoes. The market people seemed to like her, perhaps because she knew what she was buying, and they never took advantage of her. Next time she shouted "Tomat," and gradually she learned the names of things.

Meats were a problem which she never quite solved. That day she decided we would have clam chowder. The only recipe she'd learned as a student in Boston was the kind that is made with salt pork, potatoes, onions and milk. First she looked for the clams and glowed with delight when she found big deep sea scollops in their shells. (Anything in shells were clams to her.) Then she had to have salt pork, which didn't seem to exist in any of the shops, certainly not in the one that had a horse's head over it. I think she solved that problem in time, but that day she reluctantly settled for a chunk of bacon.

She was very eager to get some basic kitchen supplies, and we found a wonderful store with all kinds of canned goods. When we had asked earlier where we could find baking powder, we were told to go to an apothecary shop. Mother wasn't convinced, so when we got into this big store she shouted "Baking powder!" (Mother didn't normally shout, but she seemed to feel that people would understand her better if she shouted.) With great dignity, the clerk walked back to the shelf and took down a can of Calumet Baking Powder. This proved, I guess, that there were a lot of Americans in the area. The dairy store with milk, butter and eggs was right across the street from our apartment.

We almost never ate out at a restaurant in Paris, partly because it was too expensive, but also because it would have deprived Mother of her main activity and her justification for being in Paris. She loved to have me invite my friends to dinner, and they, in turn, loved to come. She was used to feeding hungry boys and always cooked ample quantities. She knew nothing about French cooking, and it never entered her mind to do things differently from the way she always had. My friends ate ravenously when they came to dinner, and Mother loved it. Her menu didn't vary much — meat, potatoes, vegetables, sometimes a salad, and apple pie with chunks of cheese. I insisted on having ordinary wine, which was very cheap. She came to like it too, though she always preferred apple cider when we could find it.

After a few days spent getting to know the area around our apartment, we both established a set routine and life style. Mother shopped every morning in the markets we had discovered, and more and more, she would venture across the river to visit Notre Dame or the flower and bird market. In the afternoon she would rest after lunch and then start preparing dinner. I usually worked in my studio until lunch and afterwards, if I had no appointments, went for a walk along the river.

I fell in love with the embankment along the Seine. On the street level the quay was lined with book and music stalls where I found treasures such as an early nineteenth-century volume of all the Beethoven piano works, including those that he wrote at the age of thirteen. There were illuminated manuscripts from the Middle Ages — and sometimes they were authentic!

On the lower level next to the river and on the boats that passed was an entirely different social group of people. The boats were often colorful and each housed a family with its dog. Often they dressed in costumes of the land from which they came, such as Holland and Flanders. Children wearing wooden shoes would play with the family dog as though they were in their backyard. Smaller boats filled with colorful vegetables came down the river. I envied the painters sitting and painting what they saw. Every place to sit or lie down was occupied by old men or drunks who had no place to go. I decided to buy a painting outfit and watch the show. I knew that I had neither the talent nor the patience to be a painter, but I was interested in art and felt that it might help me see what was around me. Mother and I began going for short visits to the Louvre on those days when entrance was free, just to see some special picture or statue that we had come to love. I was very fortunate to have found an apartment in the very center of the city and near to so many of the most beautiful and interesting places to visit. It took only a minute to walk to Sainte-Chapelle or the Louvre, and the left bank was filled with interesting shops. I found the little art galleries on the left bank more interesting, and coveted some of the pictures they sold.

Each week I would buy the *Semaine Musicale* and decide what concerts I wanted to hear. There were free tickets available for students. After the concert a group of us would frequently go to a café and talk over what we had heard. Sometimes we were introduced to celebrities and would feel very important and boast a little. (Once I met James Joyce in such a way and must confess that I more than once said that I knew him, when, of course, I didn't at all.) We did listen to the talk which was often very exciting and, indeed, concerned with important artistic matters. Mother insisted on my going out with friends in the evening, for she felt her presence might inhibit my activities. I suppose it would have, but it made me aware of the fact that I had a situation that was good for work while many students fell into the Bohemian life style of little work and much talk.

By October Nadia Boulanger had moved back to 36 rue Ballu and lessons were again under way. Her apartment was near Montmartre and easily reached by metro, but the walk through the heart of Paris was too beautiful to resist. I would go down the Seine to the Louvre, then to the Palais Royal and the Place du Théâtre Français, and on to the Place de l'Opéra, where I often stopped to get mail and money at the American Express.

The elevator grumbled its way up to her floor, and a maid would let me into the antechamber where I would wait until Mademoiselle called me into her studio. To the left as you entered her studio was a fireplace with a mantelpiece which had been turned into a shrine to Lili Boulanger, Nadia's younger sister, a gifted composer who had died very young. Across the room was a pipe organ. There were two grand pianos, one near the front window, where she gave her lessons, and the other opposite. There were more chairs than usual that were needed for the studio classes. The room was crowded and rather dark except for the front window.

When I came in, there was the usual talk: "Had I had a good week? How was my mother? What was I composing? What concerts had I gone to?" It seemed to me that Mademoiselle was always taking lozenges from a little box. I knew that she got into her studio by five or six in the morning and worked until late at night, and that she lived most of her life sitting at that window teaching or writing letters. Sometimes the maid would bring her a cup of tea and a biscuit.

She never talked about generalities at my lesson, though she sometimes showed me the latest score by Stravinsky and played parts of it on the piano and talked about it. She always got around to my music, playing it through and offering criticisms that were always positive even when they were harsh. I don't think she ever flattered her students. She certainly didn't flatter me. But she had favorites and would go out of her way to forward their reputations. Roger Sessions was very offended by that quality and resented the way she pushed her own students for prizes and undercut students of other teachers. Perhaps it is my natural timidity that has always made me feel doubtful of her reaction to my music. It may well be that I was lucky, for Mademoiselle was always honest and concerned and her lessons made me think and work. What more can one ask from a teacher?

Mademoiselle always had pictures around her. I remember particularly a large reproduction of the Delft harbor by Vermeer which she obviously loved. She once drew my attention to the effect that was achieved by making the sky such a large portion of the space, and then she made the point that time proportions in music could be examined in the same way. That was the nearest she got to generalities, and somehow such talk seemed germane to the lesson. She had advised me to enroll in her counterpoint class at the École Normale de Musique. She didn't suggest that I continue harmony. She didn't mention theory at my lessons. When I left I usually had a letter to mail or a message to deliver, but I always went away feeling challenged.

The Wednesday afternoon class introduced me to many more of her students. There was an English boy named Lennox — now Sir Lennox Berkeley. Israel Citkowitz and Elie Siegmeister were always there. We were all around the same age and often met at concerts or cafés. Now and then older American composers would attend.

Every seminar meeting was aimed at some specific idea. We were told to write a piece for oboe alone and it would be performed. I learned that the oboist had to breathe and that in writing a piece for woodwinds, one imagined the articulation with one's mouth, while with the stringed instruments one imagined the bowing and articulation with one's arm. Mademoiselle would put two students at each piano, each playing a separate part of a Beethoven string quartet. When one considers that there were no recordings, it was a practical way to approach the problem and provided the added experience of reading different clefs at a set tempo. Once Stravinsky visited the class and talked about what I later called "one-part counterpoint" — *i.e.* the trick of breaking a single melodic line into many lines and motives.

During the course of the year, Mademoiselle analyzed all of the Beethoven string quartets in preparation for a spring festival at which they would all be performed. Many of the Wednesday classes were given over to this analysis. It gave a focus to our study and suggested to me ways of handling such a seminar that I would put to good use in later years.

It was during this time that I came to feel that analysis of music should come from an aural experience rather than from a theoretical preconception. As so often in my musical growth, an idea that a teacher expounded took years for me to understand. I don't think I am slow to grasp ideas, but I certainly refuse to accept ideas until I have given them long consideration.

Mlle. Boulanger knew that I was committed to the gamble of being a composer and was surprised when I explained how I had studied the cello seriously for years. She felt that I should not give up the cello too quickly and suggested that I take lessons with a young conservatory student who would be willing to teach me for a very small fee, despite my lack of professional ambitions. His home was on the edge of the Seine, which necessitated a long boat trip. I now feel a little guilty when I think of those lessons and how much they would have meant to a young cellist. If only I had had them when I started studying the instrument! His name was Pierre Fournier.

Why are some people so much more able to learn foreign languages than others? My approach is aural rather than visual, which probably only means that I have never learned to study language properly. My lack is not entirely from laziness, though I have to admit that I lose interest quickly when it comes to learning grammar. I have the greatest respect for — indeed am jealous of — people who can write English beautifully, and I have argued with students that they would compose better music if they could learn to write an elegantly formed paragraph.

I tried to study French at the Berlitz School in Paris (though I really couldn't afford the lessons), but I seemed to get nowhere and dreaded the meetings. At last I gave up and decided to bear the smiles that always came when I spoke French. Of course, I could get along after a fashion, provided I didn't try to talk about anything interesting.

There was one time when my handicap was a help. Arnold Schoenberg came to Paris and gave a lecture on dissonance in music. He read a phonetic translation into French of his paper. The French couldn't understand a word he said (perhaps they didn't want to), but I had little trouble. It sounded like my own French! After the lecture the students went to a café and discussed not only the lecture but the whole business of twelve-tone technique, which was then in the air. Schoenberg's lecture, to the best of my memory, was only about the relative importance of dissonance and consonance.

About this same time we heard a concert featuring a work by Schoenberg and Alban Berg's *Chamber Concerto*. Nadia Boulanger (and that meant many of her students) didn't approve of these composers. Her students referred to them as the "Schoen Berg" and the "Sour Berg." I liked Alban Berg's work better than Schoenberg's.

Most of the orchestras that gave concerts in Paris that winter seemed to me pretty poor, but the programs were often interesting. I went to as many free concerts as I could. I was more interested in the music being played than in the performances, and since I knew so little about contemporary music, there was a lot to hear.

Sometimes concerts turned out to be very funny. There was a soprano who commissioned Ravel and other important French composers to write songs for her and to accompany her at the premieres. It is impossible to describe her voice except to say that we practically burst trying not to laugh. The composers who accompanied her were suffering as we were. The lady seemed totally oblivious to the audience's reaction.

Then, of course, there was the premiere of Antheil's *Ballet mécanique*, a work that used airplane propellers and mechanical pianos and seemed belligerently American. It was a rainy day and we all had umbrellas. We students sat in the balcony and could look down on the audience as one by one they opened their umbrellas — quietly, not making a sound. We students had a field day discussing the work, and there was talk of taking lessons with Antheil. It came as a surprise to me that audiences hissed and cheered sometimes right in the middle of a work. We decided that the French weren't really a very musical people but that they loved a show and insisted on being a part of the action. Even orchestra players, especially the timpanists, seemed unwilling to do what the conductor wanted. It must have been misery for a young conductor.

While I went to most concerts by myself, Mother did occasionally go with me. There were very cheap tickets for the top balcony at the Opéra, and almost anything was new to us. Naturally I was eager to hear the Wagner operas even if they were given in French, which sometimes — especially in *Die Meistersinger*— resulted in very strange mixtures. I can't say I developed into a Wagner enthusiast. We very much enjoyed going to the opera and sometimes were thrilled by performances of such works as Ravel's *Daphnis et Chloé*. We saw a beautiful performance at the Opéra-Comique of Debussy's *Pelléas et Mélisande*.

Although we couldn't go to all of the performances of the Ballets Russes, we loved those that we saw. Koussevitsky came to Paris and conducted a series of orchestral concerts in which works by Aaron Copland and other American composers were included. These concerts were very memorable, not only because of the beautiful performances but because of the works that were played. They began to give me a perspective on American composers that I had never had, and also an awareness of the orchestral challenge to a composer.

My brother Nat arrived in Paris in late September with a girl he had met on the boat. We rented bicycles and made a trip up the north bank of the Seine to Rouen and back along the south bank. Gus and Mollie also visited us in the fall. They had rented rooms with kitchen privileges in someone's house in Berlin and were having trouble adjusting to life there. How they envied us the privacy of our apartment! They were the first to actually look at a picture on our dining room wall and roared with laughter when they discovered it was filled with naked ladies. They felt we should turn the picture to the wall, but Mother and I thought it gave a nice Parisian touch to the place, even though we had never looked at it.

On walks through the streets of the Left Bank I had become fond of several modern painters exhibited in small shops. Had I then realized their worth, I could have paid for my year in France if I had bought their paintings. But even at the low prices, I couldn't afford such a luxury. We loved to go to the Flea Market just to look, not to buy. Many students bought pictures there for their apartments. For twenty-five cents I bought two very small panels painted on wood and signed "Bernard." The market was filled with all kinds of brocaded curtains, copper pots and pans, pictures, and even furniture. Earlier I found an artist's box filled with tubes of paint, a palette and bottles of turpentine and oil and some blank canvases. I never turned out a picture worth looking at, but I enjoyed many lovely sunny afternoons trying.

Gus and Mollie were eager to have us visit them in Berlin at Christmas. Mother and I counted our cash and decided that if we traveled third-class we could just manage the trip. We started out on a train that was going not only to Berlin but also farther east to Poland. It was crowded with people carrying Christmas presents, food for several days, and an incredible amount of smelly baggage. We were lucky to find two seats together. People had to stand in the aisles all the way to Berlin.

After a day and a night on the train, we were awfully glad to find Gus and Mollie waiting for us at the station in Berlin. We had a wonderful reunion because we were all a little lonely. Gus had tickets for performances of Stravinsky's *Firebird* and *Petrouchka*. At last I could see what the music on my records had been written to accompany. The orchestral performances far surpassed those we had heard in Paris.

My brother wasn't a part of a student group as I was in Paris, and I think he missed that experience very much. At the same time that I was turning from playing the cello to composing, he was moving from playing the violin to musical scholarship. Looking back, it seems a pity now that he hadn't registered for courses at the university. However, that had not been possible, given his background. American universities had not yet established graduate programs in musicology.

The great libraries in Berlin were the only outlet that my brother could find for his new interests, and it was during this year that he became so committed to the study of music history. Berlin seemed darker and colder than Paris. I was glad to get back home and to work.

We must have visited every old church in Paris, with Notre Dame, St.-Denis and Ste.-Chapelle taking first place, but St.-Germain-des-Prés, St.-Etienne-du-Mont, and St.-Gervais not ignored. Some churches had a special attraction, such as a beautiful organ or choir, or an historical interest like St.-Sulpice or St.-Clotilde or La Madeleine, or the Panthéon and St.-Julien-le-Pauvre.

Taking advantage of special student railway rates, we made most of our trips outside Paris to see old towns with famous cathedrals like Chartres, Beauvais and Rouen. Having lunch in these smaller towns was our only introduction to French restaurants with *prix fixe* menus. Since we made these trips on weekends, we often ran into small-town fairs. I remember one in Beauvais where the town square was filled with booths selling china, farm produce and even farm animals. Mother bought a coffee set which she treasured to the end of her life.

We made one other venturesome trip with Gus and Mollie to Italy for Easter. My father must have financed it, because we surely didn't have the funds for such a trip. To our surprise, third-class rail travel turned out to be very comfortable, not crowded and difficult as we thought it would be

The train went to Geneva and we stopped for the night at Montreux, and walked to the castle of Chillon not far from the station. The next day we went through the Simplon Tunnel into Italy and on to Milan. We changed trains there and had time to walk to the cathedral from the station. We arrived in Florence in the early morning and met Gus and Mollie at the small pensione we had chosen.

Mollie insists that we saw every church in Florence. I think she was right. We were typical American tourists, on the go every minute and relatively ignorant of everything we saw. We had lots to talk about.

The next day we took the early train to Siena and after lunch a local train to Orvieto, where we had a wonderful dinner with the famous local wine. We arrived in Rome in the late evening. The pensione we had decided on was near the central station, very simple, but pleasant and remarkably quiet.

Gus and I decided to see the city at night and found a bus that took us to the Spanish Stairs. We climbed to the gardens above where we could look out over the lights of the city. We stopped at an outside caffè and had wine while we talked about our studies during the year. He and Mollie were returning to Carleton College and he looked forward to teaching his course in the history of music.

Our visit to Rome was limited to one day, which meant that we could visit only the Forum and St. Peter's. We returned to the pensione for dinner completely exhausted. We took a different route on returning to Florence, stopping in Assisi. That was the high spot for me of our visit to Italy. Fortunately, we had a longer time there. We gathered things for a picnic and took the bus to the Monastery. After we had visited the church and heard beautiful singing, we climbed up the hill and picnicked looking out over the valley.

Since we were all tired and low on cash, we decided to spend the remaining day in Florence. Mother and I would take the night train directly to Paris, and Gus and Mollie would take a train to Venice and then to Berlin.

Our coach went to Paris with only a short stop in Milan. At dawn we were traveling along Lake Maggiore and during the day we had beautiful views of the mountains. We arrived in Paris at about midnight, took a bus to Place St.-Michel, climbed the stairs, and let ourselves into our apartment. How wonderful it felt to be back! We had enjoyed Italy, but we loved Paris.

Our last two months in Paris were very busy and very happy. It was the concert season and also the time of year when the markets were full of spring produce. I felt that I had learned a lot from Mlle. Boulanger and couldn't help but be jealous of those students who were planning to spend another year with her. I hadn't composed anything that was worth keeping, but I knew how serious a decision I had made and how much I needed to work. Nadia Boulanger had filled my head with ideas about music, about teaching, and about how to study. She had made me feel that a composer contributed something very important and that I had an obligation to give myself totally to whatever I did in music. Being an American was not a handicap, but a great opportunity. I may have gained some sophistication, but not at the expense of my real roots. I was still awkward, still timid, but underneath I had a sense of confidence and knew what I wanted to accomplish.

61

A prejudice had developed in my mind — one that I was only vaguely aware of and can hardly trace in memory. I had somehow discovered the music of the seventeenth century and fallen in love with its clarity, imagination and simplicity. What had been the influences? My brother had talked about the great libraries of Berlin. I had discovered the Bibliothèque Nationale and especially the Bibliothèque Ste.-Geneviève, both only a few blocks away. Mademoiselle had shown me the *Fiori Musicali* of Frescobaldi and encouraged me to analyze every note. I had found the works of Corelli and Tartini in the music stalls along the Seine.

I fear, too, that I had come to dislike much of the German music of the late nineteenth century — composers like Reger, Bruckner and to a lesser degree even Mahler, whose music seemed to me overly complicated. 1927 was a year when Stravinsky was embracing neo-classicism. Though I didn't respond very enthusiastically to those scores, they probably still influenced me.

We left in June with Gus and Mollie on a boat that docked in Boston. My father and Martha had driven east to meet us. We looked forward to visiting old friends of my parents in Bryantsville, south of Boston, before driving west to Minneapolis.

CHAPTER VI

1928 - 1930

Bryantsville was the little town where my father had served as pastor during his doctoral studies at Boston University. The Lewises, their best friends, still lived in the old house where they had always lived, and the town and woods looked just as my mother had described them to me when I was a child. On arriving we all went down to the shore and bought a big bucket full of littleneck clams and had a lunch of steamed clams. It was a new experience for Martha and me. I loved them, but Martha had trouble getting them down. Still, it was a perfect introduction to New England.

I had hoped that Gretchen and I could be married that summer. I didn't want to live in the Midwest and thought the best thing would be to get a job on the East Coast, but I had no idea how Gretchen would feel about all this.

About this time I heard that Tilton School for Boys in New Hampshire was looking for someone to direct a new music program. Immediately I made arrangements to meet Dr. George Plimpton, the school's head, in Boston. When we met at the Copley Plaza Hotel, he instantly offered me the job. I was to organize a glee club, play for the chapel and begin a program of general musical activities. Though Dr. Plimpton was very well intentioned, he had no clear idea of what he wanted, except that he wished the school to become known for encouraging music. I have no memory of what salary I was to be paid, but it must have seemed adequate. I was to live in a little house on the campus and to use it also for musical activities.

Since Tilton was on the Boston and Maine Railroad, with direct trains to Boston, Dr. Plimpton suggested I enroll at Harvard and spend a few days each week doing graduate study in music. I found a room near the campus where I could live during the days I was in Cambridge and soon arranged to study composition with Edward Burlingame Hill.

When I got back to Minnesota, I found that Gretchen was vacationing on a lake only a few miles from our place on Lake Mille Lacs, so I immediately went up to visit her. She was studying violin there with Valborg Leland, who was temporarily filling my brother's position at Carleton. I discovered that Gretchen affected me just as intensely as she had before. I don't remember our talking about getting married, but I must have told her about my job at Tilton and my plan to study part-time at Harvard. In retrospect I can easily understand her reluctance to move to Tilton. A new faculty center had been built at Carleton, and she had a very nice room there which she hesitated to give up. The possibility of living in Cambridge never entered our minds.

Our decision to postpone marriage another year depressed me but in no way altered my feelings about Gretchen. It was much later that I recognized her profound interest in scholarship and her desire to learn languages that were basic to her development. (Perhaps even she didn't quite understand this at the time.) She was a fine teacher, enjoyed her work and colleagues at Carleton — more good reasons not to leave Northfield. So I returned east alone, determined to make the year a profitable one.

Tilton was a curious town. A "Mr. Tilton," who had made his money selling leather goods to the Union Army during the Civil War, built a large home in the style of a French château, and across the valley from his house he constructed a triumphal arch under which he planned to be buried. From Italy he imported a lot of metal statues of classical figures with which he lined both banks of the river. He had several mistresses and built small houses for them along the street. It was said that one was still living in a house which was always shuttered and dark. She never went out and people said she was insane. Mr. Tilton learned that triumphal arches weren't so good to be buried under, and so he built himself a proper mausoleum of white stone.

His grandson lived in the big house with his charming wife who loved music and helped me to organize a town chorus. They were delightful people and very active in the life of the small town and the affairs of the Academy.

The town of Franklin was just across the river. Franklin had always voted Democratic, but because old Mr. Tilton was a militant Republican, Tilton became a separate town. The friction between the two towns still continued, mainly over the building of a fence around the graveyard, which they shared. Tilton wanted a stone wall but Franklin wanted an iron fence. I wonder if they ever settled this problem, for there was no fence at all when I was there.

The small house in which I lived had very little furniture and no rugs or pictures. The front room, where I was to teach, had an upright piano, a table and some chairs. I slept in the dining room and in back of that was a kitchen and a bathroom. The four boys who lived on the second floor and ate in the dining hall were none of my concern. The main Academy building (from the nineteenth century) had a large tower in the middle, with dormitory wings branching off each side, and housed the chapel, the dining hall and a large social room. The faculty and their wives lived on each floor of the dormitory and supervised the boys. There was a new gymnasium which served also for dances. Nearer the street a new administration building housed the library, science laboratories and classrooms. It was a pretty campus, located halfway between Concord and Laconia.

I found teaching boys of that age very gratifying. If they are at all interested in music, their enthusiasm is contagious and they are willing to give their best efforts. There were several piano students, but only one was really gifted. He was working his way through school by washing dishes and eventually entered the Massachusetts Institute of Technology. There was another boy who played violin well. While I could not pretend to teach him, I organized a piano trio and we played Niels Gade's *Piano Trio* on a concert.

Because so many boys could play wind instruments, I was able to organize a jazz band. I got out the orchestrations we had used on the boat and we went to work. Fortunately, one boy had a drum set that he could bring from home, and he turned out to be very good. Most American boys at that age liked to play jazz. If one used good arrangements, everyone could participate. We always had an audience when we practiced. There was even an increase in the number of dances scheduled in the gymnasium, since the school no longer needed to hire a dance orchestra. The glee club did so well that we were invited to sing on one of the Boston radio stations, which pleased Dr. Plimpton very much. Though most of the music we sang was light, we did perform a few motets and madrigals for the chapel services. Since there was no school song, I wrote one (now probably long forgotten) and made an arrangement for the glee club. I organized a town chorus, mostly of women, but with a few men, some from the glee club. On one concert we performed Debussy's *La Damoiselle élue* and some choruses from Handel's *Messiah*. So life in Tilton was busy.

Life in Cambridge was busy too. My lessons with Edward Burlingame Hill were held in his studio on the top floor of his home. Hill always composed standing up. He was a lovely person, kindly and perceptive. He didn't have Nadia Boulanger's teaching gifts, nor did I learn as much from him. However, his orderliness made a big impression on me. It was after working with him that I came to realize how valuable a well-organized studio is for a composer, how it expresses his way of working and how people value an artist to the extent that he values himself. During that year (1928) I had one lesson with Georges Enesco and another with Gustav Holst, both of whom visited Harvard. Holst talked to me about his recording of *The Planets* that had meant so much to me and of his interest in a purity of orchestral sound. Enesco was very impressive and made me feel again how much there was to learn.

Because of the limited number of days that I could be in Cambridge, the only class that I could take was Walter Piston's instrumentation course. Like Mademoiselle, Piston taught his course by asking the students to write small pieces for each instrument and then having the pieces performed. It was a good device, but very time-consuming. I often wished that he had talked more about the problems of each instrument.

Like Gretchen earlier at Radcliffe, I came to love Boston very much. I would arrive at North Station at about noon and immediately go to Peroni's or Dine's and have a fifty-cent dinner of clam chowder, crabmeat salad and frozen pudding. My room was in a drab old house very near Memorial Tower, so I spent as little time there as possible. Though I knew only a few students, and none well, I was invited almost every week to play string quartets with Sprague Coolidge. Most of the players performed better than I, but none enjoyed it more. We worked on several of the early Hindemith string quartets and on Turina's *L'Oración del Torero*.

Social life in Tilton was almost nonexistent, with the result that I went on long walks through the beautiful New Hampshire countryside, smoking my pipe and dreaming about things that I wanted to do. Sometimes I got involved in student activities. At Thanksgiving I went with a group up Mt. Kiasarge and spent the night on the top in a cabin built for hikers. It was very cold, and the top of the mountain, which is solid rock, was extremely slippery. The boys were scared to death, and so was I. Still, we managed to get to the cabin and build a warm fire in the wood stove. Getting down the next day was worse because we were not properly equipped for the glaring icy rock. But once we reached the tree line where there was snow on the ground, it was easy going.

The boys played a trick on me when the school hill had a nice bed of snow. We went skiing in the afternoon. I had never worn binders in North Dakota and actually knew nothing about skiing, but I managed to have a good time. After dinner they suggested we ski down the hill in the moonlight and talked me into going first. I didn't know that during dinner they had built a jump part way down the hill. What amazed me more was that I went over it and kept my balance right to the bottom!

The Christmas holiday in Minneapolis and Alexandria was a very unhappy time due to the total friction that now existed between my parents. They were both bitter and Father was suffering from very serious hypertension. I fear that I was gloomy when I visited Gretchen, because I had come to doubt if we would ever be married. I was as deeply in love with her as ever, but I felt that she saw no future for us. I was glad to get back to Tilton.

Next spring I received a letter from Roy Dickinson Welch, head of the music department of Smith College in Northampton, Massachusetts, inviting me to a performance of Monteverdi's *L'Orfeo* at the Academy of Music. Dorothy Smith must have written to him about me. I loved the Monteverdi score and was very eager to hear the performance.

The weekend was most pleasant. Roy Welch and his lovely wife Sylvia went out of their way to be nice to me, introducing me to many of the music faculty at the party they gave after the performance. As I was leaving town, I stopped at the florist's and had flowers sent to Mrs. Welch to thank her for their kindness to me.

It never entered my mind that they were looking me over for a job at the college. The offer came as a complete surprise. I was to sit in on the class that Jacques Pillois would give to the first-year students in harmony, and then I was to teach three other sections exactly as he did.

I also received, at the same time, an offer to head the music department at a large boys' school in Pottstown, Pennsylvania. When I phoned my father and asked him which job I should accept, he replied: "Smith, and thank God for it!" So I told Professor Welch that I would love to join their faculty and informed Dr. Plimpton that I would not be returning to Tilton.

I had made several friends at Tilton. A boy from a nearby farm took care of the furnaces at the school and was passionately eager to learn music. Every morning when he arrived, I would give him a short lesson, which he would quickly absorb. He was big for his age and a little awkward. Whether he ever made any use of the music he learned, I don't know, but his parents were appreciative. I often saw them when I went for long walks. They had in their barn an old grandfather clock that they hated, though it had been handed down to them through generations. I thought it was very beautiful, so they insisted on giving it to me. I persuaded them to let me pay twenty-five dollars for it. A note inside the clock states that it was made by Eli Terry in 1809. Its wooden works had to be replaced and a new ogee base restored to the bottom. It still stands in our house.

Another boy named Philip Gibbs had been pressing me to visit his family in Attleboro, Massachusetts, to learn what a shore dinner was and how to eat a lobster. One weekend we drove to his home, and what a meal we had! I learned how to eat all of the lobster meat and also what elegant bisque can be made from the shucks. His father had invented fiber-reinforced tape for sealing packages. Philip went to the Wharton Business School and is now head of a big company his father started. He is married with eight children.

The summer of 1929 is a jumble in my mind that I cannot sort out. My brother Nat had been married. At one point we drove to Chicago, stopping at Cicero to hear the Coon Sanders' Jazz Band. Nat had bought a big secondhand car and was driving to New Orleans to work for a trade journal of some sort. Gretchen had decided that she wanted to study for her doctorate at Columbia University and planned to go east in the fall. Gretchen and I went east together by train, she to study at Columbia and I to teach at Smith College. I found a room in a big, old-fashioned rooming house that served meals, and moved into my studio, with a beautiful Steinway grand piano, on the top floor of Sage Hall.

Nothing that I had ever experienced could have prepared me for the sophistication of Smith College's faculty and students. Had I not worked with Nadia Boulanger, the seriousness of purpose and the professional level of the music faculty would have overwhelmed me.

Sage Hall in 1929 was a revelation. It was beautifully designed for its function. An impressive front entrance led into a concert hall. The entrance to the teaching part of the building was at the back of the auditorium and led to the first floor and the main office, where Mrs. Leary could tell you in a second what you wanted to know. It was here that the faculty gathered between classes and picked up their mail. Along the corridor and across from the office were four of the largest studios, each with two Steinway grand pianos for the piano faculty. In the first was Arthur Locke, in the second John Duke, in the third Solon Robinson, and in the last Raymond Putman. All were fine concert pianists. At the end of the hall was a large elevator for moving pianos, and doors that led into a four-story wing housing all the practice rooms, most furnished with small Steinway grand pianos. This practice wing was constructed in such a way that one heard very little of the sound in the rest of the building.

The basement, below the office and studios and facing on the Mill River, was divided into classrooms, each with a Steinway grand and blackboards on which the music staff was painted. The basement under the concert hall was given over to a very large classroom for courses in music history and appreciation. Across the hall was a large record collection, carefully housed and indexed, and guarded by Ruth Agnew. Up some stairs were the concert hall restrooms and also Roy Welch's study.

The second floor of the main building had three studios. Leland Hall, a novelist and a very fine pianist who taught music history, had the first; Mabel Garrison, the famous opera singer, had the second; and Miss Rebecca Holmes, who taught violin and conducted the school orchestra, had the third.

Across from these studios was the music library. First came a small seminar room which held the complete works of many composers, important collections such as the *Denkmäler,* and an invaluable collection of duplicate scores that could be used in teaching small classes. Next to this room was the office of the librarian. Beyond that was the large reading room with long tables for readers and book collections along the walls.

The studios on the top floor had dormer windows and were darker and hot in the summer, but wonderfully private and remote. Doris Silbert had the studio at the top of the stairs. Next came the studio of Marion De Ronde, who taught cello. Werner Josten, the professor of composition, was adjacent. At the very end was my studio. Across the hall was first a seminar room with other historical collections and next to that a large room that was used either for big seminars or for social occasions.

One has to keep in mind that Smith was an undergraduate college with an enrollment of about two thousand girls. Music had started as a conservatory at the college but had developed into a department following more the Yale example than the Harvard one. Credit was given for performance lessons. The standards were very high, thus attracting very talented students.

Some distance from Sage Hall was the John M. Green Auditorium

69

which housed a fine pipe organ. It seated over a thousand people and made an ideal hall for the Concert Course that brought several large symphony orchestras and famous performers to Northampton.

Northampton was a lovely quiet town with a long musical tradition. The Academy of Music on the main street had seen many great theater companies in the past and had sponsored concerts by such artists as Jenny Lind. Across the street was the old church of Jonathan Edwards. Forbes Library housed one of the great collections of the nineteenth century with an excellent collection of old music. On Round Hill, located on the opposite side of the campus, was one of the finest schools for the deaf in the country and also many beautiful homes. Across from the college, separated only by Paradise Pond and the Mill River, was "Dippy Hill" with its state mental institution.

It was eight miles across the Connecticut River to Amherst College and the "Cow College" — now the University of Massachusetts. To the south, only a few miles over the notch, stood Mt. Holyoke College for women. There were no superhighways then. Driving north, one came to the beautiful old town of Deerfield. If one drove west on a road that wound through the Berkshires, one passed through lovely villages and came ultimately to Pittsfield and (at a later date) Tanglewood.

The girls dressed very casually in sweaters and skirts, bought at Saks Fifth Avenue but left out in the rain, it was said, to acquire the proper messy look. It was something of a hazard to teach an eight o'clock class because the students would put a raincoat over night clothes and arrive at the last minute. Come Saturday and Sunday, they dressed up for the arrival of the boys visiting from Amherst, Williams or Dartmouth. The students were very bright and many worked very hard. I spent several hours attending Jacques Pillois's classes. (I observed that the girls didn't like being pawed by the old roué.) His harmony teaching was dreadful. It quickly dawned on me that there was nothing in his classes that I should imitate, so I tried to find a serious way to teach those elementary classes.

When I occasionally meet someone who was in my class, she tells me that I scared the students to death. (Not as much as they scared me, I'm sure!) They usually admit that I was very serious about teaching them. Roy Welch never criticized me for not following Jacques Pillois's example. (I suspect he and everyone else on the faculty knew perfectly well what had been going on.)

A New England college like Smith has its own very special social quality which can be difficult for a new faculty member. One is pretty much ignored and left to one's own devices; nobody is unfriendly, but relationships are left to form naturally. The teaching schedule encouraged a freedom of action. Since all of my classes were on the first three days of the week, I could concentrate my work, or be away from the campus. I started teaching at eight on Monday and was finished by noon on Wednesday. Then I could visit Gretchen in New York City or she could come to see me in Northampton. But usually I got into my studio and worked.

I soon got to know Rosamond Foster who also lived in my rooming house. She introduced me to Roger Sessions, who was married to her sister Barbara. I knew all of the music faculty and they were all friendly. However, Roy Welch and Doris Silbert were especially kind to me. Leland Hall probably helped me most professionally that year. The stock-market crash in the fall made me wonder whether I would be kept on at Smith.

A Piano Trio was the first of my works to be publicly performed. It was premiered in Cleveland by the Denoe Leedy Trio and reviewed by Arthur Shepherd in the *Plain Dealer.* I couldn't possibly afford to be at the performance. Shepherd's extremely critical review bothered me a lot, so I wrote to Herbert Elwell of the Cleveland Institute, who had suggested the work. Shepherd soon replied in a forty-page letter! He had re-examined the work carefully, finding some things that he liked very much and others that he did not care for. He also gave me advice as to what direction he thought my music should take. It was a wonderful letter revealing a very great man. Leland Hall, who knew the work and how much I wanted to hear it, organized a trio to play it publicly in Sage Hall. Doris Silbert wrote a long review for the *Northampton Gazette* praising the work.

The fall of 1929 was, of course, an important historical moment in the history of the United States. Fortunately Mr. Morrow, a trustee of Smith College, had put all of the endowment into government bonds and the college weathered the storm of the stock-market crash better than most institutions. A pianist, new to the faculty, and Jacques Pillois were not reappointed, but to my surprise I was. Perhaps Doris Silbert's favorable review had been partly responsible for my reappointment. I took over some of the elementary music courses and was given my own course in musical analysis.

It was obvious to both Gretchen and me that we were so emotionally involved that we should get married. I don't think Gretchen was happy at Columbia. It seemed to her a big factory devoid of contacts with either faculty or students. Her living conditions were grim and the big city increased her sense of apprehension. So we decided to be married at Christmas and move into an apartment I had found on Prospect Street.

Unfortunately, she became quite ill in the late fall and decided to go back to Alexandria. I accompanied her as far as Philadelphia and then saw her leave. On arriving home, she went into the hospital almost immediately for all sorts of tests, only to find that that she was suffering from nervous exhaustion.

That was bad enough, but it was a relief to know that it was nothing more serious. I moved into the apartment and spent almost as miserable a spring as could be imagined. Sometime in February Gretchen went to Battle Creek Sanitarium in Michigan. I went out by bus at the end of March to visit her. It was unusually warm weather and she was able to go for walks with me in the park and sit in the sun. She felt that she was better and that we could plan to be married during the summer and drive east.

When I got back to Northampton, I rented a little white house that would be available for the following academic year. I began to feel that at last my life was going to take shape.

CHAPTER VII

1930 - 1932

GRETCHEN and I were married at her home in Alexandria, Minnesota on September 3, 1930. It was a lovely wedding. Mrs. Ludke had banked the living room with fall flowers that she had collected to protect them from the frost. She had found fresh strawberries and prepared a beautiful wedding luncheon. Our families were all there — Father and Mother, Gus and Mollie, Nat and Flora, and Martha and Walter Davidson with their new baby. Mr. Ludke had given us a new Studebaker as a wedding present, and Mrs. Ludke had bought lovely dresses for Gretchen at a resort branch of Young Quinlan.

In the late afternoon we left with a clatter of cans tied to the back of our car for our first stop at St. Cloud, seventy miles away. Fearing that the drive would be too hard for Gretchen, we had made reservations on a boat that took three days to go from Duluth to Buffalo.

On the boat we had a nice outside cabin, deck chairs and a comfortable place in the dining room. The boat wasn't crowded and the weather was beautiful. It was wonderful not to have to drive through the many cities along the way and to have a restful conclusion to all the days of planning for the wedding.

After landing in Buffalo, we drove only a short distance, stopping at Batavia for the night. Gretchen didn't feel well the next day, so we only drove to Syracuse, then to Albany and finally Northampton. We both felt relieved to find our little house that I had rented was adequately furnished and clean. We had several weeks before the school year started to get acquainted with each other.

A faculty wife faces a difficult period of adjustment unless she comes from the same area. Not only is there very little social life, as I had discovered during my first year at Smith, but the age difference is more obvious than in a larger university. There were brilliant people teaching on the faculty and charming women among the faculty wives, but it took time to get to know them. Some of the faculty wives, who had independent means and who eventually were to become our close friends, seemed at first stiff and arrogant. The adjustment was hard for us, but it was really something that could be solved only with the passing of time.

Mrs. Neilson, the president's wife, made a formal call, but Gretchen had no idea who her guest was until she looked later at the calling card. At first Mrs. Neilson seemed overpowering, but in time we found her charming and friendly. I must admit that Gretchen wasn't well and we had to refuse most invitations. Also, she had neither the strength nor the opportunity to pursue her own interests. Even so, we had a good deal of activity because, as music faculty, we had free tickets to the concert series and went to all the recitals of my colleagues. Solon Robinson and his wife had cocktail parties, which was something new in our lives.

My professional life was the same, but my teaching schedule was heavier. I not only had a new course to teach, but shortly after the start of school, the teacher of Keyboard Harmony became pregnant and I was asked to take over her course, one that I disliked.

My introduction to the analysis of music had developed from my following a recording with a score and marking as I listened to points that seemed important. Later I would try to figure out why each point was interesting. It never entered my mind to read a book about form and match what I heard with what the book said. This method of aural analysis was reinforced by studies with Nadia Boulanger, who used to play a work, demanding that we analyse it as fast as she played. That meant that you had to listen carefully and have at the tip of your tongue the terms to describe the musical event. Roy Welch once asked me to analyse a work for his class. Instead of looking up the analysis in Tovey's *Essays*, I listened carefully and made the class listen carefully too. Such a procedure would have been impossible without recordings.

At this time I found in Leland Hall a very sympathetic musician, a person with ideas that seemed to me truly germinal. He argued that the important things to answer when listening to a work were: "Is it high or is it low?" "Is it loud or is it soft?" "Is it slow or is it fast?" "Is it long or is it short?" Then there are many questions derived from simple factors, such as: "Does the music move rapidly from high to low?" "Is the loudness abrupt or gradual?" He pointed out that Beethoven tended to be abrupt, while Mozart tended to be gradual. "What is the relationship of slow to fast?" he would ask. Listen to the way Bartók leads to the cadencing of sections by slowing down. These factors may not lead to a definitive analysis of a work, but they went further than just naming a bunch of harmonies and cliché cadences.

I began to be known as something of a rebel, which led Arthur Locke to warn me against being critical of colleagues. I am everlastingly grateful to him for talking to me about that problem, since I had no desire or intention to be critical of anybody. It is all too easy to be critical of one's colleagues when you are excited about a new idea. How many colleagues would sit down privately with a young teacher and explain that fact? Smith College had a civilized music faculty, almost free of jealousies and gossip. That was partly because of the tone set by the administration of the school.

William Allen Neilson was one of the great college presidents of his day, and Marjorie Hope Nicolson, who had been one of my lecturers in Freshman English at the University of Minnesota, was as brilliant a dean as ever lived. Both were always available to anyone who wanted to see them. When I asked Neilson if it would be a good idea for me to commute to Yale and study musicology, he said, "Well, Finney, you're a composer aren't you?" Yes, damn it, I was a composer! But how often does the President of a college recognize your ambition? Neilson was a great Shakespeare scholar and Marjorie Nicolson was a leading thinker in the History of Ideas and an authority on Milton. Roy Welch was a brilliant teacher and an excellent administrator. I was lucky.

I had no desire to teach composition. Werner Josten was an excellent teacher, and there were three or four students with real talent. I often wished that I could show Werner my compositions and get his criticism, but he avoided that kind of contact. John Duke, a gifted composer of songs and the pianist who had premiered Roger Sessions' *First Piano Sonata* in New York City, was willing to talk about his works and to look at mine.

I remember most vividly his playing and talking about the Sessions sonata — how desperately Roger worked to meet the concert deadline, sending John a measure or two every day or so. The composition had originally started with what finally became the link from the first movement to the slow movement. John thought the work almost unplayable and tended to be critical of what he thought was a turgid style. I found the style "neoclassic" (How I hate such terms!) and influenced by Stravinsky. I thought the sonata beautifully designed, though I could see why John felt as he did, his own compositions flowing so naturally from his pianistic sense. He performed a piano sonata I had written before my *Piano Sonata in D minor* (published in 1937 in *New Music*). This earlier work was influenced by the Sessions sonata, but in my effort to simplify the texture, I produced a rather sterile statement. John Duke performed it beautifully and, as he always did, entirely from memory.

Gretchen and I decided to spend the winter semester of 1932 in Europe, and Roy Welch, who had received a Guggenheim Fellowship, suggested that we live in Vienna at the Strasser home in Hietzing, where they had found rooms. There was an attic room that we could rent very cheaply. (Hietzing is a wooded residential suburb of Vienna only one stop beyond Schönbrunn.)

The fall passed quickly. After the Christmas festivities we sailed to Italy on the S.S. Roma. We hadn't realized when we booked passage that the ship was scheduled to stop at Casablanca, Gibraltar, Algiers and Palermo before landing at Naples. In Algiers we bought beautiful Moorish tile for a table. It filled a suitcase which I carried until we got back to New York. We spent several days in Naples, not only sight-seeing but also working. Beginning with my earlier student trip to Italy, I had developed a great love for the music of the seventeenth century and had begun to think about copying out manuscripts in European libraries. This new enthusiasm didn't mean that I had less interest in composing, but that I had found in the simplicity and the emotional directness of baroque music a guide to what I wanted to achieve. In the library of the Venice Conservatory I found many interesting manuscripts of unpublished works. The copying of a flute concerto by Francesco Mancini became so time-consuming that I began to think of the possibility of using photography. When we got to Vienna, I looked around for a camera store and discovered the Leica. I was amazed at what it could do. Though I couldn't afford to buy one immediately, I was determined to follow through with my plan. Little did I know what I was letting myself in for!

We took a night train from Venice to Vienna, arriving on a crisp morning. The house — typically Viennese and charming — was very comfortable and served lovely meals. The Strassers were Jewish. The wall in front of their house was already covered with swastikas. A son and a daughter had left for England because of fear of the political situation.

I had planned to study with Egon Wellesz, but he was spending the winter in Cairo. Roy Welch, knowing that Alban Berg lived only a few blocks away, phoned him and arranged for me to meet with Berg the next day. So I went with my scores, rang his bell, and a maid let me in.

Alban Berg was a large and very friendly man. His lessons were like long visits, not organized, but filled with new ideas and suggestions. His piano where he gave lessons was in the living room near the entrance to the house. It was the only room that I saw, and it was furnished as a studio, except that in one corner was a table with many chairs where we always had coffee. He explained that he couldn't meet me every week because he would frequently be out of town, but that he would see me as often as he could. Actually, I was able to see him only eight times during that winter and spring of 1932. My lesson was at three in the afternoon and at five we stopped for coffee. Afterwards we often walked together to the train that connected Hietzing with Vienna. He had a swinging stride and talked all the time. Seeing him was always a pleasure because he was so gracious and friendly.

At my first lesson I showed him a sonata for violin and piano. His reaction puzzled me and taught me something very important. The theme of the first movement had eleven notes of the scale in it. He was very excited about that and pawed through the work, looking for that twelfth note as an important climax point. I knew nothing about twelve-tone technique and hadn't even realized that my theme used eleven notes of the twelve. He explained that he thought I had omitted it in order to make the climax more important.

I learned that I had organized the movement intuitively with no plan in mind. He thought I should know something about twelve-tone technique and advised me to buy Schoenberg's *Wind Quintet,* which had just been published, and to analyse it note by note. He got out his copy and showed me the row on which the work was based. Then he took music paper and copied the row in the four forms it could take: straightforward in black, the retrograde in blue, the inversion in red, and the retrograde-inversion in green. Then he told me that I should make the transpositions on all twelve levels of the scale.

He pointed out that I could either number these levels from one up to twelve, or I could use the diatonic levels (I, N, II, iii, III, IV, MT, V, vi, VI, VII, LT). I look back on this advice as very significant, because in the second suggestion (which I followed) he related the levels of transposition to their tonal implications. It is important to remember, of course, that Schoenberg's *Wind Quintet* is actually very traditional in its formal organization. The diatonic transpositions of the row are more revealing than the chromatic.

Berg thought of the twelve-tone technique as an expansion of the tonal tradition. He never spoke of "a-tonality." Certainly what I got from his teaching was an expansion rather than a revolution of ideas. This expansion moved from the old triadic concept to a new concept of pitch polarity. Berg never again referred to Schoenberg's work or to my analysis. He had given me a suggestion and the rest would be up to me.

The next thing he did in that first lesson shows his sense of humor. He got out Wagner's *Tristan und Isolde* and showed how in the first phrase of the Prelude all twelve notes of the scale had been used, but with some repetitions. He pointed out that one could find two possible rows, depending upon whether one included the harmonization. He chose the row from the melody and said we would now recompose the phrase allowing no repetitions and using the row to dictate the harmony as well.

He played what he had written and leaning back with a smile said, "The Wagner is a good deal better, isn't it?" What effect did this have on me? What did I learn? Well, I learned how one could go about composing music using a twelve-tone row technique that resulted in a harmonic pattern which was contrapuntal and yet just as expressive as a tonal structure. What Berg had written had its own character that was derived from the row he had chosen from Wagner's music.

Finally, Berg asked if I'd like to sit in on the rehearsals that a very young group was having of his *Lyric Suite*. He made arrangements so that I could go as often as I pleased. Since the rehearsals were close by, I went often. I saw him again in about two weeks, and all my subsequent lessons followed a similar pattern. He was very interested in variation forms, especially when based on more than a single theme. He almost never talked about his own music, nor did I have the knowledge to ask him questions. I never met any of his other students. By summer, when we left Vienna for Paris, I felt that I had learned a great deal, but I didn't know just what. It took many years for me to realize how much he had given me.

We were very happy in Vienna, seeing many operas from the Emperor's Box at the State Opera, visiting the museums, going to innumerable concerts, eating at little restaurants, and doing all the things that tourists do. We discovered that we loved to dance and that the orchestra at the Hietzingerhof played waltzes beautifully. I spent many mornings in the Bierstube analyzing Schoenberg and looking at papers, while Gretchen practiced the violin in our room. With the Welches, we tasted the new spring wines and came home pie-eyed. We went on long walks through the Wienerwald, feeling very romantic and sentimental.

I had arranged to study with Nadia Boulanger during the summer, but planned to live in Paris, not in Gargenville. When we got to Paris, Mademoiselle put us in touch with one of her English students who had an apartment to let on rue du Cardinal-Lemoine, a block or so from Place Contrescarpe. It was a rather new building facing a little square filled with chestnut trees. There were two rooms with large windows looking across the city from Notre Dame to the Sacré-Coeur. The little bathroom served also as the kitchen. We were very lucky to get it, for we wanted to be in Paris just the length of time that the student wanted to be away.

The problem was that there was only a single bed. The idea of buying a bed seemed silly, so we bought an oriental rug instead. Each night we would fold up the rug and put the mattress on the floor and the rug on the springs. But there was a grand piano and a harpsichord and Picasso prints on the wall. The student had loaned the harpsichord to Ralph Kirkpatrick, who soon arrived to take it away with him. When he later invited us to a party, we got to know him a little and found that he was also interested in seventeenth-century music.

The chestnuts were in bloom and the streets were festive with people dressed in bright colors. I had talked to Gretchen so much about Paris that the actual arrival could have been an anticlimax for her. But it wasn't. It was our first visit together there. Every time we returned, it would be a joy.

I started composing a piano sonata which was so complex that I later made it into a piano concerto. What caused me to make it so complex? Could it have been the influence of Alban Berg and my fondness for the *Lyric Suite?* Or because the music I had heard in Vienna was usually more complex than any I had heard before? I had started the piece in Vienna, but too late to show to Berg. Looking out on Notre Dame, I would work at the piano every morning and beat my head against that piano sonata, feeling delighted if I moved ahead a measure or two. But what a heavenly place to work!

The whole area around us was interesting. Place Contrescarpe even had a Moroccan shop where we could buy unusual food. The Mosque was only a few blocks away. We often walked there to drink out of the fountain, which was supposed to have health-giving qualities. Sometimes we would have coffee and pastry at the café there and then walk in the opposite direction past the Panthéon to the cafés and restaurants along the "Boul' Mich'."

For the first time we discovered how nice the restaurants were on the left bank. Sometimes we splurged and had dinner at Delpuech, our favorite restaurant on the Place du Théâtre Français, where we could get langouste with mayonnaise and a bottle of Vouvray. Often we would walk the length of the Avenue de l'Opéra and then sit at the Café de la Paix having coffee and a brioche, making it last for an hour so we could look at the passersby. I look upon our stay in Vienna and Paris as our real honeymoon. Gretchen was over her illness and we enjoyed doing everything together.

I saw Mademoiselle occasionally, but we usually talked about teaching and not about my music. I didn't discuss my lessons with Alban Berg with her, since I felt she might be critical. Nor did I show her the piano sonata on which I was working. I again felt the strength of her personality and respected her as much as ever. Frequent lessons were impossible since she was very busy and not often in Paris. At this time it seemed more important for me to discover a routine of daily studio work that would lead to the slow accumulation of new compositions.

The months spent in Europe had given me a great deal: a routine of composing, an interest in old music that I wanted to edit and perform, ideas of musical structure which were completely new to me, and even a certain confidence in my own capacities. Perhaps I was biting off more than I could chew, a common enough experience for a twenty-six-year old. But I had energy, good health, and lots of ambition.

I left Europe with no regrets. I realized what a rich environment Smith College offered me, what a wonderful music library it had, how many excellent amateur musicians lived in the community, and how distinguished the faculty was. What's more, my teaching schedule had been reduced. I was to teach elementary harmony, the analysis course, and a new course for graduate students in the realization of figured bass and the editing of old music. I was looking forward to the challenges ahead.

CHAPTER VIII

1932 - 1937

W HEN we returned to Northampton, we rented an attractive old nineteenth-century house on West Street. It was our first completely unfurnished house. Downstairs were a living room, a dining room, a kitchen with a big cupboard room off of it, and a bedroom and bath. Upstairs were three bedrooms and a small bathroom.

We had very little furniture - a wing chair and an old-fashioned spool-bed with proper springs and mattress. Our first task was to find a matching spool-bed so we could have twin beds in our downstairs bedroom. 1932 was a good time for American antiques, and we scouted the local auctions to buy our secondhand furniture. I bought eight rabbit-ear Windsor chairs for fifty cents a piece and refinished them in black lacquer. We found an old four-poster double bed, painted red with barn paint, and got it upstairs where I spent the year scraping it down to the beautiful maple wood. We had to lengthen it by two feet and have special springs and a mattress installed. We found an old maple slant-top desk and a cherry "high-daddy," both in beautiful shape. Our grandfather clock stood in the entryway. A window in our dining room looked out on an unsightly back porch, so we bought a corner cupboard made of pine, maple and rosewood, which not only blocked out the window, but also held all our dishes.

We found a cherry drop-leaf dining table with two half-circle tables for each end, making it into a banquet table, but it cost seventy-five dollars, which was much more than we could afford. Instead I bought two smaller cherry drop-leaf tables, both very old and in need of refinishing. We still have these lovely antiques that we bought very cheap to furnish our first house.

We felt more a part of the College than we had before. Almost immediately we were invited to parties where sometimes "bathtub gin" was served. I had to ask a friend what it was and how you made it, not that we served it much or even liked it. At least, we weren't quite so green about such things as we had been before! Contrary to popular belief, the faculty was not a heavy-drinking crowd, nor were there a lot of extra-marital relationships. Though "Who's Afraid of Virginia Woolf?" was later filmed at the college only a few blocks from where we had lived, I can think of no plot less descriptive of life there in the thirties. The pace was leisurely, the faculty very professional, and the students very bright.

Northampton was then a small New England village with no strong town-gown feeling. My salary as an instructor was very small, but considering that rib roast and ducklings cost nineteen cents a pound, my salary went about as far then as it ever did. We made musical friends in the surrounding towns of Amherst, South Hadley and Easthampton.

I decided to organize a chamber orchestra that would perform seventeenth- and eighteenth-century music. Roy Welch, who knew of my interest, saw no reason why I shouldn't organize a group as long as it did not use student performers. We performed works I had copied in Europe or had discovered in the library. I had to copy out the instrumental parts for the orchestra, which was made up of a flute, eight violins, two violas, two cellos, and a double bass.

The first concert, on November 23, started with Purcell's "Sonata VI" for strings and harpsichord. Monn's Cello Concerto in G Minor followed, and the program ended with Rosetti's Sinfonia in C. It was such a success that concerts of old music became a yearly part of the Thanksgiving celebration. Over the next five years we gave more and more concerts, always to large audiences. Although we always performed works that I had copied from manuscripts, we also played from printed scores such as Bach cantatas or Vivaldi and Corelli concertos for which there were orchestral parts available.

Was I a good conductor? Perhaps I could have been had I had the proper training. But without that training I had to work too hard to get from the orchestra what I wanted. Leland Hall, the local critic, wrote: "To the interpretation of this music, Mr. Finney brought the enthusiasm it demands, and he imparted this to those who played for him. The audience responded....The music flowed on naturally as the brook flows, sang as the birds sing, and for a while one could revel in the feeling that music is something one may enjoy and need not understand."

I was approached to do more conducting, but only once, some years later, did I venture elsewhere. That was when Arthur Fiedler of the Boston Pops had a heart attack, and I had to conducted my *First Symphony*. Certainly it was a thrill to conduct such a beautiful orchestra, but I had forgotten to put out the cymbal part — and didn't even miss it! I decided then that I would rather hear my music conducted by a professional. Still, I do have some regrets.

At the Yaddo Festival of 1933, John Duke performed my *Piano Sonata in D Minor*. I made new friends and renewed friendships I had formed in Paris in 1927. It was there in Saratoga Springs that I first met John Kirkpatrick, who expressed interest in my piano music. Afterwards, every piano work that I composed up to 1950 was written for, edited by, and performed by him. He became a very close friend, especially after he and his wife Hope joined the faculty of Mt. Holyoke College.

In 1933 I met and became friends with the violinist Gilbert Ross, who was teaching at Cornell University. We persuaded him to join the faculty of Smith College in 1934, where he remained until he accepting a position at the University of Michigan. It was Gilbert who was responsible for my appointment at the University of Michigan in 1949. We have edited Tartini works together, tried our hand at cutting acetate records in the thirties and enjoyed arguing about contemporary music over martinis. He remains to this day my closest friend.

Editing old music has often interested composers, not always so much from a scholarly as from a purely compositional viewpoint. I had neither the temperament nor the training of a scholar, but I had great respect for the clarity of Italian baroque music, and I felt that to edit it to fit the taste of nineteenth-century German audiences was to destroy it. In realizing a figured bass, I sought to enhance rather than complicate the musical statement. The students in my graduate seminar first improvised a realization before they wrote it down. Working out the details of the score often led to an enthusiasm for some "forgotten" composer.

I found that I, too, became committed to the works of certain composers such as Geminiani and couldn't resist involvement in making modern editions. Ultimately, I had the idea of starting a Smith College Music Archives of old music. The treasurer of the college, Mr. Hyde, told me that I could have a small annual budget for such a publication — he called it "Finney's Folly" — and so I prepared Geminiani's twelve *Sonatas for Violin and Continuo,* Op. 1, the first in the series. I not only included the first edition of 1716 but showed the changes Geminiani had made in his second, revised edition of 1739. *The New York Times* (December 1, 1935) reviewed the volume and called the Smith College Music Archives "a commendable achievement, representing much research and labor." Some years later, Manfred Bukofzer, reviewing the whole series, regretted that I had not done more to show the change in ornamentation in the violin part. He was quite right. It was my hope that I had done enough so that other scholars, more concerned with performance practice, would deal with the subject. The second edition of the Geminiani seemed to me less interesting than the first, which was clearer and more simple. There was a degree of freedom in modulations (I thought of them more as "bends"), especially in movements marked "Affettuoso," which deserved greater study.

The most important event in our lives during 1933 was the birth in May of our son Ross. Gretchen was seeing a doctor in Springfield, and when the time arrived, I drove her to a maternity hospital there. The birth was slow, and the doctor didn't want me around to complicate matters, so I returned to Northampton to meet my classes.

I received a telephone call at Sage Hall that Gretchen had given birth to a healthy boy, was resting well, and could see me the next morning. I went over to celebrate with Roy and Sylvia Welch. The next morning when I saw Gretchen, she showed me the baby. He had lots of dark hair; I was told it would not last, but it did. He always had long eyelashes and bushy eyebrows. We thought he was mighty handsome from the very beginning.

For the first week or so a nurse lived in and took care of the baby and our maid did the house work. I hated having so many people around, but it all cleared up in a few days and we settled into our family routine: changing diapers, feeding and burping the baby even in the middle of the night. I learned that when he looked at me with a beatific expression, he was about to throw up.

I heard of someone in Holyoke who, because of the depression, wanted to sell a brand-new Mason and Hamlin grand piano. I bought it for five hundred dollars, one hundred down and forty each month, without interest, which was only a little more than I had paid to rent a piano. I usually composed in my studio in Sage Hall, but I wanted a nice piano at home so we could play chamber music with our faculty colleagues and friends.

Gretchen took Marjorie Nicolson's course in Milton during the winter and found it very interesting. She was also very impressed by how the large class was taught. Miss Nicolson was a little overpowering as an individual. (She was also dean of the college.) During the winter Marjorie invited Gretchen to join her graduate seminar, which met at the Dean's house every Wednesday afternoon. I suspect that Marjorie sensed that Gretchen with her graduate training at Radcliffe, Berkeley and Columbia, was a born scholar and had a command of language that justified her ambition. She may also have noticed that she was at a very crucial point where she needed encouragement and freedom from her demands as a housewife. Columbia had been a bitter disappointment to Gretchen.

We got to know Marjorie gradually. For two years Gretchen went every week to her seminar, always returning with a big piece of the cake that the Dean's housekeeper made. Once Marjorie phoned me and raked me over the coals for not appreciating Gretchen's talent. I was taken aback, but in retrospect I realize that it was a wonderful thing for her to have done. I don't think I was aware of which talent was the most important to Gretchen: playing the violin or scholarly research. In any case, I didn't realize how essential it was for her, at that moment, to break away from the routines that children and husband imposed.

In the first seminar, on Seventeenth-Century Literature, Gretchen chose Milton's "Lycidas" as the subject of her paper. In trying to explain the complex structure of the poem, Marjorie compared its form to Sonata Form in music. I blew my stack at that and insisted that if its form had any relationship to musical form, it would be to seventeenth-century music. So I brought home works of Monteverdi and early operas. When Gretchen discovered that Milton had called "Lycidas" a monody, she became hooked. She was on the track that in twenty years lead to her book *The Musical Backgrounds of English Literature, 1585 - 1630*. Her trip to work in the New York Public Library left me to look after the children. Of course, they got sick, so I wrote *The Game of Harmony* to amuse them. Harcourt, Brace and Company's sales, mostly to women's music clubs, were adequate to supply me with two suits a year. We have always referred to the book as my "two-suiter."

I have not kept any works that I composed before 1933. The decision to settle on 1933, made many years later, was largely imposed on me, since my first published work, my *Piano Sonata in D Minor* (1933), had already been issued in Henry Cowell's *New Music* in 1937.

Once a work is published, it is difficult to disown it, and probably unwise. I composed works after that date that I have not permitted to be published, which was no great problem since publication was rarely available. Photocopies of some of these works are perhaps in libraries here or there. The truth of the matter is that I was involved in so much musical activity that I had not yet reached any real creative stride. But even so, my development would have been even more difficult and painful had I not been in such a wonderfully stimulating and creative environment. Certainly, no "publish or perish" attitude existed at Smith College at that time.

The Depression had hardly touched the college, thanks to the financial wisdom of the administration and the trustees. I was very busy, not so much from my teaching schedule as from the diversity of things I wanted to do. The other work that I composed in 1933 was my *Concerto No. 1 for Violin and Orchestra*. Since then it has gone through a lot of revision, mostly in its orchestration. Though I recognize its faults, I am proud of the work even now. Gilbert Ross gave the only performance, in 1950, with the University of Michigan Symphony Orchestra. Only in the last movement, "Medley," do I find a slight suggestion of the direction I was headed in. The first two movements show my love of the Brahms *Violin Concerto*, but not his skill. The last movement uses a banjo tune "Pretty Polly" and a fiddle tune that I had known for years. In this work a dichotomy became evident: I was confronted with the ambition to compose music with professional skill but also to write music that reflected my American roots.

During the mid-thirties there was a growing feeling that the United States should isolate itself from the political tensions in Europe. One effect of this hysteria was an increased emphasis on American history. A younger group of the faculty wanted to organize an inter-departmental major in American Studies. We were all friends and frequently met to "chew the fat" over a mug of beer. I was interested in giving a course in "Music in America;" Pete Larkin, "Art in America;" Newt Arvin and Dan Aaron, "American Literature;" Bill Christian, "Religion in America;" Ray Billington, "American History;" Otto Kraushaar, "Philosophy in America;" and Dick Ballou, "American Education." It was a distinguished group with friends at Harvard and Yale who visited and gave us their ideas. Each person offered his course in his own department, and the student planned her program with the help of an advisor. This experiment was probably unique in the academic world at that time, and most of these men went on to outstanding careers throughout the country.

To teach a course in "Music in America" was much harder in the 1930's than it is today. There were few recordings, few scores, and only a few studies by men like Oscar G. Sonneck and John Tasker Howard. Howard's *Our American Music* was available as a text, but I felt it lacked an overall view. I wanted to find a focus that could be achieved in a semester course, one that had resulted from long talks with my colleagues and from reading American history and literature. My ignorance was appalling and my scholarship nonexistent, but since the whole subject was so meaningful to me as a composer, I brought a genuine enthusiasm to my teaching which perhaps communicated to the students.

Two problems stood out in my mind: to get students to listen correctly to the American music of the seventeenth and eighteenth centuries one must know the music composed in Europe at the same time. One must also try to understand the diversity of American composers in terms of frontier society. There was the "tinkerer" who experimented; there was the expert who aimed at doing something better than anyone else; there were the propagandists and the cultists; and there were the humorists and the theatrical people. America reflected not only the diversity of them all, but its folk music echoed the diversity of its population.

Assigning the students critical texts to read offered no solution, because music was an art of feeling, not of the exposition of ideas. Besides, few such texts existed. Somehow the music had to be heard. At best, one hoped that the students would gain some slight understanding of how people felt when they sang psalms and hymns, folksongs, or Civil War songs, or that they would come to know what Moravian chamber music or *The Ainsworth Psalter* sounded like. The course was doomed from the start, but it might open up a vast area for scholarship. It might lead to some understanding of the dichotomy that the American composer faced.

I had to get out my guitar and remember the songs I had sung as a child and learn a few that I had not known. Digging out Waldo Selden Pratt's *Music of the Pilgrims*, I learned to sing several of the Psalms with my guitar. Once when Carl Sandburg came to Northampton, he spoke of the Pilgrims as unmusical. He came to our house and I sang him some psalms and he taught me the "Riddle Song" ("I gave my love a cherry that's got no stone"), which I hadn't known. I organized a performance of eighteenth-century Moravian chamber music and learned to play some Gottschalk piano pieces and to sing the songs of Francis Hopkinson. I made the class sing psalms and choral works by Billings and Conrad Beissel from scores projected onto the blackboard. Instead of having an examination, each student could write a paper or give a short recital. In one class we performed the music of A. P. Heinrich, and in another arias from W. F. Fry's opera *Leonora*. But the program that most delighted me was by a student who made a strong case for the jazz musicians of the twenties and actually played a wire recording she had found somewhere in New York City. We did several of Ives' songs from the collection of *114 Songs* that Ives himself had given the library, and a movement from one of his violin sonatas.

It was during this period that my brother Theodore and I started going to the annual convention of the Music Teachers National Association (MTNA). Though Smith College was a special member of some sort, nobody had ever attended these meetings. We found ourselves enjoying the musicologists the most, not only because they gave interesting papers, but also because they knew the best restaurants in the convention cities and always planned an evening get-together away from the meeting hall. I gave some papers for the American Music Section of the MTNA and once organized performances for the meetings. Once when we met in Cleveland, Arthur Shepherd invited us to his home to hear him and the Walden String Quartet perform his *Piano Quintet*.

In 1934 the musicologists organized a separate society — the American Musicological Society — and Smith College joined the next year. Glen Haydon, whom I had known in Vienna, tried to explain to me the breadth of musicology, but I was never completely convinced that a composer belonged to such a group. I suppose that's why eventually I lost interest in it. Actually, I have never been a very good "joiner" of anything, and had it not been for my brother Gus, I might not have joined the A.M.S. in the first place. But I liked and respected the people: Gustave Reese, Otto Kinkeldey, Charles Warren Fox, and the others.

1935 was a year of many changes at Smith College. Roy Welch left to develop a music department at Princeton University. His home was rented by Gilbert Ross, who came to teach violin. Roger Sessions commuted between New York City and Hadley where he rented a little house. Frederick Jacobi lived in Northampton and commuted to teach composition at Juilliard, and his wife Irene, a fine pianist, joined in all kinds of performances, even playing concertos with my chamber orchestra.

Gretchen and I spent the summer of 1935 in Paris, staying at the Hôtel du Danube on rue Jacob. The Ludkes took Ross for the summer, an imposition for which we never quite forgave ourselves. (Ross got impetigo and Gretchen was very worried.) I was working on my *First String Quartet* at the time. The score was finished, but I was not happy with it. I deleted the first two movements, put the third movement first and composed new second and third movements. Even when I look at the score today, I can't figure out what problems were bothering me. Of course we enjoyed Paris, but we were glad to get home and get our lives back to normal.

I studied that fall with Roger Sessions, and one of my lessons was the most important I have ever had. Perhaps that was true because of the trouble I had experienced in composing my string quartet. When I took my *First Sonata for Violin and Piano* for him to criticize, he spent the hour examining it page by page, saying very little. When he came to the last page, he backed away, frowning at it, whipped back to the first page, then back to the last again and said, "Hmm! Now, we'll have tea." Barbara served us a lovely tea, and we had interesting talk, but what on earth had he thought about my score? When I got home I was puzzled. I began to imitate his action, and suddenly it dawned on me that nothing on the first page made the ending inevitable. From that lesson I learned that a composer mustn't delay making clear what his piece is going to be all about. The very first measure or phrase must capture the listener and move him through a time-space to an inevitable ending. It taught me that a student learns not only from his teacher's words but also from his actions.

I have never been able to define what made Roger a great teacher. It was partly his kindness and partly his serious attitude towards his work. He wasn't always very articulate. He might put his finger on a bass note and say "Hmm. Line." If you knew how much importance he put on the bass line, you knew what he meant. At about this same time I drove with him down to Brooklyn to hear a performance of his suite from *The Black Maskers*. On the way home he talked a lot about his new *Concerto for Violin and Orchestra* (some of which was composed on the top floor of Sage Hall) and how it differed from his *First Symphony*. Roger was never inarticulate when talking about music generally.

No one has performed as much of my music as Gilbert Ross. He premiered my *First Sonata for Violin and Piano* at The League of Composers in New York City. I wrote my *Second Sonata for Violin and Piano*, my *Fiddle-Doodle-ad*, and my *Duo for Violin and Piano* for him. With the Stanley Quartet, he premiered my Fourth to Seventh String Quartets. He commissioned and performed my *First Piano Quintet* which he recorded along with my *Sixth String Quartet*. It was a wonderful addition when he and his lovely wife, Gertrude, arrived in Northampton.

Fred and Irene Jacobi had many distinguished house guests, and we were often invited for musical evenings. I remember especially the

Pro Arte Quartet who played works of Anton Webern. They played everything at least twice. I had heard Webern's music in Vienna, but never so well performed. It never made the strong impact on me that Berg's music had, but I became very fond of the *Five Movements for String Quartet*, Op. 5.

Fred was always very liberal with his time and gladly looked over my scores. His advice was always very practical. "Could the instrument play such a passage?" "Was the movement too long?" "Did enough happen to interest the audience?" I remember showing him one piece that was intentionally very static with almost nothing happening for several minutes. I explained that I wanted the piece to be boring. "Oh, no!" he said. "You want to give the impression of monotony. Never be boring!"

Mrs. Neilson asked whether I would be willing to give one of my chamber orchestra concerts in the President's House every fall. The house was beautifully suited for such a concert. There was a big entrance room where the orchestra could play and a winding staircase on which many people could sit. At one end was the spacious living room and at the other end the President's study. Mrs. Neilson thought that such a concert would be festive and a nice way to bring together the faculty. I always included a concerto, and on one occasion Irene Jacobi played a Mozart Piano Concerto.

It is my memory that Werner Josten, who taught composition at Smith, took over the college orchestra when Miss Holmes retired, but he became ill and asked me to assume that responsibility. I built it up into an orchestra that could perform both classical works and such modern works as Prokofiev's *Classical Symphony*. I persuaded performers from nearby towns to join the group. One year Bob and Carol McBride came down from Bennington, adding an oboe and a French horn. We gave the concerts in John M. Greene Hall.

The Jostens were always very nice to us, and it was in their home that we once met Mrs. Franklin D. Roosevelt. They often invited us to their summer home for a week. Though Werner's studio was right next to mine, he never talked about the work he was writing and was not willing to criticize my music, unlike Fred Jacobi.

In 1936 I was thirty years old.

The Composers' Forum-Laboratory asked me to bring down a group to New York and give a concert of my works at the Federal Music Project Headquarters on West 48th Street. (This was the Second Series in the concerts that Ashley Pettis directed.) A slip of paper in the program asked the audience to write down questions for the composer to answer in the discussion that followed. John Duke performed my

Piano Sonata in D Minor, Gilbert Ross and Irene Jacobi my *First Sonata for Violin and Piano,* and the Northampton String Quartet my *First String Quartet.* The audience was large, but I would guess that ninety percent came to find shelter from the cold November weather. Many went to sleep, but some had come to hear the music. The discussion at the end was lively and prolonged, since nobody was eager to leave the warmth of the hall. I felt that the Forum served the double function very well at a time when young American composers needed an audience in the city and when unfortunate people needed shelter.

I spent the spring holiday at Yaddo in Saratoga Springs composing the music for a dance-drama to be performed during the commencement exercises. I lived in the Dutch Tile Room in the old farmhouse that we called "The Brothel." (It had been one in the days of Edgar Allan Poe.) Josephine Herbst and John Cheever were both in residence. When Miss Herbst learned she had received a Guggenheim, she rented an old horse and rode it bareback from the stables to the mansion. I had a studio over the garage, and one day the cook rushed in and told me a tree had fallen on the Swedish forester and could I please rush and help him. I was able to lift the tree a little, and when the ambulance came they freed him. He was as tough as nails and survived without injury. Elizabeth Ames, the Director, came to apologize for the interruption to my Muse. My stay at Yaddo was productive and the dance-drama ("Man and the Masses") got finished and produced.

The other great event of this period of five years was the birth of our second son, Henry. Like Ross he started the process in the middle of the night and took his time about coming. He was a very plump baby with very blond hair and looked more like a baby should. Once again the doctor had to find a formula for feeding him, and we had a nurse in the house. I adjusted to the routine more easily this time, and Henry was very cooperative, eating well, burping beautifully and causing the minimum of nocturnal disturbance.

My works were being more widely performed. In February of 1936 Frederic Tillotson and Norbert Lauga played my *First Sonata for Violin and Piano* at the Longy School in Boston. There was a lot of partying, and I had a chance to again meet people like Piston and Hill. All the papers carried reviews, but one, written by "A.V.B." especially interested me. He wrote:

> The refreshing thing about Ross Finney's Violin Sonata is that it abandons the constantly modulating, over-rich texture of the impressionist for a much more concise, sharply etched style. This music retains, however, the impetuous forward movement, its use here being related to the momentum for its own sake of Stravinsky and

Hindemith. Again one feels a kind of racing from one end of the movement to the other, if somewhat more healthy. And there is again not much leisure to glance at what is going on as one hastens forward, if anything is indeed there to be glanced at. This is well-made music nonetheless. It adheres to a fairly tonal idiom without being too reminiscent.

I have never had much interest in criticism, but I think this critic heard the problem that concerned me. I was glad to find out, many years later, that "A.V.B." was none other than Arthur Berger.

When we drove west to visit our parents, as we did several times during this period, we always followed Route 20 to Buffalo, then proceeded across Canada to Sarnia, and on across Michigan to Ludington, catching a night boat that arrived on the west side of the lake in the early morning. Then we drove across Wisconsin to Minneapolis where my parents lived, and on to Alexandria to visit Gretchen's parents.

We often drove during the evening. We had an enormous basket where we put Henry so he could sleep. On one trip my mother gave us a little black scottie named "Toddy" that we had for many years. Mr. Ludke always gave us a big box of goodies from his grocery warehouse to take home with us.

Father died in 1934, but shortly before his death he was able to see Ross, his only grandchild. Both my brothers were now professionals. Theodore M. Finney, after completing his *History of Music*, became head of the music department of the University of Pittsburgh in 1936. Nat S. Finney was working on the *Minneapolis Star*, but soon moved east to become manager of the Washington Bureau of the Cowles Papers.

We had come to know Archibald and Ada MacLeish who lived on the hill above Conway, only a few miles from Northampton. Archy and I loved to roam the woods and gather mushrooms. Afterwards we would have a wonderful steak fry with the mushrooms we had gathered. Sometimes we would flop in the woods and talk, and once I got a terrible case of poison ivy. I set several of his poems to music during this time. In 1934 the *Five Poems of Archibald MacLeish* was awarded the Connecticut Valley Prize by the Wadsworth Atheneum and the "Friends and Enemies of Modern Music" in Hartford. John Duke and Mabel Garrison performed them at the festival in the Avery Memorial Auditorium. (It was at this same festival that Virgil Thomson's *Four Saints in Three Acts* was premiered.)

In the fall of 1936 I applied for a Guggenheim Fellowship to spend a year in Europe composing. The following April I was notified that I had been granted a fellowship, and almost at the same time received word that I had been awarded the 1937 Pulitzer Scholarship in music. I found that I could, indeed, have both at the same time! The Pulitzer, given for my *First String Quartet,* which had been performed by the Gordon String Quartet, paid fifteen hundred dollars, with medical insurance under a Columbia University Group Insurance. The Guggenheim paid five thousand dollars. We decided to take our car with us to Europe and settle in some place in Switzerland or southern France, both of which were midway between Paris and Italy.

CHAPTER IX

1937 - 1938

WE left for Europe in August sailing on the S.S.
Europa, tourist class but with our Studebaker on
board. Gretchen's Aunt Lane went with us, partly
for a trip to Europe and partly to help Gretchen
with the children. It was a complication that didn't
work out, because we made every effort to avoid
big cities, frustrating Lane's ideas of a European
tour. Our trip was pleasant enough on the boat.
Henry was less than a year old and Ross, at four,
could wander freely asking questions about everything he saw.

We arrived at Cherbourg, unloaded our car,
and packed it for the drive to Switzerland, where
we thought we might spend the year. We avoided
Paris, taking a southerly route to Mont-St.-Michel,
and spending the night at St.-Malo.

The drive down that route was wild, sheep all
over the road at unexpected places, horse-carts
and wagons, people walking to market — a mess
to drive through. Mont-St.-Michel was unbelieva-
bly beautiful, but it demanded a lot of climbing
which Ross loved, of course, but Henry couldn't
manage. Still I wouldn't have missed it for anything. We decided not to cope with a restaurant
meal, and instead had a picnic after we crossed

over to the mainland.

Because of the August holiday, we had a hard time finding a hotel in St.-Malo, and what we did find was in the center of town and very noisy. The boys were hungry, everybody was irritable, and I was exhausted from the driving and felt that our trip was not going to be as idyllic as I had imagined. When we got up the next morning, things seemed brighter, and we were over our low spell from the night before and eager to be on our way.

In order to avoid big cities, we drove south into Brittany and then east, through country as beautiful as anything France has to offer. We stopped in Bourges for the night and had our first proper French dinner after a quick visit to the cathedral. The next day we drove to Geneva and saw the Alps for the first time. Sight-seeing was difficult, and we were in a hurry to get settled for the year at Gstaad where the Jacobis had lived when their children were young. When we arrived there, we were appalled by the prices and a little put off by the stiffness of the place. In fact we couldn't find a reasonable hotel and had to drive to Gsteig, where we found one that we could afford, with a sensational view of the mountains. We decided to stay a few days and catch our breath and figure out what we were going to do.

Our second choice had always been the French Riviera. I wanted to be where I could work, and the formality of Switzerland bothered me. What's more, the winter would be cold, and we had no interest in winter sports. So we decided to return to Montreux and cross over into Italy via the Little St. Bernard Pass. Crossing the mountains was very exciting and not as hard as I had feared. All went well until Aosta, where our car died on us. Finally we found that we had been sold dirty gasoline and would have to have our carburetor cleaned and a new filter installed. I suppose we stopped for the night, but my memory is of driving to Ventimiglia and entering France at Menton.

We fell in love with Menton-Garavan at first sight. The beautiful mountains protected the villas from the northern winds, and the old city, perched on the western point of land, dominated the bay. It seemed to us cozy, protected, and scenic, and there were many small villas that looked as though they would fit our family needs.

We stayed several days in a small pension, perfectly comfortable, except at night when the mosquitos swarmed into our bedroom. Poor Henry hadn't been protected that first night with netting, and he was a sight. The weather was stifling. I feared that it would be that way all winter, but we were told that in early September it would change.

We hunted for a villa that we could rent. The prices were cheap enough, but the villas were enormous and often perched on the top of a cliff overlooking the sea. After only a week of hunting, we found exactly what we wanted: a small villa with its gardens completely surrounded by walls and fences and a lovely terrace overlooking the sea. All the rooms faced south onto the terrace, which was completely protected from the north. The living-dining room and my studio were on the first floor with the kitchen at the back. The bathroom was halfway up the stairs, and the second floor had the masters bedroom and three small bedrooms for the children. We rented the villa until June and moved in.

The first thing we did was to hire Josette to be our cook and housekeeper and her sister, Louisette, to take care of the baby. They were with us the entire year, and we were devoted to them. Josette did most of the shopping and all of the cooking, serving us wonderful dishes that were part Italian and part French. Since there was no refrigeration, she shopped every day, and what we didn't eat she took home to her family. Josette slept in a little back room near the kitchen, and every morning after getting the fresh *croissant* and *petit pain* from the gate, delivered warm from the bakery, she would bring our breakfast to us in our bedroom, dress the children and feed them downstairs, often on the terrace. We bought canned "Lait Gloria" for Henry, though Josette thought it a great extravagance. Both women were very kind, always cheerful, and during the entire year there was little friction.

There was a "Collège" in the center of town in which local children went to school from nine in the morning until four in the afternoon with about an hour and a half for lunch. We found that they would take Ross even though he couldn't speak a word of French, and that he could walk home at noon and have lunch with us. It seemed an awful thing to impose on a four-year-old, but there was a class-room just for that age, and everybody seemed very nice and friendly. So we got him the proper smocks and Josette filled his lunch box, and we drove him to school. There was a café on the sea a block from the school, and we would meet him there every afternoon and drive him home.

It was a toss-up the first month whether Ross would be able to take it. Fortunately he liked the school very much and the French kids liked him. Whenever they saw him they'd waive and call "'ello, Ross!" which in French is one of the most beautiful sounds you can imagine. But in the late afternoon when he got home, he would climb up on an old table under the fig tree and play train with the branches. The main train line ran a block below us, and he could see it from the window in his room. Josette talked French to him, but if we did, he would tell us to stop and sometimes burst into tears. Naturally we worried, until suddenly, instead of talking English as he played train, he began to speak French, as though he were playing with one of the French children in his school. It took him about a month to make that adjustment, which was probably the length of time that it took him to adjust to the school. The children had their recess on the beach, playing games and yelling at the top of their lungs. We would see Ross right in the midst of it having the time of his life, so we knew that he had made the adjustment and was happy with the school. Fortunately, he was in excellent health and began, now and then, to walk the mile to his school, meeting friends on the way.

The school was no kindergarten. His classes, he explained, were in addition and subtraction, language, writing, etc. All the children were Catholic, so he imitated their habits during the religious periods. There was to be a program when all his class would dress as poppies and say verses and sing songs. When we went to the program, we could hardly pick him out from the French children. We judged that he was not always cooperative at his school, since when he shouted to us "Donnez la main!", he gave our hand a brisk slap. He loved to wear a blue sailor suit his mother had made for him, and a black slicker and rain hat to match. No one else had such an outfit, and he thought it was quite American.

Almost every morning Louisette would leave with Henry in a stroller and go for a long walk along the *plage*. Sometimes we would meet them, and he wouldn't recognize us until we spoke to him. One day Josette announced, excitedly, "Madame! Henri marche!" Soon he was crawling and walking and falling down on the terrace, dressed, like all French babies, without diapers. He made great friends with our cat, which we called Madame Olivier. That cat was blind in one eye, certainly not an attractive animal, but it came with the villa. It was not a pet but welcomed us as a part of the menage. At first we worried that it would attract other cats and might scratch the children. "Mais non," said Josette. "Au contraire!" It kept all the other cats off the property and the fights we sometimes heard at night were Madame Olivier driving other cats away. There were cats all over the mountain, and we would be overrun by them were it not for our cat. So Madame Olivier was treated well and fed every day by Josette, and Henry was never bothered by her.

Villa Noël was not on a street. We had to park our car at the bottom of the paved footpath that led with steps up from the street to our villa, and then on to the boulevard above. The wall of our neighbors to the east was covered with bougainvillea. Below us, and next to the railway which was invisible except from our upper windows, was a villa that belonged to a Russian count. All we knew about him was that he liked parsnips. We entered our villa through an iron gate which was kept locked and where all morning deliveries were made. The gate entered into a lower garden where there was a handsome persimmon tree. From the garden, steps led up to our terrace that had a balustrade and looked out onto the Menton harbor. We ate most of our meals there at a metal table with chairs and an umbrella to protect us from the sun. There were, of course, a few rainy days when we ate inside and enjoyed the heat of our radiators.

Gretchen's aunt had a room at the Hôtel Angleterre on the plage where our street ended. She had a lovely view and liked the little hotel, but soon she decided to head north and visit a few places before going back to the States.

We were never bothered by mosquitos. We had no screens, but being up the mountain meant that we usually got a breeze from the Mediterranean. The stagnant weather was over and the fall flowers were pungent after the rains. It was a beautiful climate, and we understood why Menton was called "La Perle de la France." We loved to sit on the terrace in the evening after the boys were in bed and smoke our pipes and listen to the nightingales. I must explain that I smoked only a pipe and could find cheap Virginia pipe tobacco, but American cigarettes for Gretchen were very expensive. Once as a joke I bought her a very cute woman's pipe made of real briar. She didn't think it was a joke at all, but started smoking it instead of cigarettes. It became a part of our lives from that time on.

Right next to our favorite café, where we always met Ross, was the town market, which was especially attractive during the fall when so many fruits and vegetables were on display. We shopped for flowers and berries and lovely small green beans and peas and ripe tomatoes and now and then seafood that looked especially tempting.

Sometimes we'd drive to Nice or Monte Carlo to see an opera or a movie, and when we returned late at night, there would be waiting for us a lunch that Josette had prepared: a ham sandwich and cocoa or a salad of lentils and chard. There weren't many trips that we could make by car, because we were right at the Italian border, and the roads north didn't go anywhere and were very mountainous. We had to drive west either on the coast road or on the high boulevard. I loved the Nice Opera. It was a quaint, old-fashioned, Italian opera house and gave quite good provincial productions, mostly of French operas but sometimes of imported productions that came from northern Europe. More frequently we went to Monte Carlo for dinner and the Ballets Russes.

In the fall I made my first trip to see Gian Francesco Malipiero in

Asola. I had written to the maestro and received a nice letter from his wife, Anna Malipiero. She explained that the maestro didn't really give lessons, but if I could come to their villa at nine in the evening on a certain date, I could spend the evening with him in his studio while he was working. She gently suggested that it would be nice if I could leave with her a payment (very small) so that the maestro was not aware of it.

She told me how to get to Asola by bus from Vincenza and the name of the pension in Asola where I could stay. Since there was a bus that left at six in the evening, I made plans to leave Menton in the early morning and stop at Verona and Padua en route. I especially wanted to see the old seventeenth-century theater in Verona, and in Padua I wanted to go to the library in which the Tartini manuscripts were housed.

I loved Verona and think it one of the most interesting cities in Italy. The Olympia Theater was built with the stage rising towards the back and the streets radiating from the front. This vista makes possible conversations that can be heard by the audience but not by characters on one of the other streets, a situation that explains many of the theatrical devices used by early playwrights.

The Tartini collection is housed in the library of "Il Santo," as St. Anthony's Basilica in Padua is known. The situation was typical of many small Italian libraries. The librarian had spent his life organizing and guarding the collection, hoping one day to do the definitive work on that composer and his music. He was not eager to have anyone else study the music in detail and made it very difficult for visiting scholars to work in the library. The years had gone by, and he had for various reasons never gotten around to doing the study he had planned in his youth. I had my Leica in Menton and hoped to make arrangements to photograph as much as I could, but it was obvious that I would not easily get permission. (I must admit that I have lots of sympathy in retrospect for the old man. Why should a young American just thirty be given such permission anyway? Oh, well! I was young.)

Asola had been the home of Robert and Elizabeth Barrett Browning. It is a beautiful old village located on the top of a hill from which one can hear the bells in the towers (most of which are leaning) in the surrounding lowlands. I had time for a bath and a short nap and a Spartan dinner before appearing at the maestro's villa at nine.

Anna Malipiero let me in and we had time for a nice long visit. I told her about the Tartini manuscripts that I had been unable to see, and she said she'd write to the Vatican authorities and try to get special permission for me. She was English and a devout Catholic and knew every nook and cranny of the countryside around Venice. I slipped her my payment, because, as she explained, she had no idea when I'd be leaving, and she'd be in bed. The maestro would let me out.

Malipiero's studio was the main room of the villa. Its walls were lined with books. There was a large table-desk covered with manuscripts and a large grand piano at which he worked. He gave me a copy of one of his operas (I can't remember which) to study while he worked, and then he ignored me completely. I have no idea what he was working on at the piano. Finally at about midnight he said we'd take the cats for a walk. So we went down into the basement where there were dozens of cats. They gathered around us, and we started off along a path into the countryside. The cats were quite unlike dogs on such a walk, because they kept in formation, tagging along and stopping when we stopped.

We talked about all sorts of things, always in French or English because he could not bear to hear me murder the Italian language which he loved so much. I have never kept a diary, and my memory is not adequate to give details of our conversation. I remember his stopping once and saying, with a grand gesture as though he were in an opera: "You may not have tradition, but you have liberty!" We were talking about the opera he had given me to examine, the production of which was giving him difficulties.

Malipiero was a rather small, wiry man, quite gray, with sudden gestures and unexpected silences. I told him about my eagerness to see the Tartini manuscripts and that his wife was going to try to get permission for me. He said she wouldn't succeed. I said, "Well, if she does I'll take you both to lunch in Vincenza, and if she fails, I'll take you both to lunch anyway."

When we got back to the villa the cats stood in line each to be greeted by name and stroked before being returned to their room. He spent a few minutes looking at the score I had brought, saying very little. The only critical remark he made was that I had written too freely for the trumpet — that it couldn't do anything except "tink, tinka, tink." Then he let me out, and I returned to the pension at about two in the morning.

I saw him several times during the year. Anna Malipiero got permission from the Vatican for me to study and photograph the Tartini manuscripts, and I was left completely alone in the library. I photographed the collection (except for orchestral parts) and developed the film in my hotel room using the night pot to make developer and a pitcher for the fixing solution. The photographs came out quite well, considering all the problems.

Of course I took the Malipieros to lunch in Vincenza, but the maestro would not have lunch before two in the afternoon, and so we spent an enjoyable hour walking around the city. Finally we had dinner at a very special restaurant, and it was worth waiting for. They put me on the train that arrived in Menton in the early morning. I feared I might have trouble with customs at the border because of my photographs, but I didn't. I had trouble with a copy of Milton's *Paradise Lost* I had purchased. I never found out why.

That was the last trip I took to Italy! Anna Malipiero wrote that the police believed I may have taken photographs of military establishments in Padua, and it might be dangerous to return. I feared it may have caused the Malipieros trouble, but she said it had not. With Gilbert Ross I edited one of the concertos, but I never found time to do the bigger study I had planned.

(Since I have mentioned my youthful naïveté, I might add that I made a trip to Pirano a few miles south of Trieste and photographed some of Tartini's manuscripts of theoretical works. Everyone there was very nice to me and interested in the contraption I had made for photographing music, but I left under a cloud, because I caused a short circuit which burned out the lights of the City Hall.)

As we approached the Christmas season, Gretchen and I decided to make a trip to Paris to find presents for the children. We made reservations on the *wagon-lit* and left in the late afternoon, arriving in Paris the next morning.

I had finished my *Sonata in A Minor for Viola and Piano* and was eager to show it to Nadia Boulanger. I felt very good about the ideas that had shaped the work. I had come to feel that tonality was not a matter of triadic harmony but a matter of how the musical material functioned to give spatial shape to time. It seemed to me that much of late-19th-century music, especially German, failed to accomplish such tonal structure for the very reason that composers depended on a triadic explanation of the process and failed to listen to the tonal implications they had set up. To be able to use melody so that it expressed the functions of form without destroying what the French called "la ligne" had been my greatest concern in the sonata, and I wanted to talk to Mademoiselle about my ideas. After meeting with her, I came away feeling that the slow movement was all wrong and completely rewrote it.

Christmas was a great success at Villa Noël in spite of the fact that Josette roasted the turkey we bought without removing the oil sack. We tried to make the holiday as American as we could, but finding a tree to decorate was a hopeless task. The boys liked their toys, and Ross spent hours playing with the French electric train we gave him. It was quite cold and the mountain above us was covered with snow. Even our cat stuck close to the house for warmth. The little coal stove in the kitchen was kept warm all the time, making the small radiators warm enough to take the chill off the rooms.

The flowers on the terrace seemed to thrive in spite of the cold. In early January the sun came out, making it possible to have dinner out of doors if we dressed warmly. The sea was stormy and waves burst over the sidewalk along the plage, making it a little dangerous to walk along the sea wall. Once Gretchen almost ran out in the street in front of a bus. That still gives me nightmares.

January and February were sunny, but the mornings were chilly. Henry was all bundled up in his stroller and looked like a ball of wool when we saw him with Louisette on their walk. Ross seemed to prefer his slicker even if it wasn't raining. He had warm clothes under his smock because the school wasn't heated. The children got chicken pox. Fortunately it didn't develop into anything serious.

In February Gretchen made a trip to Rome. She stayed at a pension at the top of the Spanish Stairs and worked most of the time in the Santa Cecilia Library. While she was working on an article about *Comus* she became interested in the early oratorio and its relationship to Milton's *Samson Agonistes*. It was very cold in Rome and she was glad to get back to Menton, where spring was already beginning.

I particularly recall the smell of the pepper trees that were all around us on the mountain and the yellow mimosa starting to form little yellow balls of blossoms. The evenings were fresh on the terrace, making our pipes even more enjoyable. The song birds sensed the spring, and the frogs began to croak.

In March an American battleship anchored in the bay and we could see its lights reflected in the water. A couple of sailors rang the bell at our gate and visited us for no reason other than they were lonely and couldn't speak French. Ross and Henry were delighted. Later I paddled Ross in a kayak out to see the ship, but suddenly realized that it was too dangerous and turned back. After a few days the ship left, and Menton returned to normal.

Gretchen left to spend the Easter holidays in London at the British Museum. She travelled *wagon-lit* and spent a day in Paris en route. In London she stayed at the pension she knew on Russell Square near the library and worked hard on her *Comus* paper.

Easter was a much bigger event in Menton than Christmas. Great big ginger cookies decorated with colored frosting were in all the bakeries. We bought several and hung them in our garden on the persimmon tree. We thought it would be nice to send Gretchen a big box of fruit and Easter goodies, so we packed one with tangerines and cookies and candy-covered almonds which Ross so loved, and sent it off. She actually received it and enjoyed the smells of southern France that it carried.

Everything ran well, with Josette outdoing herself cooking things we liked. Once she served us a beef stew which we thought delicious though it had a kind of sweet taste that was a little different. I thought it was probably made with horse meat but decided to say nothing about it. After all it tasted good, and Ross liked it, and it was seasoned with all kinds of herbs and had lots of spring vegetables in it. For the first time Henry sat up to the table and ate some of what we ate.

A rabbit casserole was our favorite dish, and Josette explained its problems in detail, showing us that the head of the rabbit must always be visible when you bought it because otherwise it might be a cat. She cut up the rabbit in pieces, covered it with lots of Dijon mustard and chunks of butter and cooked it in the oven. She probably added some wine or cognac and herbs. The result was a dish with a wonderful gravy which one sopped up with bread. Once when she was cooking and had a little glass of cognac waiting to be added, Henry drank it all and wandered around with hiccups for a time.

When Gretchen returned the weather was at its most beautiful. The market was a riot of color with its display of early spring vegetables. We were leaving at the beginning of June, and the thought depressed us and made us take frequent trips to Monte Carlo and up into the mountains that were covered with wildflowers. Gretchen found a dressmaker and ordered several dresses with that distinct French look. But finally we had to pack up the car and head north.

We drove to Cannes and then north through Grasse, Digne, Gap, Grenoble and Chamonix to Argentière, where we spent a few days in a little hotel that looked out over the glaciers of Mont Blanc. Then we crossed into the Rhône valley and north to Montreux and through Interlaken to Lauterbrunnen, where we left the car and went up to the little town of Mürren, with its breath-taking view of the Jungfrau across the valley. It was early spring with the flowers just starting at the edge of patches of snow. After a few days we drove to Lucerne and finally into Germany.

En route to Strasbourg we had car trouble and left the car at a garage to have the carburetor cleaned while we had lunch. We came back to find that they had taken the car apart just to see how it was made, a typical German behavior at this time. Troops of boys in uniform, marched in the street and sang the "Horst Wessel Lied." We gladly left Germany.

We spent a day in Strasbourg visiting the cathedral and exploring the canals. In the cathedral Ross marched up to the altar and crossed himself. It was obvious that some of his schooling would stay with him. Though we didn't look forward to having the children in a big city, our plan was to drive to Paris. But this plan was suddenly changed when a man on a bicycle drove too close to our car and was spilled. He was tipsy and fortunately not hurt, nor was his bicycle damaged. So we gave up the idea of visiting Paris and turned north into Belgium, driving to Middelburg in Holland to rest before going on to London. In Veere, a few miles north on the coast, we found a lovely hotel with a big garden in which the children could play without our worrying. The food was simple but very good. We could hear the bells of Long Jon tolling across the fields, but not loud enough to keep us awake at night. Henry was a little better on his legs and could play some with Ross. Suddenly there were lots of children playing in the yard, all speaking different languages, but somehow communicating very adequately. It was nice to rest and watch the children play.

Finally we drove to Bruges for a night, crossing by ferryboat from Vlissingen. Next day we loaded our car on a boat at Ostende and crossed to Dover. We were lucky to find a room at the Garden House in Cambridge where we could rent a boat and pole along the Cam through the colleges. The only thing I remember about London was that Henry demanded that catsup be put over everything he ate for "un petit peu de goût." Our main concern was to get our car to Southampton and load it on the "Bremen" for our trip back to New York.

When we got back to Northampton, we rented a house on Massasoit Street next door to where the Calvin Coolidges had lived, and moved in before driving on west to visit our parents.

CHAPTER X

1938 - 1944

THE next few years were difficult for everyone. The tensions of the Great Depression had passed, but in their place were tensions that had arisen from the growing political problems in Europe. We were conscious of the Nazi military preparations because of our trip through Germany, and we began to fear that the United States could not avoid involvement in another European conflict.

During our year's absence many of our closest friends were attracted away to important positions, and we missed them very much. The environment was slowly changing. William Allen Neilson retired as president of Smith College and was followed for an interim year by Mrs. Dwight Morrow, and then finally by Herbert Davis, a famous English scholar. Roy Welch stayed at Princeton University and built the music department into one of the finest in the country. Marjorie Nicolson held a visiting appointment at Columbia University for a year and then accepted the permanent appointment as head of the graduate division of the English Department. Hallie Flanagan Davis, who had organized the WPA Federal Theatre Project, came to Smith both as Dean of the college and head of the Theater Department.

It is surprising that I was so productive as a composer during these years. I had learned a routine that kept my creative life completely separated from my teaching. The pressure to support my family led me to adding part-time appointments at surrounding colleges. Various institutions offered me interesting administrative appointments that were financially attractive, but I realized that if I moved in that direction my life as a composer would be jeopardized. I had been promoted to Associate Professor and was very happy at Smith College where we still had many friends who were professionally distinguished and every opportunity to develop our talents.

A new Dean's House was built next to the President's House overlooking Paradise Pond. The McCallum House was purchased by the college and turned into faculty apartments. A new Faculty Club, where unusually good meals were served, was established in an old house near Sage Hall, and a very lovely Alumnae House was built across from College Hall. These changes didn't take place at the same time, of course, but were near enough together to be confusing.

The Boston Symphony Orchestra gave concerts every year in Northampton en route to New York City and always played the new works that were being premiered. Roy Harris' *Fifth Symphony* was performed, and Roy stayed with us. As always, he was full of ideas. He wanted this symphony to be one continuous melodic line, making the work a song. Even if one didn't completely agree with his ideas, it was fun to hear him talk, because he was so totally committed and spontaneous. The Berg *Violin Concerto* was performed about this time and was one of the most important experiences of my musical life, for in it I found that contemporary understanding of tonal design that had so recently dominated my thinking. The ending of that concerto is as beautiful an example of function related to pitch polarity which I know.

The mood of isolationism coupled with the increased demands on my time had, of course, an effect on my creative production, both in the amount and quality of what I wrote. I had turned increasingly to "Americana," both popular and folk, not always using material that was a part of my own Middle Western background, and the result was a superficiality that made the music unconvincing. Most of these works composed between 1938 and 1942 are not now available, but several are published. Only two works seem to me of interest today: *Three 17th-Century Lyrics*, obviously influenced by Gretchen's interests, and *Fantasy for Piano*, composed for and performed by John Kirkpatrick.

There were important performances of the works that I have since destroyed. John Duke played my "Concertino" for piano and orchestra at the Boston Pops in 1942 and at a festival the same year at Woodstock,

New York. My "Overture for a Drama" was performed at the Eastman Festival in Rochester, New York, and by the New England Conservatory of Music under Quincy Porter. I remember this latter performance with some amusement since the tuba player had to report suddenly for military service and a substitute took over without rehearsal and was lost throughout the piece, blasting out bass notes at the most unexpected moments.

The Fourth Series of the Composers' Forum-Laboratory (March 1, 1939) included my *Sonata in A Minor for Viola and Piano* and my *Piano Trio in D Minor*. John Duke and I shared a concert at the World's Fair in New York on which my *Fantasy for Piano, Five Poems by Archibald MacLeish* and *Piano Trio in D Minor* were all performed.

Pearl Harbor marked an immediate change for me, just as it did for everyone else of my age. My *Piano Sonata No. 3 in E*, also composed for John Kirkpatrick, marked an abrupt return to the musical ideas that dominated the composition of my *Sonata in A Minor* for viola and piano. My *Symphony No. 1 ("Communiqué 1943")* blended those two interests without actually using any folk material.

I had visited Dimitri Mitropoulos in Minneapolis and had shown him my "Overture for a Drama," which he hadn't liked very much. But he was very taken with the slow movement of a sonata for cello and piano I had written and said if I would arrange it for string orchestra, he would perform it. This resulted in *Slow Piece*, which the Minneapolis Symphony performed in 1941.

Mitropoulos took the time to explain to me why he did not like my overture. He felt that I doubled too much, extinguishing the tone color of the instruments. He thought that a work should either be very popular or very complex, a viewpoint with which I did not agree. He was the first person to convey to me that to compose was to perform and that a composer should hear and physically feel his music the way a conductor does. His performance of *Slow Piece* and the audience's reception were gratifying, and I went home feeling a little more like a professional.

President Davis gained the undeserved reputation of wanting to see the United States join in the European conflict. When the first faculty meeting was held in the new Alumnae House, the faculty was tense for two reasons: (1) they were afraid their isolationist viewpoint would be ignored by the president, and (2) a dreadful hurricane was raging outside, with trees crashing all around. Of course it was better for us to be inside than out, but our academic calm was somewhat shaken. (When we finally finished, I found that my car had not been damaged, but that Elm Street was covered with branches and fallen trees. When I got home, I discovered that no damage had occurred there.) I liked Herbert Davis very much. He was a civilized and charming person. It was true, however, that he tended to say yes to every request and to get himself embroiled in all sorts of misunderstandings. His wife was an equally lovely person, convinced that faculty parties should be completely unplanned and informal, which of course never works. Hallie Flanagan Davis viewed the college environment as a "living theater project," which sometimes antagonized the faculty. The old "benevolent despot" atmosphere was gone and with it some of the comaraderie of the faculty. I got more involved in faculty shows, which were fun but also a great waste of time. Time was becoming the most precious item of all, and it remained so during my entire academic career.

My sons were becoming more and more active and demanding. It seems to me I was always in a hurry. I remember walking down Elm Street with Ross holding my hand and practically flying through the air to keep up. Were the times that frenetic, or had I not yet learned to say "no"?

It was not only the pressure for more income that made me take on added commitments, but also, I suspect, the gratification to my ego. I taught at Mt. Holyoke College from 1940 to 1944, and was chairman of the theory department at the Hartt School of Music in Hartford in 1941-42. I taught composition to a few local people, putting anything I earned into my "sock." I sang madrigals with an Amherst group and conducted the Smith College Orchestra.

Perhaps this is as good a place as any to explain my "sock." I had decided that if I had to teach in a college to make a living, then any money "rolling-up-a-hill," as they say, would not go into the general hopper but would be spent on something that would be fun or would forward my reputation as a composer. Therefore such money went into a sock that I kept in my dresser drawer. When I had accumulated twenty bucks, Gretchen and I would drive to New York for three days. We would stay two nights at a hotel, go to a supper club, see a couple of plays, and return the third day with presents for the boys. No concerts! Over the years my "sock" has grown into a sizeable bank account and includes all the money I make as a composer from ASCAP, publishing royalties, commissions, etc.

John Kirkpatrick joined the faculty of Mt. Holyoke College around this time, making closer a friendship that has lasted for years. John Verrall, whom I had known in Minneapolis, also joined that faculty. We decided to start a press for contemporary music written by composers in the Connecticut River Valley, and named it The Valley Music Press. The first publications were my *Slow Piece* and Verrall's *String Trio*. My

Piano Sonata No. 3 was published in 1945, with John Kirkpatrick's editings. Many of the young composers we published were friends (at least before we published them) such as Robert Palmer, Elliott Carter, Hunter Johnson, John Duke, etc.

I have had a special feeling for little presses, though I have come to realize that they are not always as helpful for the composer as I had first hoped. The two colleges jointly financed our venture, which is now called The New Valley Press and is entirely sponsored by Smith College. The problem is always distribution, and how to make the music available through music stores so that they can make a profit. At least I learned a lot about publication. I also owe both Kirkpatrick and Verrall a great debt, because they, more than any others, kept me from sinking too deeply into the Americana phase of my work.

In 1940 Gretchen and I decided to build a house. We found a lot on Ward Avenue that had a lovely view of Mt. Tom. It wasn't wide, but it was very long, running all the way back to the Mill River that made Paradise Pond. We had been thinking for some years of plans for a house, and were interested in modern, pre-fabricated houses. In fact, such plans had been mailed to us in Menton, and the French police had visited us thinking we were involved in some kind of fortifications! Perhaps fortunately, nothing worked out, and we finally got in touch with a Springfield contractor whose architect did the plans for us.

It was a rather conventional New England house with redwood clapboards which were left their natural colors and oiled. Each boy had his own room with shutters on the inside that could be closed to darken the room at bedtime. Our bedroom had a bathroom and also a fireplace with comfortable chairs in front of it and large clothes closets on both sides. Big windows looked out on the twin oaks and the view towards Mt. Tom. My studio was at the end and over the heated garage, and I bought an upright piano that was close to my desk. There was a guest room. On the first floor under our bedroom was a large living room with a fireplace and a big plate-glass window looking out on a terrace that framed our view. Off of the living room and back of the garage was a screened porch opening onto the back terrace. At the other end of the house was a dining room connected to a breakfast room and the kitchen. A bathroom and a maid's room were across the entrance hall. A big basement contained the laundry, the boy's playroom, and a utility room.

It turned out to be a very comfortable house and also a very good investment. We planted hundreds of little pine trees below the hill and back to the river, only a few of which lived and matured. But that lot is now filled with pines.

For the first time we had neighbors and a wonderful place for the boys to play. The back hill had a big patch of blackberries. Our best friends were Robert and Jane Remy, a young architect and his wife who built across the street. There were many lovely houses on the street such as the new house that Mrs. Coolidge built after the president's death. Each day I would walk to school on the path that wound along the river to Paradise Pond. Ross' grade school was a block away. It was a typical New England small-town atmosphere.

Smith College started a summer music school in the thirties and I taught many summers for a salary of fifty dollars. During this session I taught composition to a small but talented group of students. We all enjoyed the summer, even though the pay wasn't very good. Gilbert Ross conducted the orchestra and Victor Prahl the chorus. Though not large, the student body was very stimulating since it was largely made up of older people who found it an enjoyable way to spend the summer. We sent the boys to Little Sirecho Camp up the Connecticut River in northern New Hampshire. That way the boys had an outing and we had a chance to relax.

About 1940 we persuaded President Davis to offer the Neilson Chair to Alfred Einstein, who was stranded with his family in Italy. Things were dangerous for him, but unless he had a job, he couldn't be admitted to the United States. He arrived with his ladies: his wife, his sister and his daughter. He couldn't speak English well, and so his seminar, which was on the Italian frottola, was taken only by members of the faculty.

The first evening was a scream! He started to read his lecture, his three ladies seated in the front row ready to help him with English. Several of the faculty members immediately protested. We didn't want just to hear about the frottola; we wanted to know what the music sounded like. So without further ado a performing group of singers and instrumental players was organized. Instead of a lecture, it became a free-for-all, in which we edited and made parts for performance. Einstein loved this procedure, and would talk informally about the music after we had performed it several times. I immediately persuaded him to do the next volume of the Smith College Music Archives on the frottola.

Alfred Einstein had a wonderful sense of humor and was totally free of pomposity. He was intrigued and delighted when some youngsters called him a "nincompoop," and when someone told him "not to tear himself out of shape" over something, he could hardly stop laughing. He made a collection of things he had picked up as he walked across the campus on his way home — class notes, gloves, examination papers, an assortment of everything that one can imagine. He worked in his small study in the practice wing of the music building, and loved to have us stop in and talk to him about the Mozart book he was writing or about anything that was on our minds. He had just heard a performance of my *Bleheris*, a setting of a MacLeish text for tenor and small orchestra. He admired the simplicity of the setting and urged me not to worry about criticism — remarks which, coming from Berlin's most eminent critic, were encouraging.

Taking our cue, he planned his next seminar, on the Italian Madrigal, to have much less talking and more singing. At that time he was working on his monumental three-volume study of the Italian Madrigal that was to be published by the Princeton University Press in 1949. He had copied hundreds of scores of early Italian instrumental and vocal music and eventually gave the entire collection to the Smith College Music Library. Students began to enroll in his seminar and to do their graduate theses under his direction.

Everett Helm was making an edition of Arcadelt's chansons for the Archives and visited us, typing all night in our guest room, much to Gretchen's displeasure. (He had been a student of Gretchen's at Carleton College.) He asked me for a letter of recommendation "To Whom It May Concern" and proceeded to use it to try to get a small, visiting job that Einstein then held at the Hartt School of Music. He didn't succeed, of course, but it taught me never to write such letters that could be used in ways that I would not approve.

Attitudes changed abruptly after Pearl Harbor. The children of F. P. Wilson, a friend of President Davis and a famous English scholar, came to live in the President's house at the outbreak of the war. Isolationism was by then, of course, a dead issue. Everybody had a garden. The college made plots available at the bottom of Dippy Hill, and I planted my own garden. I also started to raise chickens at the bottom of our hill, and Ross and Henry took care of them. I hate chickens — that is, raising them, not eating them! They stink and they are cannibals. The boys got up very early and fed and watered them, and every week went through the process of preparing one for Sunday dinner. I doubt if they look back on the experience with pleasure, but it taught them the routine of work and gave them more respect for farmers.

We had also started a small garden at the bottom of our own hill, but because of a woodchuck we got little produce. We never did succeed in exterminating that woodchuck, but the boys enjoyed our attempts. Working on our garden on Dippy Hill gave nobody any pleasure, but it produced quite a lot of things to put by for the winter. Our chickens, however, began to lay eggs like crazy. I didn't feel we should sell them, so we ate a lot of them and stored the rest in waterglass for the winter.

The children went to their summer camp by train, but when we visited them, we took our bicycles in the baggage car to Windsor, Vermont, and went the rest of the way on our own power. We spent the night at the Hanover Inn across from the Dartmouth campus and had dinner on the terrace listening to the men sing songs (mostly arrangements by Fred Waring) while they trained for the service. The next day we stopped at Haverhill, New Hampshire, at an old inn where we had wonderful New England baked beans. From there we visited Little Sirecho Camp. Henry was almost too young for camp, but Ross worked his way through by doing camp jobs.

Several summers we were able to save up enough gasoline to drive to Gloucester for a week or two, renting a cottage near the glue factory. We all loved to eat crab meat and sun on the beach, and the boys loved the sand and the water.

During the year Gretchen attended first-aid classes and made blackout curtains for the house. The Alumnae House was turned into the headquarters of the "Waves," and the girls, dressed in fancy uniforms, would sing "I need a guy to tie my tie." The boys from Amherst and everywhere else were enlisting, and there were many marriages. The students at Smith were restless, of course, and so were the younger members of the faculty.

Gilbert Ross spent a year at the University of Michigan. When he returned for the summer, he had been offered a permanent job there, but wasn't sure whether to accept it because of some unpleasant friction with the previous violin teacher. He did finally decide to leave, and so I lost one of my closest friends. Others left to become officers in the army or navy. Archibald MacLeish thought I might be interested in the Office of Strategic Services (OSS) because of my photography experiences in Europe. Since I was pretty near the limit of the draft age, it seemed wiser to wait and see what happened.

The effect of our involvement in the conflict was immediately apparent in my work. I wrote my *Symphony No. 1 ("Communiqué 1943")* very rapidly in the weeks following Pearl Harbor. It is a work so directly reflective of the feelings and attitudes of a young person at that time that people today don't quite understand it. Young people today have no knowledge and, indeed, no sympathy for the feelings of that earlier generation. Perhaps one would call it a "dated" work, but it was sincere and to a small degree programmatic. I think it was also well written, except that the orchestration demanded later revision.

The dichotomy that had been bothering me for a decade now

dissolved into insignificance. The movements of the symphony are all built as free variations on a single thematic idea which has its roots in American song. The work demanded to be the way it was; it had its own life and its own shape. I conducted three movements at the Boston Pops in 1944, but the whole work was not premiered until 1962 when it was also recorded by the Louisville Orchestra. Their recording is good, but the work, by then, belonged to the past.

Almost immediately I composed *Hymn, Fuguing, and Holiday*, using as a theme for the variations the hymn tune "Berlin" by William Billings. Everything in the work is in some way a variation, sometimes fairly traditional, sometimes very free, reflecting the ideas that Alban Berg had generated in my lessons.

In the spring of 1944 my neighbor, Bob Remy, and I had to go to Springfield to undergo our physical examinations for the draft. Our pullets were laying so many eggs that, although we gave away as many as we could, we also ate them scrambled, in omelets, in custards, and in every other way Gretchen could devise. So I came down with a beautiful sulphur rash. You can imagine how I looked when I stripped for the examination. Everything went well until I came to the psychiatrist. He asked, "What do you do?" "I teach at Smith College." "That's a girl's school, isn't it? What do you teach?" "Music," I replied. With each question he got glummer and looked with more concentration at my rash. When it was all over, Bob and I found that we were both rejected. Our wives laughed at us. They were delighted. The only difference it made was that I went into OSS at a much higher rank and with a higher monthly income than I would have had as a Private First Class.

CHAPTER XI

ENGLAND 1944

I had known for some time that I would probably join the Office of Strategic Services in some capacity whether I was drafted or not. I was asked to serve with the Interdepartmental Committee for the Acquisition of Foreign Publications (IDC) and went to Washington in June to be inducted into that service. I had no idea, of course, where service would take me. They talked a lot about China, but I didn't think they could be quite that stupid since I had no qualifications at all for service in the Orient.

IDC was set up to serve any branch of the government — any request for published material all the way from medical books to maps, and from scientific papers to song copyrights etc. We had not only to locate the printed material, but also often to photograph it as well. Therefore part of the job required me to set up a photographic laboratory. Newspapers were basic, but so were city directories and even telephone books. I had to go through another physical examination. We were given lectures on how to "cover" our main activity. When they learned that I sang American folksongs with a guitar, they urged me to take the instrument with me, since it would serve as an excellent "cover" for what I was doing. I didn't feel I'd be very contributive to IDC. I was no linguist, but I would give it my best.

That spring was also complicated by an offer to head the music department of Connecticut College for Women in New London. Gretchen and I visited the campus and found much that pleased us. I wasn't really interested in administration. In fact, the University of Illinois had once approached me to head their School of Music and conduct their orchestra, but I felt even then that such a position would end my career as a composer.

Finally I was called in July to New York City for embarkation. Marjorie Nicolson invited us to stay with her while I went through all the details of getting my uniform (I was a civilian Captain), my papers and passport, my gas mask and military equipment. Then I had to report on a certain night at one of the naval piers, with no idea when or where I would sail.

I wasn't permitted to send any letters that included the name of the ship, but I did write Gretchen that she should read about President Wilson's trip to Europe at the end of World War I, and it didn't take her long to figure out that I was on the old S.S. Washington.

I was on the top deck in a stateroom for about eight men but with little deck space. The ship was packed mostly with paratroopers who had their hair shaved off except for a ridge right down the middle. They looked like Indians and were a rambunctious lot, all boys about eighteen acting tough to hide their fears. They sang all the time and often very well. One quartet of black paratroopers sang with remarkable originality. It was a delight to listen to them. But when the whole ship got going on this Paratroopers' Song (Sung to the tune of "Glory, Glory Hallelujah") the air vibrated:

(Chorus)

Gory, Gory, What a hell of a way to die,
Gory, Gory, What a hell of a way to die,
Gory, Gory, What a hell of a way to die,
He ain't gonna jump no more.

(Verses)

Is everybody happy? Cried the Sergeant looking up.
Our hero meekly answered yes and then they stood him
    up.
He yawped right out into the blast, his static line
    unhooked.
He ain't gonna jump no more.

He counted loud, he counted long, he waited for the
    shock.
He felt the wind, he felt the clouds, he felt the awful drop.
He jerked the cord, the silk spilled out and wrapped
    around his legs.
He ain't gonna jump no more.

Risers wrapped around his neck, connectors cracked his
    dome.
The lines were snarled and tied in knots around his skinny
    bones.
His canopy became his shroud, he hurtled to the ground.
He ain't gonna jump no more.

The ambulance was on the spot, the jeeps were running
    wild.
The medics jumped and screamed with glee, rolled up their
    sleeves and smiled,
For it had been a week or more since last a chute had
    failed.
He ain't gonna jump no more.

He hit the ground, the sound was "SPLAT," the blood went
    spurting high.
His comrades then were heard to say "A helluva way to
    die."
He lay there rolling 'round in a welter of his gore.
He ain't gonna jump no more.

There was blood upon the risors, there were brains upon the
    chute.
Intestines were dangling from his paratrooper's boots.
They picked him up still in his chute and poured him from
    his boots.
He ain't gonna jump no more.

When the ship joined the convoy, things quieted down a lot. There
hadn't been any submarine attacks for some time, but you could never
predict what might happen, and regulations were strict. Fortunately the
weather was beautiful all across the Atlantic, and the trip, as far as I
know, was totally eventless.

I had a small spot on the deck and took the occasion to read *War
and Peace*, which I'd always wanted to read but had never had time to
tackle. I forget how many days it took the convoy to cross to Liverpool,
but it seemed no time at all. Lights had not been allowed on ship so
arriving in complete darkness didn't seem strange. We boarded a train
for London and arrived in the early morning.

When I immediately went to the office of IDC on Brook Street near the Embassy to get my check and my billeting, I found that some guy in Washington had failed to take care of anything. We were all in the same boat and mad as hell. I met Harold Deutsch from the University of Minnesota who was to be head of the OSS Research and Analysis office in Paris and Ralph Carruthers, from the New York Public Library, the head of IDC in London. They were my bosses, and I liked them both. Ralph looked pale, but who wouldn't, working all day in a subbasement?

My per diem was nineteen dollars a week, and Ralph told me that I could either join several other men and rent a flat or, if I preferred, find a single room in or near London. He thought it would be wise to be near the office for a week or so until I had all the necessary PX and ration papers and had established an account at a bank. Someone I met at a restaurant said he had a room across from Claridge's and above a very good pub and that the room next to his would be vacant in a day or so. On inquiring, I was able to get a relatively quiet room on the third floor with lots of light. The door to the building was on Molton Street only a block from IDC. It wasn't cheap, but it was less than any West End hotel. The pub in the basement became, and has remained, my favorite in London.

Meals were extremely expensive anywhere and mostly "bubble-and-squeek" (boiled cabbage and potatoes) and sausages made primarily of cereal. But the food at the pub wasn't at all bad. For the moment, at least, I could get by until the snafu in Washington had been cleared up.

Since nobody had any idea of what I should be doing, it was suggested that I spend my time seeing the sights. Every night there were buzz-bomb raids. The alert would wake me, but what was there to do? A buzz bomb was a totally random thing and you could as easily run into as out of its way. I finally just stayed in bed and listened to them. When it stopped buzzing, it would fall and explode. There had been a few V2 explosions. The only warning they gave was a "woosh" and a second later a "bang." There was no point in worrying about them since it would be too late when you heard anything.

Most people hardly gave the bombing a thought, but there were quite a few who had been sleeping in the underground tube stations for years. Though these stations were a sad sight, the trains ran on schedule, and nobody complained of the crowding. I couldn't help but admire the fortitude of the people. The streets were dark and there was more danger from falling than from bombs.

The financial officer advised me to take out a special checking account that the Chase Bank had for Americans. It made funds available until the financial problem got ironed out.

I found that I could buy powdered coffee and crackers and cheese and figs at the PX and have breakfast in bed, saving quite a bit. I went to see what damage there had been around the British Museum, so that I could write Gretchen about it. Everything looked drab, but in most places bomb damage had been cleaned up.

I caught my thumbnail on a light switch and developed a bad infection. I had to go to the medics who explained that because of the pervasive dust of the bombings, very slight wounds became easily infected. He ran a scalpel under my nail, and I passed out. It made me realize what a hell of a soldier I'd make! I gained great respect for the medics. They didn't waste any time or minimize the problems.

After I had finished all the paper work at the office, I decided to go to Cambridge. I had been told to make a target list of all the important bookstores, publishers, etc. in Paris, with addresses and telephone numbers. Everything would be cheaper in Cambridge, and Herbert Davis had given me the address of Professor F. P. Wilson who, because his house in London had been badly damaged, was living there with his family. The Wilson children, who had lived in Northampton during the early war years, had returned to England. Also, August was a holiday and rooms might be easier to find. I certainly would have no trouble locating the reference books I needed for making my Target List. I was lonely in London and longed to see someone I knew, so I packed my bags and made the short train trip in the early morning, allowing myself the entire day to get settled.

It didn't actually take long. I went to the English Speaking Union and they directed me to a Mr. Duncan who had a boardinghouse right next to the entrance to Trinity College and across from the "Blue Boar" pub. Mr. Duncan looked like the English Butler in a play. He had a suite of two rooms on the second floor which he would rent by the week (breakfast included) until the University started in October. There was a nice large living room and a small bedroom, both costing less than the small room I'd had in London.

He was delighted when I showed him my ration allowance, and told me I could have a "proper breakfast" every morning with such an allowance. I found I could rent a piano and a bicycle for about three dollars a week. By the end of the day I had moved in and was feeling more cheerful than I had for some time. I telephoned the Wilsons and they invited me to tea the next day.

It would be impossible to exaggerate my debt to the Wilsons. They made me almost a member of the family and invited me to picnics and dinners, even though it must have been hard for them to get along on their rations. They lived in a pleasant house on a street where every yard had roses in front and a garden in back. Their garden wasn't large, but Mr. Wilson took great care of it. I have never known nicer people. He was, of course, a very distinguished scholar, known the world over for his study of English Proverbs, and she was a bright, sparkling lady, full of laughter and good sense.

The children were just like their parents. Two of the boys were very solemn and studious; the other boy and Elizabeth were more like their mother. I had brought boxes of Hershey chocolate bars, "Milky Ways," and gum from the boat PX, and also one orange which I had saved. Mrs. Wilson carefully peeled the orange and gave one section to each person, saving the peeling for a pudding which turned out to be delicious.

We had picnics and bicycle trips, but I especially remember one picnic when we went swimming in the Cam east of town. While the river wasn't very deep, it was adequate for swimming, and since the temperature was eighty, which the Wilsons thought very hot, we all found it refreshing. I had brought K rations as my picnic contribution, and everyone enjoyed them. There were rich soya crackers, fruit bars, hard chocolate bars, cans of concentrated potted meat, small packages of cigarettes, and powdered coffee and sugar. I became very fond of K rations, especially the kind that contained pressed ham and eggs, and since I was always hungry, I tried to get them whenever I could.

F. P. Wilson told me about a library that I would never have discovered by myself, where I could find all the directories that I needed for my Target List, and he made arrangements for me to work there any time I wanted. As a result the work went much faster than if I had stayed in London. It was very close to where I lived, and I often went there mornings.

The military progress on the continent was slower than we had anticipated. There could well be several weeks before the IDC office could be established in Paris, and because of this delay my financial situation remained vague, to say the least.

I was lucky to be in Cambridge where there were no bombing alerts and the night sounds were college bells ringing the hour. On foggy days I could even hear the Ely Cathedral bell some few miles away. We heard the bombers leave for raids on Germany and return to the airports that were all over the countryside. Life seemed much pleasanter than in London, and I didn't mind the extra weeks in Cambridge. Ralph Carruthers came down and stayed over, sleeping on the couch in the living room. He was making a business trip to explain how things were going and to check on local operations. He explained that I would have to return to London, probably in September, to purchase the uniforms I'd need for France. He was interested in my Target List and thought it would be very valuable when I got to Paris. He was afraid I would be offended when he told me that my work in France would involve a lot of field trips, and that an army officer would be sent over to head the IDC office. Field work appealed to me a lot more than an administrative desk job. It seemed probable to him that we would not move until late September, so I might as well enjoy Cambridge and my work in the library.

I had asked the English Speaking Union for introductions to musicians who lived in Cambridge. They made two suggestions: a Mrs. Clegg, who held string-quartet evenings twice a week, and a Spanish composer named Roberto Gerhard, who lived in a house on the edge of town. They telephoned both and made dates for me to meet them. Mrs. Clegg invited me to tea. Her house was some two miles from the center of town, and when I arrived, I wondered if I had the wrong day, because there was no sign of anybody making plans to receive guests or serve tea. Finally I was ushered in to meet Mrs. Clegg. She was a very strange person and not at all cordial. She seemed to have a chip on her shoulder about Americans. I was thinking I'd better get out as fast as I could when suddenly, because of a rather sharp remark I made, she changed completely. Perhaps she had been baiting me for some reason. At any rate, she made tea and was very pleasant, asking questions about me and telling about her life.

She was a cartographer, and her husband, who had been a professor, had died in the early thirties. Her two children had been in Canada all through the war. She urged me to stay for the evening and play chamber music. They were going to read the Schubert Quintet with two cellos, one of my favorites. The first violinist, an American soldier formerly with the Indianapolis Symphony, had suffered shock during the invasion of France and had been sent back to head a local PX. He was an excellent musician and a very pleasant person, who came loaded with cans of Planter's Peanuts and a container of peaches. A violist and two cellists arrived, and Mrs. Clegg played second violin. I listened at first, but finally was permitted to play the second cello part. We stopped at about eleven, and because of the blackout, Mrs. Clegg urged me to spend the night. I had an excellent sense of direction and looked forward to the long walk back to my digs. We spent many evenings playing quartets and I always enjoyed the group that gathered.

My introduction to Roberto and Poldi Gerhard was very different, and it was important to me all the rest of my life. Roberto had been a

Ross Lee Finney, 1968

My parents Ross L. Finney and
Caroline Mitchell Finney

Theodore, Ross Lee and
Nathaniel, 1907

At age four, Normal, Illinois

The "family orchestra" (Gus, Nat, Mother, Slats)

At my cello, age nine, Valley City

Grandmother Matilda Mitchell
in Fayette, Iowa

Right: With Nat, Valley City, 1913
Below: Father, RLF, Nathaniel,
Theodore in Minneapolis, ca. 1922

RLF, Gerald Greeley, Theodore
Finney, Minneapolis, 1922

Carleton String Quartet, 1925

UNIVERSITY MUSIC HALL
Thursday Evening
FEBRUARY 5th
Auspices: Mrs. Carlyle Scott

First American Tour of
Mlle.

NADIA BOULANGER

Distinguished French Organist, Pianist and Lecturer

Management: GEORGE ENGLES
Aeolian Hall :: New York

BALDWIN PIANO

Above: Brochure for Nadia
Boulanger's first American tour,
1924
Right: In Paris, 1927
Below: Note from Nadia Boulanger
to Mother, 1927

LES MAISONNETTES
GARGENVILLE (S.O.)

My dear Mrs Finney,

We will enjoy a great deal, Mother and I, if it is possible for you to come for the tea Wednesday at 4 b c.

Let me say to you how I am happy to have your dear, gifted son as student and believe me to be, my dear Mrs Finney, very sincerely yours

Nadia Boulanger

In Tilton, NH, 1928

Tilton School

Presents

Friday Evening at Eight o'clock, Pillsbury Hall

MISS RUTH ABIGAIL ADAMS
Soprano

and MR. ROSS LEE FINNEY, JR.
Piano

❧ ❧

Prelude, Aria, and Finale,	*Ceasar Franck*
ROSS LEE FINNEY, JR.	
The Lost Heart,	*Finney*
The Piper,	*Head*
RUTH ABIGAIL ADAMS	
Slow Piece,	*Finney*
Dance Study No. 2	*Finney*
ROSS LEE FINNEY, JR.	
L'Invitation au Voyage,	*Duparc*
Lamento,	*Duparc*
Mandoline,	*Debussy*
RUTH ABIGAIL ADAMS	
Rhapsody,	*Brahms*
Ballade,	*Chopin*
ROSS LEE FINNEY, JR.	
The Little Shepard's Song.	*Watts*
Now Sleeps the Crimson Petal,	*Quilter*
The Answer,	*Terry*
RUTH ABIGAIL ADAMS	

LYRISCHE SUITE

FÜR

STREICHQUARTETT

VON

ALBAN BERG

PARTITUR

Aufführungsrecht vorbehalten — Droits d'exécution réservés
UNIVERSAL-EDITION A. G.
WIEN Copyright 1927 by Universal-Edition LEIPZIG
Printed in Austria

Alban Berg

Above: Souvenir from Alban Berg, 1932
Left: At work in the rue Cardinal Lemoine, 1933
Below: Northampton, 1934

Gretchen Ludke Finney, 1932

Above: Gretchen and Ross in
Menton, 1937
Right: With Henry and Ross,
Northampton, 1937
Below: Henry, Mother and Ross,
Washington, DC, ca. 1940

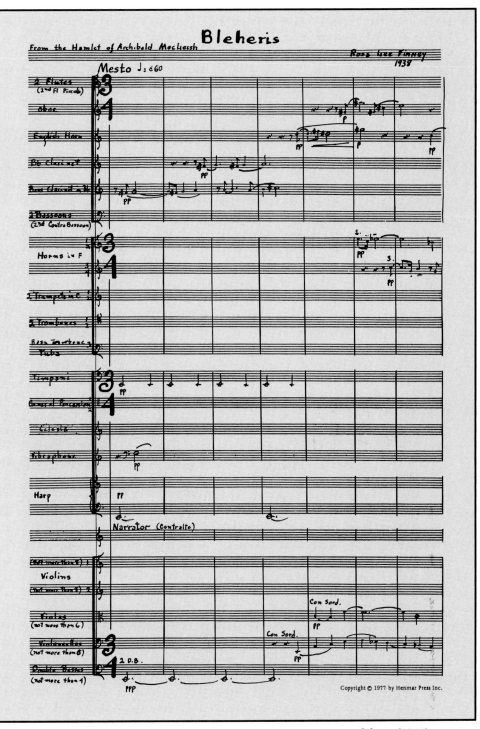

Bleheris (1937)

Above: The Barbershop Quartet
of Smith College: RLF, Dick
Ballou, Otto Kraushaar, John
Duke, ca. 1940
Below: With Dimitri Mitropoulos,
1941

To Mr Ross Lee Finney
very appreciatively
and friendly
D. Mitropoulos
1941

OSS, Paris, 1944

Stanley Rubint and RLF
in southern France, 1944

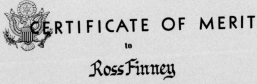

Above: Valley City
Right: 2015 Geddes Avenue,
Ann Arbor
Below: Chappaquiddick

Dedicated to the Memory of Serge and Natalie Koussevitzky

SYMPHONY No. 2

ROSS LEE FINNEY

Symphony No. 2 (1958)

Above: In my studio, Ann Arbor, 1968
Right: Athens, Greece, 1960 (*left to right:* John Papaiannou, Ross and Gretchen Finney, Daryl and Peggy Dayton)
Below: Gilbert Ross in São Paulo, 1958

Left: With Henry Cowell, Chicago, 1962
Below: In our Ann Arbor garden, 1961 (*left to right*: Ed Coleman, Gerald Humel, Roberto Gerhard, Robert Ashley, Leslie Bassett, Sherman VanSolkema, Poldi Gerhard, David Bates (*seated*:), George Cacioppo, Roger Reynolds)

Roger Sessions, 1965

Walter and Evelyn Hinrichsen,
ca. 1966

At work and at play

Above: Erick Hawkins in
"The Joshua Tree" (1984)
Below: With Don Gillespie at
23 Bank Street, New York, 1989

Weep Torn Land (1984)

Above: Fiftieth Wedding Anniversary gathering, September 3, 1980 (*left to right*: Catherine, Henry, Helen, Dorothea, Laura, Ross; *kneeling*: Nathaniel, Christopher)
Left: Nat S. Finney, Washington, DC, ca. 1949
Below: Theodore M. Finney, University of Pittsburgh, ca. 1938

student of Schoenberg, and Poldi was Austrian. Because of my study with Alban Berg, we had an immediate contact and talked about Vienna and music far into the evening. Roberto made his living writing music for the theater and for the BBC. His own interests in contemporary music were a little foreign to English tastes of that time, especially to the academic tastes in Cambridge.

He longed to talk about twelve-tone technique and found me a very interested listener. I had the feeling that the problems he faced were not unlike my own. His Spanish background was important to him and to a degree came into conflict with his study with Schoenberg, just as my study came into conflict with my interest in Americana and my Midwestern background. I valued my many meetings with Roberto as much I had valued my study with Boulanger, Berg and Roger Sessions. He was working on a violin concerto, as I had been, and though I had none of my scores with me, our talk was very meaningful and satisfied a great need that I felt.

I was called back to London for a few days to get all my papers for the establishment of IDC in Paris. Since Washington had finally come through with the proper directives, I needed to buy uniforms and equipment should an immediate departure date be set. Harold Deutsch took the occasion to gather the entire group together and talk to us about what we would be doing.

The young lieutenant who would head the IDC office had arrived and I had a chance to get acquainted with him. Jack had been a student of French at Princeton University, which was all textbook learning and not much more useful than mine. He didn't strike me as a heavyweight at all, but he was very pleasant and we got along fine. I made him realize that I had no ambitions at all and would cooperate in anything that had to be done.

Everyone was impressed with my Target List, though Deutsch had a very valuable suggestion, pointing out that I hadn't looked into the many Bulletins that were issued by the various French Institutes. When I returned to Cambridge, I immediately plunged into this project. I especially liked a young soldier named Stanley Rubint, who was to be connected with IDC and had a splendid command of languages and a wonderful sense of humor. I also met Bernie Aronson, who was to establish and direct IDC's photographic laboratory. He was a big, explosive, unpredictable person, with his own life style that seemed to take him from one brothel to another, but never, at least as far as I was concerned, troubled our good-humored relationship. He was a Navy man, and I got the impression that the Navy did well by its personnel. He could hardly wait to get to "Par-ee." The group at the meeting was large, and I must admit it was a very distinguished company of men. We were told that we should always refer to our activities as "Research and Analysis," which I suppose in a broad sense it was.

When I met the financial officer again to try to get my affairs in order, I found that there was still a snafu. I had been given the list of equipment that I should buy at the PX on Oxford Street, all to be financed by Washington. That led me on a shopping spree. It was a long list, with everything from underwear, shoes and winter uniforms to a trench coat (which I loved) and an officer's cap. The works! But the finance office learned, too late, that I would have to pay for some of the items listed as being required. I wouldn't have bought some of that stuff if I'd known that, and I was miffed! "Snafu" was becoming a basic word in our vocabulary.

I had to get all my insignia and have them properly sewed on my uniform, a job that was technically beyond my capacity. Joanna and Elizabeth Wilson came to my aid, and also showed me how to wear my uniform properly. I had bribed them with a few things from the PX.

I found that I could have my old room in London for the few days I had to be there, and I enjoyed myself rediscovering and introducing friends to the pleasures of my favorite pub. We even had high tea at the Savoy! There were no buzz bombs, but the first night there was a terrific explosion nearby, and the next day I saw a big hole where a building had been.

Everybody tried to persuade me to go along on an excursion to Edinburgh, but I returned to Cambridge to get my uniform in shape so I could show it off to friends there. I was glad I hadn't given up my rooms at Trinity, since it would be several weeks before we would be leaving.

The Wilsons took very seriously the project of getting me properly into my uniform. It was a regular army-officer's uniform except that it had no captain's insignia. But I had everything else, including dress shoes and combat boots. I was told that the boots would never feel right until I walked in the Cam and let them dry out on my feet. That wasn't true, because when I put them on they fit me perfectly and were always comfortable.

The Wilsons loved my bribe, and we planned a bicycle trip along the old Roman road all the way to Ely. For the rest of my stay in Cambridge, I wore my uniform just to get used to it. Mr. Duncan the "Butler" could hardly believe his eyes and served me a "most proper" breakfast. Mrs. Clegg had found a cello that I could use, so I was always included in the chamber-music evenings. The change that bothered me the most was having soldiers salute me. I didn't know what to do at first, but finally saluted back as best I could.

Roberto and Poldi Gerhard completely ignored my uniform and acted as though I didn't look any different. I felt very silly riding my bicycle, and I did find the uniform hot. Summer uniforms were not permitted in the European Theatre of Operations (ETO), which was probably a good regulation since no one can figure out how to dress for the English weather. Fortunately, I had both regular pants and dress pants and didn't have to worry about getting dirty on picnics.

Every day I worked hard at the library filling in the publications that Harold Deutsch had suggested. I had missed a great deal, because the French go in strong for Institute and Government publications. I compiled a long list of names of offices and people who might be useful and got more and more involved with scientific and commercial bulletins. Actually, those last few weeks in Cambridge were the most decisive for my Target List, and when I got to Paris, I was very glad indeed that I had taken the time to do the research.

The last week of September was finally set as our departure date. The week before I had an especially festive final dinner with the Wilsons. Joanna had prepared an exceptional lamb roast, and after dinner F. P. Wilson got out some whiskey which he must have been saving for a very special occasion. They urged me to visit them on my return at their London home, which they hoped to have in condition before the next academic year. I returned my piano and bicycle, packed a box of Arthur Ransome's books and mailed them to Ross and Henry, and returned to London for our departure. Of course we didn't leave on schedule — nobody thought we would. But we did finally depart for Paris on a DC-3 before the end of the month.

CHAPTER XII

FRANCE 1944 - 1945

WE flew from London to Paris on a DC-3 civilian transport, not a military plane, as I had feared. If the night had been clear, we could have seen the Normandy beaches. The route had been dangerous a month earlier, but there were no German planes around and everything went smoothly until we got to the Le Bourget airport. The runway had been badly bombed and was filled with craters which the pilot was able to avoid with a beautiful serpentine landing.

We were driven immediately to headquarters where we were given papers for billeting. The choice was between a very fancy hotel near the American Embassy or an old hotel, the Hotel Powers on rue François 1ᵉʳ near our office. I chose the latter because I figured that as more American military officers arrived in Paris they would want to be in the modern hotel near the Embassy. Also the Hotel Powers was in a much quieter area. I settled on a room one floor above the last stop of the elevator, again because it was less convenient and at the end of the hall. As it turned out, my planning was wise, for I was able to keep that room for my entire stay.

The room itself was a joy — a bit Edwardian,

but with nice substantial furnishings. There was a big bathroom with all the conveniences except hot water. The windows faced the Seine and from a glassed-in balcony one could look out over the city to the Eiffel Tower. The room had a southern exposure so that even in winter the sun warmed it. All that was needed was a piano, which I was determined to find. My mess, a few blocks away, had been an attractive restaurant and though short on provisions, was improving daily. I didn't mind the omelets concocted from powdered eggs, or the spam, especially when the chef turned it into a meat pie or served it with a special tomato sauce.

My office was on the third floor of a building on rue Pierre Charron. Mary, our WAC secretary, had already arrived. She was a mannish lady, slightly too plump, who bustled hurriedly from place to place. Jack, the Lieutenant, hadn't yet arrived. Bernie Aronson was already out on the Boulevards and away from the office, and in the meantime nothing was being done about the photographic laboratory. We had the space and the equipment, but everything awaited Bernie's know-how. Stanley Rubint was the most active and contributive person in the office, performing all sorts of jobs that demanded his linguistic talents. He had been born in Hungary and was educated in Spain. He fought in the Spanish Civil War and later emigrated to the United States.

Our first assignment was to clear out German offices. IDC was routinely involved wherever there were books or documents. We formed a team consisting of myself, Stanley Rubint, Bob Hall in the map division of OSS, and Hankins who was an authority on Slavic cultures. We would set out at eight in the morning with a jeep and a couple of trucks to bring back materials that we wanted. Our goal was to get through three establishments a day. We worked very well as a team because we enjoyed each other and could usually find something to laugh about. But it was hard work and far removed from our special concerns.

We got our vehicles, of course, from the motor pool, but I had the same driver every day. He was an excellent driver and could easily get us wherever we wanted to go. But he was a character, constantly talking to himself with non-stop profanity.

Though most of the jobs were dirty and demanded little thinking, we had to be constantly on the alert for booby traps. At the Chamber of Commerce on the top floor we found a locked safe which we obviously needed to open. The odds were high that it would be wired with explosives and to open it in the room was unwise. After considerable argument we dropped it into the courtyard, and it blew to smithereens. No harm was done, but not much good either, since we never discovered what was in it.

The Cité Universitaire was our spookiest job. The engineers had cleared out most of the mines, but hadn't found all of them. At a business office on the Avenue de l'Opéra we found lots of important material, and I picked up the only firearm I ever carried. In a desk I found a tiny, pearl-handled pistol about five inches long that must have been intended for some Fräulein's protection. I "liberated" it and carried it for the entire time I was in France.

We had a list, of course, of specific items wanted by IDC such as special maps and directories or even editions of popular songs like "Lili Marlene" (needed by the Alien Properties Custodian). Our interest was entirely in printed matter. One warehouse was filled with German propaganda publications. At the end of the day we would leave the material we had collected at the proper office, taking to our own office only material that was on our list. By the end of the day I was exhausted. Perhaps we didn't need to work so hard, but we were eager to see the end of the assignment and return to our own work.

One job stands out in my mind. We had a call from G2 (Intelligence) asking us to clear out the house of an anthropologist who had been murdered by the French underground. The French military didn't want to go near the place, but thought important documents might be in his library. We drove out to the suburb on the left bank of the Seine across from the Bois de Boulogne and finally found his house. There was a big library that had very valuable maps of Japan, giving depths of surrounding waters. The bedroom presented a strange sight: a table covered with bottles of sleeping pills and many black-edged notes with "MORTE" printed on them.

When we examined the books written by this anthropologist, we could understand a little of what must have happened to him. They started with magnificent studies of the tribes of northern Siberia, obviously the work of a dedicated scholar, and then gradually became smaller and cheaper, turning anti-Semitic, and finally degenerating into pure Nazi propaganda. They traced the downfall of a great mind.

We loaded all the important books onto the truck along with other documents, some badly rain-damaged, that we found on the ashheap outside the back door. Much of the material, such as maps of water depths, went to the Navy, but all the rest was taken to the Anthropological Museum at the Trocadéro. I asked them if I could have two things: a Coptic or Armenian tryptich with Negroid Biblical figures and a volume with musical neumes on vellum, bound in camel hide and of Near Eastern origin. The museum was delighted to give them to me in return for all the other things I had rescued.

I wore my combat clothes, which would get filthy by the end of the day. Before going to dinner I would have a cold bath and get into my dress uniform. We had no liquor ration, but I had traded five packages of cigarettes for a bottle of cognac. The bars were expensive and not very good, but the bar next door to the hotel was festive with pleasant music, and we sometimes gathered there to relax a moment. Usually I preferred a drink on my balcony overlooking the city. If I was not too exhausted, I would sometimes go to the cinema around the corner after dinner.

After a week or two we had cleared out the German offices and could turn to other jobs. I began to visit bookstores and publishers to find material that had been requested from Washington offices such as the Surgeon General's. At about this time I met John Marshall, who represented the Office of War Information (OWI) and was involved in giving the French offices American publications issued during the war — almost the exact opposite of my job. I liked him very much indeed, and we realized that we could be helpful to each other. He was more knowledgeable than I and gave me some valuable introductions.

One of the major problems that I faced was how to deal with collections of civilian property the Germans had stored in warehouses. Obviously liquor and tobacco had quickly been dealt with by the military, but there was a store on the rue de Rivoli with a large collection of pianos which seemed to belong to nobody and was beyond our capacity to move.

I was introduced to a helpful young fellow who belonged to the French Civil Service. For the first time I learned that there was a government that functioned all the time regardless of what party was in power. Since they would know what to do with the pianos, we passed the buck on to them. In the process I asked if I could borrow a small piano for my room and it was immediately delivered.

A young fellow I met invited me out to his place for dinner and to meet his official friends. His home was a little cottage on the southern edge of Paris where he had a big vegetable garden and fruit trees. He showed me his cellar where his winter vegetables were carefully stored and his fruit individually wrapped in newspaper and laid out on long shelves. I was asked to bring my guitar, and after dinner there was a lively gathering at which they all had fun imitating Marshall Pétain's speeches. It was a long evening, too. The métro stopped running at eleven and we had to wait until it started up again at six in the morning. I discovered that it wasn't uncommon for younger people to spend the whole night together because of the transportation problem. I must say, it drained my energy, and I tried to avoid such parties. These young people were all worried because they still faced military service and feared they would be sent to the Far East.

I wrote to Ralph Carruthers in London that I thought he should come over and get the photographic laboratory functioning. Bernie and Mary fought like cat and dog, which was both annoying and funny, since neither of them got any work done. Ralph came over and in his gentle and very able way got Bernie working in the laboratory. He ignored Mary, which was probably the most effective thing he could have done. He also set up the field trip that Stanley and I were supposed to make in October.

Stanley and I started out in mid-October to make a report on business conditions in southern France — wine and cognac, shipping, industry, etc. Two areas were of special interest: southwestern France and southeastern France. The American forces had come north up the Rhône valley to Lyon and then, via Dijon, connected with the army in northeastern France. The invasion from Normandy moved south of Paris and then turned north. As a result American troops had completely missed the region, especially around Toulouse, which was almost a separate country with its own army that had moved into France at the end of the Spanish Civil War. The area was radical or even Communist in character. It didn't impose any real danger, but it was something of an embarrassment, and we were asked to make a report on it.

The southeastern area, which ran from a little east of Nice up to about Grenoble, had been bypassed by Allied troops. There was still some fighting in the effort to push German and Italian troops back into Italy. Our job, though fairly nebulous, was to contact certain individuals in Monte Carlo and eastward towards the border.

We were assigned a command car with a trailer attached and a driver who was the joy of our lives. His name was Beau, but he pronounced it "Buy." He was from Buffalo, a devout Catholic who couldn't speak a word of French but had a sense of humor and a friendly nature that couldn't be surpassed. He was delighted to be making a tour of southern France. Why not? Also, he was an excellent driver and the command car was powerful, if not speedy, and very comfortable.

Our first stop was Dijon. We had a terrible time finding a place for the night, but were finally allowed to sleep on the floor in the officers' billets and to eat at their mess. The next day we reached Aix-les-Bains and found it so pleasant that we spent two nights. A hotel was being set up as a rest camp, and the soldier in charge let us have rooms together without regard to rank. He had been left to set up the place and had been elected mayor of the town. Everybody liked him.

The camp was an engineering unit which had gone through tough fighting all the way from Anzio up to the invasion of France. One fellow had the job of getting a brewery running. At Anzio he had had a terrible time getting hops until he heard that all the mules nearby had dysentery. He soon found that the hops that had been sent were being mistaken for fodder. He was having better luck in France and was determined to turn out the best beer in Europe. The Mayor had liberated from the Germans a warehouse full of cigars and motorcycles and made them available to the soldiers on leave. He had opened the baths and set rigid rules regarding the treatment of local girls and families.

Both Beau and Stanley were determined to take baths. I couldn't blame them, for none of us had had a proper bath since arriving in Paris. It was my first experience with such a place, and I found it extremely relaxing after all the long hard work.

Stanley's directives were different from mine, and I had no idea what investigations he was supposed to make. He insisted on our next stops being Privas via Valence, and then Aubenas. That trip I shall never forget. We went along a secondary road that went over a pass into a valley that the Free French had pinched off, not allowing the Germans to enter. The American army going up the Rhône hadn't bothered to go there, so we were the first Americans to arrive.

We were given very special treatment. The main industry of Aubenas was to store *eau-de-vie* in great casks in caves for proper aging. We visited the caves and had to taste from the newly opened casks. An old man who welcomed us showed off a pair of gloves that an American soldier had given him in the First World War. The men drank our health and we theirs. I have no memory of coming out of the caves — until the next morning when I awoke in a proper bed but with a headache to end all headaches.

From there we crossed over to Digne and followed the road south. We ran into an accident where the narrow, winding road crossed a mountain stream. To avoid hitting a child, an army truck had run into the end of the bridge, and the vehicle hung in a precarious position. The driver was in shock but not seriously hurt. We took him to a farmhouse nearby and they gave him *eau-de-vie* and a big bowl of soup. Beau pulled the truck back onto the road, and we were able to leave. A little farther on we came to a ford where the bridge had been blown out and a small car was stuck in the middle of the river. Beau drove around the car and pulled it to the other side. Except for those events we reached Cannes without trouble.

We had a lot of work to do in this area and fortunately had no trouble finding billets. The Hôtel Negresco in Nice had been turned into a rest area for both enlisted men and officers. I had a lovely room and bath facing the sea, and Stanley and Beau had pleasant back rooms.

I met an accommodating two-star General at the Negresco who told me where I could get needed rations. He gave me a requisition, and Beau drove me to the ration depot where we got not only cases of C and K rations, but several big crates of "10-1" rations, which means enough food for ten men for one day. It contained cans of ham, cheese, beef, butter, jam, real coffee, etc. — enough supplies for the rest of our trip.

Nice had been occupied by the Americans for only a short time. The hotel had just been commandeered for a rest camp and everything was in transition. We took C rations to the cook and asked him to serve us dinner. The waiter brought it with a flourish to our table in a great silver tureen. The wine we had given him was served in crystal glasses. All he had added was a salad and French bread.

We were told that it was possible to drive to Monaco and perhaps a little beyond, but not to Menton, and that we would not find a billet or gasoline in Monte Carlo. We decided to keep our rooms and return to Nice at the end of the day. Stanley had a few special targets, but because I had very little to do in Monaco, we quickly finished and returned by the lower road where we could see if the villas had been damaged.

I got out of the car at Eze, the better to examine a villa we had been asked to report on, and stepped on a mine. It must have been defective or it would have blown off my legs. I suppose it was what they call a "Bouncing Betty," which only throws shot around. One fragment hit me high in the back, so Beau drove us to the army hospital in Nice. After making X-rays, the surgeon, using a local anesthetic, operated and got out a big slug that had stopped just short of puncturing my lung. He gave me a lot of penicillin and taped me up so that I looked like a General Electric refrigerator. After they put me to bed, they gave me a glass of rye whiskey, which I remember as tasting better than anything I'd had to drink since I left home. I slept like a log.

The next morning I explained that I had appointments in Marseilles and Toulouse and that if it were possible, I'd like to be released. The doctor thought it would be OK provided I went immediately to the medics in Marseilles, and he gave me penicillin to take at certain intervals. Marseilles was not like Nice or Cannes, but we soon found a billet (nothing like the Negresco) and ate K rations.

In the morning, I went to the medics, and they dressed the wound.

It wasn't at all infected, so they thought I'd be able to do my jobs in Marseilles and go on to Toulouse the next day. They urged us to take more time for the trip so that I could rest. I was given more penicillin and sleeping pills. I actually had no further targets in the area after Toulouse and Bordeaux, but Stanley had several nearer the Spanish frontier that he could do by himself, leaving me to rest in bed. From the start Beau had been trying to get us to go through Lourdes so he could buy charms for his friends. We had assured him that we would do that, and now we had a good excuse.

A secondary road took us to Arles and north to Tarascon where we were able to cross the Rhône to Nîmes. I wasn't able to do much sight-seeing but would wait in the car while the others did. Still, one can see a lot from a car. The farms we passed, looked, I thought, just as they had in Roman times. We spent the night in Nîmes. Stanley had to visit Montpellier.

I felt better the next day, making the short drive to Carcassonne where we became sight-seers, going to the best hotel and taking the best rooms they had. In fact we were the only guests in the hotel. I was half starved and wanted a bath, but I managed only a spit-bath. Stanley arranged everything, getting our rations to the chef and organizing a special dinner with wine and cognac and coffee.

What a dinner it was! I couldn't believe my eyes when I saw the table. The spam and cheese had been turned into a gourmet's delight, and something had made the beans very special. The salad was obviously home-grown. We bought the wine locally, a lovely rich red wine similar to Hermitage. There was a kind of fruit-chocolate desert: a "charlotte de fruits et chocolat." I could not believe that those fruit and chocolate bars in K rations could become anything so elegant. After cheese and crackers with cognac, we had our coffee on the terrace.

The chef, who was also the waiter, treated us as though we were VIP guests. We learned that he had been the top chef on the S.S. Normandie and had returned from New York to Carcassonne where he had formerly lived. The meal and a wonderful night's sleep made me a new man. Beau drove Stanley somewhere the next day and I spent my time seeing the old city.

The following day we made the short trip to Toulouse where we had to find a hotel and a restaurant in which we could eat, since there was no American billet in the city. We finally got settled as best we could, and I made an appointment to see the Mayor in the late afternoon.

He was a burly man, dressed in an old field uniform. He glared at me and took out a big revolver and whammed it on his desk. I reached into my pocket, took out my little pearl-handled revolver and whammed it on the desk. Then we both burst into laughter! I had no trouble from then on. We had a long fruitful talk, and he introduced me to the young editor of the communist newspaper, who just happened to be there. The editor, who spoke excellent English, invited us to his home for dinner, explaining that there wouldn't be much to eat.

His wife was a lawyer, and they had two children. The family came from Paris and had been active in the underground. They were still known by their underground name of "Gallois." Madame Gallois spoke fluent English, too, and was very nice. One child was four and the other eighteen, both boys and very lively. Stanley and Beau were with me and we made a hopeless crowd for them to feed. I got out one of our "10-1" rations and we all pitched in to make dinner. The Gallois family had never seen a "10-1" ration, and they were ecstatic. They contributed the wine, and we had a feast.

Toulouse was a rather forlorn city, crowded with refugees and uncertain what the future would be. There was, of course, a political struggle going on between the communists and the various other forces in France. I had made contact with what was, at the moment, a very separate province of France, but it certainly was not my job to do anything but observe and report. The Gallois were planning to come to Paris, and I arranged to meet them there. I found them pleasant, but had to be very careful about what I said and fell back on the old "research and analysis" gimmick.

We left the next day for Bordeaux, where Stanley got sick. I did as much research into industry as I could. (There was plenty of wine and cognac but no bottles!) We drove east to Rodez and stopped there for the night, during which Stanley had another stomach attack. I found a big *bonbonne* that just fit in our trailer and had it filled with *eau-de-vie*, and we poured wine into a small *bonbonne* that would fit nicely into our command car. Our next stop was Clermont-Ferrand, where I found a wonderful file of maps showing sand and gravel deposits along the Rhine. After a night in Vichy, where I found nothing of interest, we returned to Paris.

November and December are often cold months in Paris, but the winter of 1944-45 was especially severe with no fuel to heat buildings. While my hotel room was cold, our office was colder, and Mary, who had to sit at her desk all the time, suffered the most. The mess was nice and warm since the kitchen opened directly onto the dining area. The sergeant, a friend of mine, exchanged wooden boxes for my cigarettes, so on very special occasions I could have a fireplace fire in my cold room.

I gave a party for our office to which I invited Harold Deutsch and the enlisted men who had gone on my field trip and also those who had worked with me in clearing out German offices. I kept my *bonbonnes* in my room and felt that I should share my liquor supply. The party was a great success. We sat around the fireplace relaxing, playing the piano and singing songs.

Around mid-November Fred Kilgour came in from Washington and Ralph Carruthers from London for a special meeting of IDC. They both loved Paris and were a bit jealous of us in spite of the cold. We spent almost every evening in my room after dinner discussing how things were going and what still needed to be done. I felt that Fred and Ralph understood the office problem that Mary and Jack and Bernie created, and hoped they might iron out some of the difficulties.

Naturally we planned some festivities for them. I had been saving the "Lili Marlene" copyright matter for just such a time and realized that though we never would solve the problem, we could at least have fun trying. I decided that we should interview Suzy Salador, the nightclub singer who had a place on rue des Petits-Champs which had operated all through the German occupation.

Suzy was an amazing person, who even at the age of sixty could sing "naughty" songs dressed in almost no clothes. She had run the front part of her place for Germans and in the back had maintained a way station for downed airmen getting back to England. The walls of her saloon were covered with priceless paintings of her as a young girl by Renoir, Cézanne and many other great French painters of her time. She spoke English and was fun to talk to, but of course hadn't the vaguest idea who owned the copyright to "Lili Marlene." She sang in a typically French fashion, and Fred and Ralph would surely be enchanted.

We made the more normal rounds, the Lido and the Folies-Bergère. I had never been to those places. (I couldn't afford them as a student.) Later I came to realize that the naked women, of which there were plenty, were not so much the major attraction as the staging, the costumes, the fantasy and humor of the script which took your breath away. Nothing in French art had greater elegance. Perhaps it was vaudeville at its very best.

Because of the "visiting firemen," November turned out to be a very busy month. The top office had been very pleased by the collection of maps I had found (those giving water depths around Japan and those from Clermont-Ferrand showing sand and gravel deposits). I had come to know Louis Chereau of Le Matériel Téléphonique, an engineer with a degree in law. At lunch at our mess he revealed that he had a complete file of all the patent abstracts that had been published during the past ten years, which I could photograph if I wished. Did I ever wish! It is amazing how many things the French have invented and then been unable to exploit. I asked Louis Chereau why this was true. He argued that the French can't follow a design without deviating a little at some point. This habit is both their virtue and their fault. It leads to new discoveries, but it ruins any manufacturing process. There were a great many patents in jet propulsion that would surely interest our engineers. Louis Chereau was one of the most brilliant minds I had ever encountered. He was very nice to me, inviting me to his home near the Invalides for dinner. I believe he thought I knew more about science than I actually did. To be truthful, I had never heard of a patent abstract before.

Another valuable contact I made was with M. Tellemont who owned Masson, the publisher of medical books. When I talked to John Marshall of OWI, he mentioned that some publishers had saved files of publications in the hope that their American clients would want them after the war. I found that M. Tellemont had kept in storage five sets of everything Masson had published during the war and was very eager indeed to renew contacts with the Surgeon General's office in Washington. We could furnish transportation and insure payment and they would save us the miserable job of packing everything. Masson had published several valuable books on tropical medicine that I knew would be of immediate interest.

M. Tellemont invited me to dinner at his home and asked me to bring my guitar. His apartment was on the Boulevard St. Germain near the "Deux Magots." He was a charming and dignified, elderly gentleman and his wife was equally pleasant. He had a son who was active in the business and three daughters whose husbands were all prisoners of war in Germany at the time. They all spoke English. The apartment had an Edwardian elegance that reflected the conservativism of the whole group. They had a farm near Tours which had been somewhat damaged during the Normandy invasion, but had supplied them with all sorts of produce. After a lovely dinner I sang songs for about an hour, feeling almost as though I were back at Smith College.

About this time we began to discuss the possibility of making a field trip to Strasbourg, which had recently been liberated. Certainly such a trip should be made, but I was embarrassed to realize that in Cambridge I had not included Strasbourg in my "Target List." There were more compelling reasons for my reluctance to make the trip. I feared that the very hard work of clearing out German offices would be more than I was up to. Though my wound was almost completely healed, I had developed a hernia which forced me to be careful about lifting anything heavy. I couldn't come right out and say so, but I had grave doubts that the efforts of Fred Kilgour and Ralph Carruthers had actually solved the Paris office's administrative problems. The many contacts I had made with publishers and scientists would certainly be left dangling if I were away, and I doubted whether in Strasbourg I would find anything important enough to justify my absence. It was a great relief when we decided that Stanley Rubint would be the best person for the trip (with help from Bob Hall and perhaps Hankins, and with Beau driving the command car, if at all possible).

It was at this time also that I became known as "Colonel Rose Le Finger." Suddenly a poster appeared at the Sorbonne announcing lectures on scientific developments during the war years. M. Joliot-Curie would talk about France and M. "Colonel Rose Le Finger" would talk about the United States.

Perhaps the confusion was caused by my miserable French, especially when talking on the telephone. When someone called to ask if I would give a lecture, I tried to explain that "I would like very much to, but I don't know a thing about scientific developments anywhere and will have to refuse the invitation." In trying to be polite I evidently hadn't made them understand that I wouldn't do it. So I was in a pickle! When I went to the Embassy to explain my embarrassing situation, they were very understanding and assured me that they would take care of it for me and find someone to take my place. But from that point on I remained "Le Finger."

Towards the end of November, I came back to my usually cold room after dinner to find heat in my radiator and lots of warm water. It was the day before the team was to leave for Strasbourg, so I invited them all to come up and celebrate by having a warm bath. Each of them soaked about an hour. Then we sat around drinking eau-de-vie and talking about the trip they were to make. (The trip very nearly ended in disaster when they ran into snipers firing from trees and barely escaped being captured.)

There weren't many requests for our services in December, though, because of the German breakthrough in Belgium. It was certainly the most unpleasant period of the year. We were all worried about the Strasbourg team. I finally decided to develop my own contacts and office routine.

We missed Stanley very much. He was the most able person on the staff and knew how to organize his work. His status as an enlisted man rather than an officer limited his position. He would have been the best person to head the office. This suggestion had actually been made but never reached the powers that be. I have often wondered whether Stanley's having fought in the Spanish Civil War figured in the delay of the promotions he so well deserved.

Without doubt my folksong singing made it easier for me to make valuable Parisian contacts which I could use in the acquisition of published materials. About mid-December, however, I began to feel that I was the one being used. At that time we were confined to quarters because of sniping around the city, which provided the perfect excuse for refusing social invitations. I did accept an invitation to a New Year's party, since it was only a block from my hotel. It was an incredibly expensive and pretentious dinner which somehow seemed all wrong. When I discovered that our host headed a large French pharmaceutical industry and that an American general, one of his guests, was connected with a large American firm, I knew why I felt uncomfortable. I decided that I would be very choosy in the future, keeping some of the contacts like Louis Chereau and M. Tellemont, who had been useful, and ignoring others.

I must admit I had learned quite a lot about French people all the way from the Gallois family who were communists, to M. Chereau who was conservative in business but liberal in his social ideas, to M. Tellemont who was extreme in his conservatism. But I had been sent to Paris not to be educated about French society but to acquire specific materials. It was fortunate, I guess, that I came down with a very bad case of the flu and could avoid all contacts for a while.

My brother Nat wrote me many long letters about Washington's attitude towards the French government. The political branch of OSS was always interested in these letters. Therefore I would always let Harold Deutsch see them as soon as they arrived. After all, Nat had become one of Washington's leading journalists and was Harold Deutsch's friend. (Nat's valuable collection of letters was unfortunately lost when I later attempted to mail them home from Paris.) While I certainly formed ideas about French society, I avoided theorizing about politics. I did, however, get acquainted with the men in the Political Office of OSS and enjoyed them more than most of the people in my office.

It was OSS policy never to talk about the work we were doing, and I was conscientious in following that policy. It amuses me now somewhat that my memory of activities and events has been influenced by that restraint. I can remember details of everyday operations but have forgotten far more important matters. I can't imagine that any of my activities at that time need to be censored now, but — strangely — memory has stepped in as censor.

We had a direct line to Washington which was very useful during the days when communications were tight, but we always had to be careful that offices outside of OSS didn't abuse that privilege. Just the same, a little bending now and then put other offices in our debt and made my job easier. Because of the material I had found for G2, I built up good relations with them. During this period I was able to supply the army with guidebooks of Germany. My recollection is that the American Army planned to enter Germany from Italy but had the wrong guidebooks. The request for the books was made and the order filled with great dispatch. For this I received a letter of thanks from G2.

On one occasion I received a request from the Alien Properties Custodian in Washington to locate a Pfc. Walter Hinrichsen and supply him with a truck. Hinrichsen wanted to travel to Leipzig and bring out music manuscripts and engraved plates from the old C. F. Peters publishing house, which I later learned the Nazis had confiscated from his family. Since I could do nothing about the problem, I took the matter to G2, which could and did take action. (Many years later I learned that Hinrichsen had been successful in his mission and in 1948 reestablished the family business as C. F. Peters Corporation in New York.) Although there was always a certain amount of conflict between military and civilian officers, that didn't bother me much, perhaps because I wore a uniform all the time I was in France. I liked my uniform, in particular because it kept me warm during the bitter cold from December through February.

Sometime in January of 1945 I was told to appear at our Commanding General's office for the ceremony at which I was to receive the Purple Heart. The ceremony was not the ordeal I had feared it might be. Two military officers who had been dropped behind enemy lines, received well-deserved medals, and the General made a very nice short speech as he pinned them on. I began to feel embarrassed. But when my turn came, the General came right up, looked me straight in the eye, and gave a little speech about the contribution of civilian officers. It was gracious and said for everybody, not just me. The medal was much more impressive than I had imagined it would be. Of course one never wears it except on the one occasion it is pinned on. I knew that civilians were not supposed to wear ribbons, but my boss Harold Deutsch said that the Purple Heart was an exception and commanded me to wear the ribbon as long as I was in uniform.

In February, Kilgour, the big boss in Washington, and Carruthers, the head of IDC London, descended upon us again. If they thought they would find spring weather, they were wrong. It was cold and messy. My room was again in demand for meetings. The first was with Fred Kilgour alone. He was determined to fire both Mary and Jack immediately and get on with the business of setting up the IDC office in Germany. I argued that such an action at that moment would give a very bad impression and that in only four more months the Paris office would no longer be important anyway. Jack would be leaving in a few days because of his father's health. Why not simply send in a new man to do office work in preparation for the move into Germany? Fred wanted me to take the administrative job, but I pointed out that in effect I had been doing that job for some time and didn't want the official appointment. However, I did want authority to reorganize the office so we could quickly complete the filing and indexing work. I didn't think Mary would improve, but it would be too much work to break in a new person at this time. Instead of having personnel waiting in London to be sent to Germany, why not bring them to Paris and train them well?

I finally convinced him, but when he called a meeting of IDC for the next afternoon, Mary took that moment to have her hair done and failed to appear. Fred was so mad that I feared the whole thing would explode. However, he laid down the law and authorized the reorganization of the office.

I told Fred that I wanted to resign as soon as the Paris operation became dispensable, as I was convinced it would by the middle or end of the summer. I was prepared to stay in Paris as long as I was really needed, but I was unwilling to be transferred to Germany or Austria. I had already written to President Davis that I would return to Smith College in the fall. Fred was very nice about it. I think he recognized that I would soon finish the job he had hired me to do. I agreed to make one last field trip through the south of France, checking on various matters but noting especially any commercial improvements since my October visit.

We made no effort to entertain Fred or Ralph on this visit. They were too busy, and I found it hard to keep going day after day. I spent my mornings in the office, afternoons following up some lead, and evenings all too often at social engagements. Sunday was the only day that was a little lighter, but even then I would go to the office to catch up on my work. I enjoyed having the staff come up to my room and talk, but they often stayed until after midnight, which gave me too little sleep.

I was beginning to worry about Bernie. He was running a temperature of 102 degrees and all the Navy would do was give him an aspirin and tell him to forget about it. He felt he was treated that way because he was Jewish. (That assumption may or may not have been true.) Stanley returned from his field trip to Cologne and came up immediately for a warm bath and a drink. It was a delight to see him, though he was feeling low. His description of that city's devastation haunted me. I realize now that my lack of energy, contrary to the medic's opinion, was a bad abdominal hernia which demanded an operation as soon as I returned to Northampton. Things got a little better with the first signs of spring at the end of February.

The spring was very hard on the French because of the scarcity of proper food. When I visited Louis Chereau, I was horrified to find his children suffering from very bad vitamin deficiency. The same was true of M. Gallois' parents, the Nichols family. I collected bacon fat, vitamins and whatever candy bars I could get and took them over to the children. M. Chereau was leaving for the States to attend a scientific congress. He had just invented the Microfiche, which made microfilm filing much easier. M. Gallois had just been chosen as one of a group of French journalists to go to Washington. I gave them both introductions to Nat in Washington. They also promised to telephone Gretchen.

March proved an excellent time to invite my many contacts to lunch at the mess. Lunch was not our best meal by any means, but my guests loved it, especially if we had canned spinach or something similar. These guests were minor officials of various ministries, many of which issued publications. I was amazed to find from a M. Dompierre, who was establishing a National Archives of Ministerial Publications, that there was no comprehensive index of the actual publications. He soon gave me lists of the ministry libraries and librarians and of publishing houses which printed government bulletins. I found that I could talk easily with these younger men who would often take me to meet the heads of the ministries. But it was always a two-way deal. I furnished them with material and they gave me material I wanted. The publications were not top secret, but were wanted in Washington to complete files interrupted by the war. For these efforts I was made an honorary member of the Société Nationale de Recherche Scientifique and will receive their publications for the rest of my life. God knows what I'll do with them! Louis Chereau was probably responsible for that.

As the weather in March became lovelier, I did a few things I had wanted to do for a long time. I called on René Leibowitz, who had been a pupil of Schoenberg and was one of the leading musical figures in Paris at that time. Leibowitz lived on the rue de Condé. It was nice to talk music, but I felt cut off — as though music was something I had composed in another life.

I also went to an orchestral concert that Charles Munch conducted, but truthfully, I enjoyed neither his conducting nor the music. One visit I did enjoy enormously. Nat had asked Marquis Childs to get in touch with me, and we arranged to have dinner at the Café de la Paix. It was a breath of fresh air to talk to someone who had just come from Washington and knew Nat.

I invited a young fellow to lunch who was an employee and close friend of the French Secretary General. M. Chamieron had been active in the Resistance. He insisted on taking me over to meet a M. Joxe who was very friendly and asked one of his English-speaking secretaries to help me in my survey of southern France. Through him I met a young M. Collet who headed the French Liaison Office and was in line for a high position in the German Occupation Government. Through this chain of contacts I made a collection of materials that our political office considered valuable. Everyone was impressed when I received an elegant formal invitation to sit in the stands put up in the Place de la Concorde for the big military review at which General DeGaulle was to speak.

It's strange the things one remembers. There was someone named Reuben who came in from Switzerland and brought me a Swiss watch. His work was always top secret and the less I knew about it, the better. And there was someone named Lester who barged in from London one day and made a big fuss about the keys to the photographic lab. Why, I'll never know.

Perhaps it is typical of the winding down of an office that last-minute activities are hectic. We were all waiting for Stanley to be given his commission, but he had to leave for Germany before the decision was made. We were nearing the end of our indexing, a point I had never expected to see. I feared that I would have to give up my room at the Hôtel Powers since I was scheduled to return to the States immediately after my field trip. That meant hours of packing and shipping. My social activity had not slackened even though it no longer served any military purpose at all. I had never had time to make many musical contacts. I would like to have seen Nadia Boulanger, who had returned to France. But there was so little time. I was on a treadmill that seemed to go faster and faster towards no destination.

We finally got things in shape at the office so that I could get off on that field trip I had promised Fred. As no jeep was available from the motor pool, I was forced to drive a small German car that Stanley had brought back from Cologne. It was a nice looking little car, but in dreadful shape. The boys at the garage had done their best to get it ready, but warned I might have trouble with it. In some ways I was glad to be going by myself. I was tired of people. Still, I would have given anything to have Beau, who was somewhere in Germany, drive me. On a beautiful April day, I started south planning to stop in Vichy. I arrived there in the evening and got myself a room for two nights at a big hotel. It seemed easier to drive to Clermont-Ferrand for the few hours I needed for my work. I didn't expect to find anything as exciting as the maps I had found there in November, but I had to see a few specific people and pick up some routine material and reports.

My next stops were Limoges and then Perigueux. Finally I reached Bordeaux where I had quite a lot to do. I didn't expect to spend a week there, but that's what happened when my car suddenly broke down. The tires were caput. In fact, everything needed fixing. The only American outfit in Bordeaux was the Navy, but I finally persuaded them to fix the car. Since they needed a week for all the repairs, I was forced to take a "vacation." That first evening I went to the opera and saw Massenet's *Hérodiade*, developed a prize stomach-ache from drinking wine, and woke up the next morning feeling like a dead cat. I decided that perhaps I did need a vacation, so I took the first train to Biarritz.

There were almost no Americans in Biarritz. Families with children playing on the beach made me feel lonely. I found a room in an old-fashioned hotel right on the ocean and a little restaurant nearby which served eggs, potatoes, and occasionally a little ham. Since I hadn't had any fresh eggs since I got to France, I enjoyed the meals but avoided wine so that my stomach would improve.

I was too lonely to enjoy the ocean, so I went by train to Pau, Tarbes and Lourdes. There was no important research to be done there, but I enjoyed seeing those cities and the striking view of the Pyrenées. At Tarbes I saw one of the saddest scenes I have ever witnessed. Looking half-starved, two prematurely aged young prisoners of war from Germany got off the train when I did. The whole town was there to meet them along with their wives. The two men couldn't stop weeping, but their wives put their arms around their husbands and laughed and joked with tears streaming down their faces. What courage the French had!

I was more relaxed when I returned to Biarritz, but I was glad when the week ended and I could start out again with my car in good shape.

Toulouse seemed a very different city from my earlier visit. It was easier for me to deal with, however, because it now had an American military establishment. Most of the French government officials were new. I visited the Gallois, but even they had changed. M. Gallois looked old and very tired. Madame Gallois bubbled with the excitement of her trip to the United States. My stomach was bothering me again. They thought it was from water pollution and advised drinking wine or beer. I called the office in Paris from Toulouse and explained my delay and my failure to find much of importance. They urged me to go to Marseilles and fly to Paris for the weekend, where my presence was required. I drove to Montpellier and found the visit worthwhile, and then I made that beautiful drive again through Arles, Les Baux and the ancient Roman countryside to Marseilles, where I left my car in the motor pool and hopped a plane to Paris.

I arrived in Paris on the fifth of May. On May 7, in the evening, there was a report of Germany's surrender. Though the surrender was still unconfirmed, all night there was a slow crescendo of activity in the streets with people clustered in groups. Small planes flew over the city dropping flares until the red and white balls of fire looked like fireworks. There were no bells or sirens — only a crescendo starting from a hush, moving to a rustle, and increasing to voices and laughter, until by morning it was almost a roar. I had to take a bus to the airport at 5:00 AM for the flight to Marseilles. All my papers were signed. I was scheduled to leave for London the second week of June, which would give me time to get to Marseilles and Nice and drive back to Paris via Lyon and Vichy where I had a few things to complete.

Jack, who had returned to Paris, was directed to go to Marseilles and help me with the last leg of the field trip. I was of two minds about the arrangement Although I had been lonely and would enjoy company, I had little confidence that he would be helpful. He couldn't get transportation on my plane and had to wait for a flight the next day. I told him I'd meet him at the airport in Marseilles. My flight was delayed because of fog, but when we got off the ground it was very clear and we could see the Alps and the beautiful vineyards and towns below and the sweep of the Rhône valley.

VE Day was in progress when I got to Marseilles. It was unlike Paris. Everybody seemed crazy — yelling, laughing, jumping out of windows, on the verge of rioting. Obviously there would be no possibility of getting any work done, so I met Jack the next day and we drove to Cannes, which had become a rest area for officers only. We were able to get rooms at the Carleton Hotel for a week. Nice had become a rest area for enlisted men only, which meant that any work we did there or in Monte Carlo would have to be done from Cannes. There was no point in trying to work for a few days since everything was closed.

Almost immediately I ran into trouble with Jack. All the way from Marseilles he had told me how and where to drive the car. I didn't take kindly to that, but I managed to hold my temper. Finally, when we realized we'd have several days of vacation, he tried to pull his military rank on me and insisted I turn the car over to him. I gave him bloody hell! In the first place, the car had been assigned to me in Paris and was my responsibility. In the second place, I was the only person with a SHAFE pass. And what a pass it was! The MPs could not stop or question me or anyone in my car for any reason, but had to provide any help or supplies I requested. And Jack thought he could travel without such a pass! Also, I knew perfectly well why Jack wanted the car. I didn't give a damn about his morals, but several couples had been killed from stepping on mines during trysts in remote parts of the beach. Perhaps I had come to the end of the line after a year of his inept behavior. We parted company, and that was the last I saw of him until he came around for the free ride to Nice and Monte Carlo.

My room at the Carleton was beautifully located and the solid food they served was just what my stomach needed. I spent my time by renting a little boat and paddling out into the bay where I could see the mountains behind the city and lie flat soaking up the sunshine. By the end of three days I had a beautiful tan and a contented stomach. Finally I was able to spend a day in Nice doing the few jobs I had on my list. Jack didn't show up for the work in Nice, but the next day when I decided to make the trip to Monte Carlo, he suddenly appeared. I had met a colonel and a major from G2 who were resting up from combat in the Harz Mountains and on the Elbe, and asked them if they would like to join us on our trip to Monaco. They were delighted, since they had no transportation of their own. We started early, hoping to have time to drive to Menton. It was a great help to have them along, because they both outranked Jack.

We found we could drive to Menton but not to Garavan where Gretchen and I had lived in 1937. The middle of Menton had been bombed, but it looked as though the city could be quickly repaired. There were explosions, probably from clearing out mines. Of course, Monaco had suffered no damage. The town seemed to be celebrating VE Day when we were there, but we were told it all had to do with some local event. A brass band was playing while we had lunch at the Café de Paris. The Casino was functioning, and after touring it, Jack stayed to gamble a little. When we returned he had a "Polish Comtesse" in tow and thought me a terrible heel when I insisted that we had to leave for Cannes.

The next day I told Jack we would go to Marseilles, spend a day finishing our work, and then head north for Paris. He was furious and insisted that he would not return to Paris for at least a week. I told him that was OK by me, but that he'd better have papers and travel orders or he would be AWOL. I suggested that he telephone the office and get the matter properly settled.

He appeared the next day and we set out for Marseilles. The work didn't take very long nor was it of any real value, so we left in the afternoon and spent the night at Aix-en-Provence. Our route took us up the Rhône via Lyon, where I had a small job to do, then to Vichy to pick up material that had been left there for me, and finally on to Paris. I decided that if I never saw Jack again it would be too soon. I stopped at the motor pool garage with the car, which was in much better condition than when I had picked it up.

Foolishly, I decided to break in a new pair of shoes which caused a big badly infected blister on my heel. At the American Hospital they took one look at my foot, put me in a wheel chair and started treatment that took several days. It was a strange experience, because the hospital was filled with civilians returning from German concentration camps, poor souls who weighed about sixty or seventy pounds. The treatment that the hospital gave everyone was magnificent. I went back to the office in about a week and had only a few days to finalize everything before flying to London.

London seemed a totally different city from the one I had known just a few months earlier. It was quiet and green, with grass nicely trimmed and flowers all around. Everybody was cheerful. I visited the Wilsons at their West Hampstead house, which had been damaged. The children were suffering from vitamin deficiencies and Joanna was in the hospital with a thyroid problem. At the PX I bought a lot of chocolate bars for the children and cigars for Mr. Wilson. I promised that when I got home I would send them ping-pong balls and some special soap and salve that they needed. It was nice to see them, though I thought it would be hard to get their house into proper shape. By the end of the next decade Mr. Wilson was at Oxford living on Cumnor Hill.

To my surprise, Fred Kilgour had made out a high priority for my return by air. I had to be ready at a moment's notice to go to the airport if there were space, even though it might just be for one leg of the trip. I got notice to rush out to the airport for a plane that would take me to Prestwick, Scotland. I waited in Prestwick for several days, until suddenly there was space and I was off for the States. We came down to refuel at Keflavik in Iceland. It looked like an awfully risky landing strip right along the shore, with lava on one side and the ocean on the other. I had breakfast in a quonset hut, and then we took off for Gander, Newfoundland, where again we landed for fuel and breakfast. We flew over the Connecticut Valley, and I thought I could see Northampton set between the white patches of tobacco fields. And then we were in New York, welcomed by the Red Cross and with a whole quart of milk that I drank down in one gulp.

It's difficult for me to remember the exact timing of events in the next few days. I telephoned our house and got no answer. So I telephoned our neighbor and learned that Gretchen and the boys were in Minnesota. And then I telephoned Alexandria, and Gretchen answered. I told her I was in New York City and would have to go down to Washington before I could go home. She said that they would take a train east as soon as they could and I should call again from Washington to find out what reservations she was able to get.

I got into Washington that day and stayed with my mother. When I called Fred, he said I could be sure that two days would be all that was necessary for me to be de-briefed. I called Gretchen and she told me the exact time she and the boys would arrive in Springfield on the "Wolverine."

I visited with Nat and Flora and Martha and Walt and had a nice long visit with Mother, who wanted to hear all about Paris. I finally got to Northampton at the end of June. Our house and car keys were with our neighbor. God, it was nice to be back in my bed! It was nice to drive my own car. It was like waking from a bad dream. I got up bright and early and drove to Springfield in plenty of time to meet the "Wolverine." Would they have been able to get a Pullman reservation? Would they have found a seat? Would they be on the train? Well, it was pulling into the station. And there they were! Oh, God!

CHAPTER XIII

1946 - 1950

IF I were asked to choose a dividing line in my composing, I would probably point to 1950. I would do so for three reasons: I started using a serial technique; I became a professor of composition and Composer-in-Residence at the University of Michigan; and I felt the effects of the war receding more and more into memory.

The five years that preceded my move to Michigan were transition years. The rampant nationalism that I had witnessed in Europe, and loathed, almost erased my interest in Americana. It became clear to me that the quotation of folksongs in my compositions could result in a trivial procedure that destroyed my musical intention. My *Third String Quartet* and my *Barbershop Ballad* for orchestra seem to me works that suffered from this fault. The experiences during the war made me feel the need of an expanded musical vocabulary, and gradually I turned to a more chromatic statement. I faced a conflict, but it seemed to me I was not alone. When I studied with Alban Berg and later talked with Roberto Gerhard I sensed that they, too, felt a conflict between twelve-tone technique and the national music that was a part of their backgrounds.

146

The four years from 1946 to 1950 were very productive, and several works I composed then continue to be performed today, such as my *Fourth String Quartet,* my *Piano Quartet,* and my *Spherical Madrigals.* The first work I finished on returning from service was my *Fourth Piano Sonata ("Christmastime, 1945")* which I wrote for John Kirkpatrick. This work, reflecting the contrast of Christmas once again with my family and Christmas in Paris during the "Bulge," is, like my *First Symphony,* somewhat programmatic. These works of that time were performed in New York, Washington, D.C., and other eastern cities.

I enjoyed returning to Northampton and valued the friendship of faculty members I had known, many of whom had just returned from service. We all felt a little restless and found it hard to resume the patterns of daily life we had followed before the war.

The first thing I did on returning was to buy two dozen baby chickens and have them caponized at the agricultural school in Amherst, with the result that by Thanksgiving we had capons that weighed up to fourteen pounds. Our sons had tapped the maple trees along the street and Gretchen had boiled down the sap into maple syrup. After that year, and because of the end of war rationing, we stopped our agricultural practices — to the delight of our neighbors.

Both boys had grown a lot and were active building a tree house in a big elm by the Mill River. Gretchen kept on with her teaching and was busy with her scholarly writing. My music began to be published by Carl Fischer and G. Schirmer in New York, but I still was interested in the Valley Music Press and the Smith College Music Archives.

In order to free summers for our work, we continued to send the boys to a camp in northern New Hampshire. Ross worked in the stable taking care of the horses, and Henry was old enough to be involved in the camp's normal activities. The boys enjoyed the camp and learned a good deal. As long as gasoline was rationed, we bicycled up the Connecticut River to visit them. Later, when we could drive the car, we rented a place in Gloucester and spent a week with the boys at the beach.

Northampton was a lovely place to spend the summer with drives into the Berkshire Mountains. Tanglewood had started, and we made many friends. I visited Aaron Copland there and again met John Verrall, who was about to leave New York City for a teaching position at the University of Washington in Seattle. He and Robert Palmer came down to Northampton to show me their music. Gretchen and I needed the summer to relax from the growing pressure of our teaching activities. I also began to yearn for a year, free of teaching, when I could devote all my time to composing.

In 1946 I applied for and received a renewal of my Guggenheim Fellowship for the academic year of 1947-48. We thought of going once again to France, but there were many reasons why this was unwise. Living conditions would still be difficult in Paris, and we doubted if we could repeat the experience of living in southern France that had been so wonderful in 1937 when the boys were much younger.

Perhaps more important to us was that Ross had entered junior high school and was not doing very well. He had failed the entrance examinations for Exeter and needed the challenge of a better school. As a result we began to think of spending the year in California.

I accepted an invitation to teach composition at the School of Music of the University of Michigan during the summer of 1947. It was an interesting challenge to work with a more advanced group of students, and the salary was attractive. Gilbert and Gertrude Ross were now living in Ann Arbor, and since they were planning to spend the summer at their cottage on Martha's Vineyard, they offered us their house. We sent the boys off to camp and drove out to Michigan.

The University was an entirely new experience for us. The social life, though very enjoyable and stimulating, left us breathless. People went out of their way to be friendly. My students were mature and hard working, most of them having just returned from military service. They were a delight to teach, aware of their shortcomings and eager to learn. I did feel the tremendous drive of the University and wondered how an artist could survive and produce under such pressure. Working in the early morning was the only way I could get any composing done.

During the summer our plan to spend the next year in California became fixed. Fred Hard, the president of Scripps College, found us a little house in Claremont and urged us to come out and play string quartets with him. He was a friend of Marjorie Nicolson and himself an English scholar.

E. Wilson Lyon, the president of Pomona College, stopped in Ann Arbor to try to persuade me to head their music department. I told him I would be in Claremont during the year and would look things over when I got there. We also met a nice family in Ann Arbor that was moving to Northampton and wanted to rent our house for the year, even taking care of our scotty. So we returned home with all our plans settled. We got our house ready to leave, collected our boys from camp, got the car in shape and packed for the long drive across country.

We set out in early September. I thought the trip would be as exciting for the boys as for me, but it didn't turn out that way. Ross got car-sick in the Berkshires and in Yellowstone Park. Henry was more interested in playing games in the car than in looking at scenery, but at least he didn't get car-sick. We visited Gretchen's parents in Alexandria and then headed west through South Dakota. In Yellowstone Park we stopped at the Old Faithful Inn, but Ross was too sick from the altitude to do much sightseeing. Probably the boys remember more of the trip than I realize. They loved Bryce and Zion Canyons and were amused with the idea of sleeping all day in a motel in Las Vegas so we could make our drive across the desert to California after dark. After drinking big glasses of fresh orange juice at stands all along the highway, we got to Claremont in the late morning and found the little house in which we would live.

Ross was able to enter Webb School as a day student and enjoyed it so much and did so well that he later easily passed his entrance examinations for Exeter. Henry went to the public school, which was only adequate but was conveniently located only a few blocks away. I rented a piano and began composing my *Spherical Madrigals* for Lee Pattison's excellent madrigal group. Gretchen had hoped to work in the Huntington Library, but it was too far away to be very useful. Her work suffered that year from lack of stimulation and research materials.

When President Lyon reminded me of my promise to consider his offer to come to Pomona College, I made an effort to acquaint myself with the faculty and equipment of the music department. I sang Gershwin's *Of Thee I Sing* from cover to cover for Daryl Dayton's course in music appreciation, delighting some and shocking others. We became very close friends with the Daytons, and Peggy Dayton, who taught at the University of Southern California, sang my *Poor Richard* songs on one of her recitals. I came to feel that to reach the standards of Smith College's music department and especially its music library, the demanding administrative work at Pomona would in effect end my professional life as a composer. So I told President Lyon that I was not interested in the job. Curiously enough, he refused to take my answer as final, with the result that we sometimes felt embarrassed socially.

We became tourists, driving to the ocean to swim and to the desert for overnight picnics. Every week we drove to a new place: the Knot's Berry Farm, which we loved, or a ghost town in the Mohave Desert. There were endless places to see. We limited ourselves to the country-side with its orchards and vineyards. During vacation we drove to the Grand Canyon. Henry and I rode mules to the bottom, and when we returned to the top, I could no longer walk. Henry loved that trip. My brother Nat and his wife joined us.

We loved to stop along the highway and buy melons, nuts, dates, wonderful olives, avocados, and all kinds of local produce. There was an orange warehouse in Claremont where we could buy a bushel of odd-sized oranges for almost nothing. We had a lemon tree in our yard that produced flowers and fruit all the time. There were small shops where we could buy homemade fabrics and interesting artistic prints and pottery. When I visit California now, I find everything has changed. Because of the heavy traffic and the housing developments there are no road stands or orchards, and hardly a countryside to speak of anymore.

In December 1947, the Kroll Quartet premiered my *Fourth String Quartet* in Cambridge at an Elizabeth Sprague Coolidge concert given for the MTNA. Of their performance in New York City the following April, Irving Kolodin wrote in the *The New York Sun*: "Finney has been especially successful in balancing the expression of his thought with the substance of it." As much as I wanted to hear the premiere, I couldn't afford the trip to Boston, nor did I want to be away from my family during Christmas.

My *Fourth Piano Sonata ("Christmastime, 1945")* was given several performances by John Kirkpatrick and other pianists. In his review of a performance in Washington, D.C., Glenn Dillard Gunn wrote: "This Fourth Sonata is a noble page." My *Piano Quartet*, composed in Claremont, was premiered by Erich Itor Kahn and the Berkshire Quartet at the Founder's Day Concert for Elizabeth Sprague Coolidge at The Library of Congress. *The Washington Post* stated that I had

> "...added a virile score to a limited field in American Music. He achieves a sense of unusual size for chamber music through the clarity and breadth of his themes. Finney is not concerned with modernity or conservativism. He writes beautiful music, music possible only in our time. That is enough for him and ought to be enough for us to hear his music frequently..."

Although I never took newspaper critics very seriously, I must admit the favorable reviews were encouraging at that time.

It is hard to realize today, when one can fly across the country in a few hours, that in 1947-48 the trip took days and was very expensive. Only by being at performances could a composer hear what he had written. Another decade would pass before the taping of concerts became common practice. No American composer earned enough from his compositions to pay for such travel. Yet, many performers were still resentful if the composer was not on hand to acknowledge the applause.

The media was becoming more and more powerful, and some composers hired managers to handle their careers. This postwar period was critical. Recordings had existed for three decades and libraries of performances had been started. Now the field of electronics influenced all aspects of composing. The electronic media were becoming more important than the print media and demanded the presence of the composer on radio and finally television, making him much more a public figure than ever before.

The business side of being a professional composer required more time, but there was very little income from the music he produced. The division between popular music and classical music widened for the very reason that the first had a large source of income and the second did not.

One of the most unexpected results of the G. I. Bill of Rights was that young people began to accept the gamble of becoming an artist, knowing that there was little hope for income from that activity. It was inevitable that young composers would rebel against old artistic habits and seek greater visibility through the electronic media.

Composers of my generation, though perfectly aware of the problems, had to be more pragmatic in their decisions. Faced with the necessity of making a living, they could establish a second career as a teacher or conductor, or like Ives, go into the completely different profession of business. The tradition of having a patron was never characteristic of American society. To a large degree my freedom of action was restricted by my family needs. I had reached the point where I knew certain things about myself. My music had to sing and to have special shape in its temporal design. The element of humor, so basic to American folk music, had to find expression. The works that I composed during this period are among my best, even though they mark the end of older interests and not the beginning of new ones.

Since I had agreed to teach composition at the University of Michigan again the next summer, we had to be prepared to leave the West Coast in late May of 1948. Having received a message to telephone Dean Earl V. Moore at the University at a set time, I put through my call in San Francisco while my family went to the "Top of the Mark." Dean Moore offered me a position for the coming year as visiting professor to teach composition and conduct a graduate seminar in "Music in America." I could arrange my schedule so that I could make frequent trips to Northampton. After talking it over with Gretchen, I decided to accept the offer.

We all enjoyed our trip east. We drove north to the Columbia River, feasting on Dungeness crabs and salmon. When we reached Valley City, North Dakota, my children looked at me as though I were crazy. I must admit that Valley City didn't look the way I remembered it. The hills weren't so big, our old house looked like a little shack, and the

Sheyenne River seemed nothing more than a creek. We stopped in Ann Arbor long enough to rent a house for the summer, and then drove to Northampton in time to get our boys off to summer camp. I had a sinking feeling when I saw our house and the lovely New England countryside. Once more I would be spending the year away from home. Ross, however, would be at Exeter and I would return to Ann Arbor every other week to teach three days at the end of the week and three days at the beginning of the next. The "Wolverine" left Ann Arbor at 7:30 PM and got into Springfield in the early morning.

The summer in Ann Arbor was very much a repeat of the year before. We had a social life that was pleasant but exhausting and a lively group of students to teach. A newly formed string quartet — it later became the Stanley Quartet — performed my *Fourth String Quartet,* which I heard for the first time. I finished my *First Piano Concerto* which Felix Witzinger had commissioned and would premiere in 1951 in Berne, Switzerland. At that time the Swiss critic wrote that "Despite the formal character of the work it still retains — and this seems typically American — a certain earthiness which recalls the days of the pioneers." The work seems to me light and good-humored, alluding in the last movement to a popular tune which was sweeping the country ("Woody Woodpecker"), but which the critic for some strange reason heard as "Büffelherden!"

The Rosses invited us to visit them at their place on Chappaquiddick. So after collecting the boys from camp, we set out with Henry (Ross wanted to visit a girlfriend) and saw for the first time the place that was to become our summer retreat for many years. Getting to Cape Pogue on Chappaquiddick is like visiting a foreign country. One ferries from Wood's Hole to Martha's Vineyard, then takes the "On Time" from Edgartown to the island, finally crossing to the eastern shore over a bridge that became famous in 1969.

We drove along the sandy beach to the lighthouse, next to which was Gilbert and Gertrude's house. I had never seen such a beautiful ocean setting. One looked southeast over the Atlantic, east toward Nantucket, north to Cape Cod, west to Edgartown and the Vineyard. Cape Pogue was a primitive landscape, dominated by the sea and sky. The dunes were covered with flowering vegetation and a few scrubby trees that had withstood the hurricanes over the years. The island had been patrolled by the Coast Guard during the war because it was an ideal landing site for German submarines.

Just west of the Ross's house was a little cottage in poor repair, almost overgrown with poison ivy and bayberry. We fell in love with it and immediately made plans to buy it if we could. We were able to enter it and found it furnished with all kinds of wicker furniture and old dishes and books. In a closet were old clothes left by the Coast Guard. There was a big stone fireplace and a front porch with a cement floor that was cracked in places. It was a mess! We decided if it were cleaned up, we could make it livable. It was nearer the shore than the Ross's house, and the beach below the bluff was a stretch of beautiful sand. (Everyone has seen our little house in the very last scene of the motion picture "Jaws.")

The property was owned by an elderly lady who was willing to sell us the cottage if we also bought the adjoining lot on which stood the stone fireplace and chimney and the cement porch of a house that had burned. She was very eager to sell, and the price was very low indeed. It was too late in the season to clean out the cottage, so we left everything for the next summer. Since we would need a jeep to get out to Cape Pogue, I bought one in Ann Arbor to use during the year.

My schedule at the University was divided between musicology and composition. Raymond Kendell had left Michigan for California after organizing a musicology department, and his salary was used to bring me to the campus. Louise Cuyler, who had finished her Ph.D. in musicology at Eastman, had recently returned to Michigan to direct the growing graduate program in musicology.

I was losing interest in musical research, but I enjoyed teaching the seminar in "Music in America" to such talented students as H. Wiley Hitchcock and Andrew Minor. The graduate students in composition were gifted and mature: Grant Beglarian, Leslie Bassett, Anita Dennison Bassett, to name only a few. Homer Keller taught the undergraduate students composition and theory. He was unusually skillful in dealing with young students. Since my appointment was only for a year, I made very few changes in the composition program. In February the dean offered me a tenure appointment as Professor of Composition and Composer-in-Residence to organize and head a composition department. My time was to be equally divided between teaching and my own creative work.

When I returned to Northampton, Gretchen and I discussed the pros and cons of making such a permanent move. In some ways the University of Michigan School of Music was better than the Smith College Department of Music, but in other ways it was not. The Smith College music library at that time was much stronger. The faculty at Michigan was larger and covered more fields. Its graduate programs attracted a more distinguished student enrollment — a more professionally oriented group. The University, one of the best in the country, would offer our sons a fine educational opportunity and its superior main library would be valuable for Gretchen's research.

The surrounding countryside was not as beautiful as New England, but Ann Arbor itself was a lovely small city. Smith College offered the two of us salary raises that would bring our family income up to what I alone would earn at Michigan. Gretchen was a little tired of teaching, and perhaps she felt it was time for me to make a change. Many of my old friends had left Smith when they returned from military service. Probably Henry Allen Moe was right when he said, "Well, Finney, you've taught skirts for twenty years." I loved Smith College and enjoyed the students there. I had never taught composition and had no strong desire to do so, but I did consider myself a good teacher and enjoyed the contact with talented, professional young composers. So, we decided to move.

We were able to sell our house immediately for twice what it had cost us and to buy a lovely home in Ann Arbor for only a little more. Gretchen came out in April and got everything settled so we could move in May.

The boys and I drove the jeep from Ann Arbor to Martha's Vineyard in June and cleaned out our little Chappaquiddick cottage. Our first job was to get rid of the poison ivy. Then we shovelled out sand and cleaned the walls and floors. The mattresses had to be put out in the sun to dry. There were beds to clean, dishes to wash, shelves to build. At each end of the living room were balconies that had a collection of such things as rolls of roofing, old tallow candles, ladders and utensils dating from the early part of the century when the house was built. Everything had to be cleaned.

The kitchen was the worst job. The pump didn't work and we had to get someone to drive down a new point. It was a great moment when we could pump water in our kitchen — good fresh water that came down from the White Mountains. An old ice chest with ice tongs had been left. The only stove was a three-burner kerosene stove. There were no cupboards. In an old privy filled with sand we installed a chem-toilet. We had to construct steps leading up to the back door. When we left for Ann Arbor, we felt that the place might just be livable when we returned after summer school. We drove to Cherry Valley in New York for the first night and took our first baths in three weeks — only to find that we all had bad cases of poison ivy.

Our house in Ann Arbor had been built by a retiring professor of botany, a Mr. Davis. The head of the School of Architecture had designed the house so as to combine qualities of the Davises' former homes in Philadelphia and Concord, Massachusetts. It was beautifully and carefully constructed using Vermont marble for fireplaces on all three floors, "Holy-Lord" hinges made by a blacksmith in Maine and handsomely paneled woodwork. The only trouble was that it had been built with a live-in maid in mind — an impractical life style after the war. The kitchen and dining rooms were on the lowest floor with doors opening onto a garden terrace. The second or street-level floor had an impressive entrance, a big living room opening onto a screened porch, a beautiful paneled library, and, at the back, the maid's room and bath. On the top floor was the large master bedroom, dressing room and bath, and three other bedrooms with bath. There were stairs leading up to a large floored attic.

Gretchen didn't want to be stuck way down in the kitchen with the front door a floor above. Moreover, I wanted the dining room for my studio. By the end of the summer we had turned the maid's room and bath into a small dining room and kitchen with a door opening onto the screened porch. We changed the old dining room and kitchen as little as possible so that if anyone wanted to use it again, there would be no problem reconverting it. We put our grand piano in the living room and my little Steinert upright piano in my studio. The butler's pantry became my manuscript room. We installed modern equipment in the kitchen and laundry room, and the large room which had been Mr. Davis's plant room became the boys' playroom.

We have never been able to keep the yard as Mr. Davis had it. There were banks of daffodils and tulips and flowering fruit trees that I could see from my studio windows and a little pool for the birds surrounded by wildflowers. Roses grew in profusion on the back fence. Most of these are gone now, and the trees that were small have grown, making the yard a beautiful woods both in summer and winter. The black walnut tree outside our back door is the most beautiful tree I have ever seen, though it demands constant attention from our tree man and is wired to protect the house. Even so, every other year it bombards us with nuts.

A white picket fence runs along two sides of the lot. We have lost several big elms, but their removal has given space for pine trees to take over. A big bed of Japanese anemones borders the walk up to our front door. Crabapple trees line the boulevard in front of our house.

It took time to make the house our own. Gretchen took over the library and filled the cases with her books. Eventually I moved the grand piano down to my studio and gave the upright piano to Leslie Bassett. The walls of my studio are covered with pictures of family and of composers I have known. All the electronic tape and recording equipment that I need has been installed. To avoid distraction I work with my back to the lovely view of the woods and face the fireplace, which I never use. The studio has been my *sanctum sanctorum*, my escape from the University and from my family. I have always worked in the morning, not going to the University until afternoon. I know that Gretchen will have tea for us at 10:30 on our porch, which is like a tree house looking out into the woods.

Summer school ended in the middle of August, so we packed things into our jeep and our car and started out for our first summer at "Chappy." Ross drove me in the jeep and Gretchen drove Henry and "Toddy," our black scotty, in the car. We drove as usual through Canada, spending the night at Cherry Valley, New York, and arriving the next day at Wood's Hole in time for the ferry that would make possible our arrival before dark, when we could all relax and have dinner with the Rosses.

We loved that summer of 1949. We worked most of the time patching holes in the shingled walls so the birds couldn't get in and build nests, repairing the roof to keep out the rain, painting everything and planning changes for the next summer.

The boys found an old sailboat with a set of sails that they could buy cheap and spent hours getting it ready to use. Both Ross and Henry could drive the jeep, and as there were no roads (and no police to object), they drove over the sand dunes near our house. They never drove to town, of course, but they became expert drivers.

It was an ideal summer place for the boys — wonderful fishing, big clam beds, lovely inlets for catching crabs, quantities of mussels to be gathered. I especially loved to find big chowder clams with my feet at low tide, and I could fill a big pail surrounded by an inflated inner tube in a half hour. Making New England clam chowder was one of my special contributions.

The boys slept on the porch even though it wasn't screened and the wind was always blowing. Fortunately there were no hurricanes that summer. We found that our fireplace drew well and we collected wood on the shore for rainy days. The Pogue Light was now automatic, so there was no longer a lighthouse keeper. When the time came to return to Ann Arbor, we closed the house carefully to protect things as much as we could from the sand that would blow in and from the field mice that would try to build nests inside.

CHAPTER XIV

1950 - 1959

THE 1950s were years of change. The impact of science on the artist increased the acceptance of the experimental over the drudgery of mastering traditional craft. Neglected figures in the American past who had championed the experimental in art became the new heroes. Students were not as socially conscious as their counterparts had been two decades earlier, and the diversity of American culture was of less interest than the vistas that technology promised. Conformity quickly gave way to an aggressive and sometimes irrational acceptance of the experimental.

The teaching artist faced a serious problem. He had to do what he could to develop the traditional craft that might in the future be important for the young artist, but at the same time not stifle the artist's struggle to find his own individuality.

To say that I was Professor of Composition and Composer-in-Residence (dividing my time equally between teaching and my own creative work) gives little indication of the true nature of the position. In a letter Dean Moore pointed out that my "responsibilities would be teaching advanced students in the creative field of music and creative work on your own part...We should expect you to take active supervision of all of the work in composition and advise with the faculty and the Executive Committee of the school as to the long-range plans of development in the field." Only in conversations had the Dean spoken of me as *Chairman* of the Composition Department. I was aware that friction might arise, especially with the Theory Department, but I decided to assume the position the Dean had outlined and wait for someone else to raise objections. Actually no real problems arose when I demanded that all applications in composition be accepted or rejected by me.

I felt strongly that composition was more related to performance than to theory and was delighted that composers in the School of Music received not only private lessons in composition but also in performance. I inherited the practice of teaching composition in private hour-long lessons. There were no class meetings, nor were courses in contemporary music offered by either the theory or music history departments. This void had to be filled. Student composers had to meet as a group. They had to know the music of contemporary composers, especially great American composers, if they were ever to develop their own individual styles, whether experimental or traditional. The entire process of composing had to be dealt with. That meant not only conceiving the work but also notating it carefully and making clear copies that could be duplicated and then adequately performed and taped. One had to find a routine and a place for work which suited the student's temperament. It was necessary through the photo-reproduction office to make available the proper paper that could be used in duplicating manuscript. (The whole duplication process was different then from what it is today.) Contact had to be made through the university radio station for the taping of performances, and the student had to be taught to listen to the tape and make revisions when they were necessary.

It became essential for the young composer to develop a good relationship with the performers and to learn that errors in his manuscript wasted valuable time in rehearsals and lessened his position in the eyes of the performers. The student had to realize that others value the composer as he values himself. He had to learn how to make performers want to perform his music. It was the student's job to build up a repertoire of scores and tapes of his music that would represent his achievement to the outside world.

To bring about these changes, it was necessary to organize adequate performances of student compositions, which up to this time had been largely nonexistent, and to arrange group meetings of composition majors devoted to the study of contemporary music.

The Composers' Forum, which was organized to give three concerts of student music each year, was given a great boost when Gilbert Ross, Chairman of the String Department, established a scholarship string quartet devoted entirely to performing works by student composers. I didn't encourage composers to perform their own works. They had to find performers and attend rehearsals when needed. There developed a great loyalty and friendship between student composers and performers that continued for many years. The young composer was urged to be proud of his work and never to deprecate it publicly whatever his self-criticism might be.

A Midwestern Composers' Symposium was organized by Northwestern University and included the Universities of Michigan, Iowa, and Illinois. Each spring a series of concerts was given at one of these universities. Each school sent performers and composers to the symposium, and the host school performed an orchestral concert consisting of a work from each institution. The students gained a great deal from this experience, though the rivalry tended to change the event into a "big-four" competition.

In my opinion the performance activities of the composition department contributed to the other departments of the school. The theory department broadened its offerings by the appointment of two distinguished composers who were also fine theorists. Paul Cooper and Wallace Berry both came from the University of Southern California, and both were interested in contemporary music. Both became distinguished composers, theorists and administrators. Performance majors became more active in performing contemporary music and often commissioned works to perform on their graduation recitals. Percussion, long relegated to a minor position as a part of the band, suddenly gained new prominence, with the best students often majoring in composition. The University Symphony Orchestra all at once realized that it was being judged nationally by the tapes of performances they gave of student works.

Instead of organizing courses in contemporary music through the curriculum committee (after all, such courses were not a proper part of the composition department), I decided to have a weekly four-hour evening seminar that focused on some specific work. It would be open to any student who wanted to come. No attendance would be taken and it would be without credit and completely informal. Smoking was permitted and coffee and cookies were available. We met at the top of the Burton Bell Tower, and the large seminar room was always full.

The first year (1949) we analyzed Beethoven's *Grosse Fuge* and

Bartók's *Fourth String Quartet* I liked to put works in juxtaposition such as Bach's *Well-Tempered Clavier* and Hindemith's *Ludus Tonalis.* While my emphasis was always on aural analysis, we all had scores and constantly referred to them. I never lectured, and I avoided critical judgements on what the students argued. I sat back and smoked my pipe and now and then would ask a question. "Why did Beethoven use that note rather than another?" "What did this point in Bartók refer back to and what did it portend?" We would follow the score as we performed such a work as Bartók's *Second Piano Concerto,* each marking with red pencil points where something important happened musically. Then we would compare our results and discuss why we felt a point was important.

I had always felt that composers learned as much from their peers as from their teachers, but I knew also that they were very often timid and almost always self-centered. My object was to organize a peer group that would function outside of the classroom as well as in it.

Some of the older students like Leslie Bassett had seen military service. Some of the younger students like George Wilson had only started training. Many were taking advantage of the G. I. Bill. Some, like Grant Beglarian, would serve in the military after receiving their degrees. The entire group — Robert Cogan, Donald Harris, George Crumb — were serious students, determined to be composers. Students majoring in musicology, like H. Wiley Hitchcock and Andrew Minor, would come to the evening seminar. A medical student once dropped in and slept through most of the meeting.

There was a secondary course in composition designed for music students majoring in other areas, but it was required only of theory majors. I felt that such a course had a great potential not only for the Bachelor of Music degree but also for the Bachelor of Arts degree. The course needed to be designed so as to satisfy performers who were interested in composition, students of music education who hoped to encourage young people in secondary schools, and students in other fields who wanted to fulfill a group requirement in music and had performance skills. It could also serve as a requirement without credit for entering undergraduate majors in composition.

To serve these functions, it had to be a microcosm of the composition department on the most elementary level. The student had to be introduced to contemporary musical thought; he had to learn something of the craft and the discipline of composing; he had to learn how to notate his musical ideas, how to copy parts, how to learn from performances of his scores, and how to react to criticism.

From the beginning, three completely extraneous ideas motivated my thinking. I wanted to give the lectures in the course so that I could have some contact with undergraduate students. I also wanted to appoint talented young composers as teaching fellows in the course. They would give very short private lessons to each elementary student, gaining teaching experience that would help them to find jobs after they received their degrees. Adding two talented graduate students to the department would focus national attention on the University's graduate program in composition. I also hoped to encourage conducting for composers, an area of study not offered in the school's curriculum at that time.

Every student who registered for the course had to be able to perform on some instrument, and the first meeting of the class was given over to the organization of a performing group. Each student explained the range and notation of the instrument they played. We were fortunate because there was usually a percussionist, and everybody played the piano a little. My book, *Making Music, The Time-Line* (C. F. Peters, 1981) gives some idea of the course's content.

Some students such as Roger Reynolds and Robert Ashley became composition majors and have made their mark as American composers. Most returned to their own fields realizing that composing music was also hard work.

I was worried about too large a registration of composition majors, not only because of the teaching burden but also because of the enormous professional gamble for the young person. There were around twenty majors by the end of the decade, and I could imagine the enrollment increasing, as it has, to almost fifty. If I was sometimes very harsh in my advice to students, it was because I dreaded giving too much encouragement to those who lacked talent or commitment.

There was an unexpected but very welcomed result of my efforts to create a peer group of young artists. A group of students interested in theater and art organized the Interarts Union and extra-curricular performances in churches or other auditoriums in Ann Arbor. These performances were always a reaction against the academic routine and for that reason were enormously valuable as a first step into the real musical world. I did everything in my power to help them, which was mostly a matter of borrowing and moving percussion instruments like the vibraphone or the celesta. Naturally, I attended most of their concerts.

The early years of those student composers who have gained a national reputation should best be forgotten, since they often passed through embarrassing phases in their search for a mature individual style. George Wilson's *String Quartet,* published by The Society for the

Publication of American Music, was a fine step forward, though it reflected too clearly his love of Bartók's *Fourth String Quartet*. George Crumb, though always very individual in his attitude towards continuity, moved through phases reflecting his fondness for Copland's *Third Symphony*, for Hindemith and Bartók, and finally, momentarily, for academic serialism. His insatiable interest in musical sounds, however, led him steadily towards his own individuality. Leslie Bassett's devotion to contrapuntal manipulation gradually found greater simplicity and meaning as he related it to contemporary music.

Students have often made remarks about me as a teacher which are apocryphal. No teacher should be a psychiatrist, but there are times when it is hard to know what is the best critical approach to take. I recall a very gifted black student from Chicago who found himself stuck, as students often do, and wanted advice. I told him of my admiration for the Blues and Black spiritual singing. I was amazed to find that I had offended him, for he said, "I wouldn't know. My mother brought me up on Bach, Beethoven and Brahms." It taught me a lesson. The stylistic development of a composer is not the business of a teacher. His advice can do more harm than good.

During this decade I faced musical decisions that changed my compositions and produced several of my best works. It seems incredible to me now that I could have been so productive as a composer when I was not only deeply occupied with my adjustment to a new environment and to the family problems of adolescent sons, but also with all the demands that fell upon me as a teacher. I had to depend on my natural energy as I never had before.

It is not surprising that I ran into medical problems resulting from hypertension. In retrospect it seems to me that I was hyperactive and exhausted most of the time. In spite of everything, I kept to my routine of composing in the morning and teaching in the afternoon.

For several years, most of my music was written for members of the Stanley Quartet — my *Sixth* and *Seventh String Quartets*, two sonatas for violin and piano, a sonata for cello and piano, another for viola and piano, and a quintet for piano and string quartet. I also composed my *Variations on a Theme by Alban Berg* for John Kirkpatrick.

Tucked in between was a setting of all thirty-six poems of James Joyce's *Chamber Music*, a work that had been so long in my mind that I wrote it rapidly, in about two months. Because of my conviction that *Chamber Music* is a large poem made up of small mosaic-like lyrics that, taken separately, have little meaning, I was not interested in having a singer do one or two of the thirty-six songs. To do the entire cycle was obviously a large undertaking such as few singers will face.

Because of the expense of obtaining permission to use the text, the songs were not published until 1985. Afterwards the critic John Glenn Paton wrote in *Notes* (September 1987): "Injustice, artistic deprivation, cultural loss — these expressions are not too strong to describe our lack of acquaintance, until now, with Ross Lee Finney's major song cycle...If 'Chamber Music' had been published soon after it was composed in 1952, the cycle would now be established as an American classic, ranking with Barber's 'Hermit Songs' and Copland's Dickinson settings."

Five works written during the second half of the decade were commissioned: A book of children's piano pieces, *Inventions*, originally published by Summy-Birchard; *Fantasy in Two Movements for Solo Violin*, commissioned by Yehudi Menuhin for performance at the Brussels Exposition in 1958; *String Quintet*, commissioned by Elizabeth Sprague Coolidge for performance in Washington, D.C., in 1959; and my *Symphony No. 2*, commissioned by the Koussevitsky Foundation and performed eight times that year by the Philadelphia Orchestra under Eugene Ormandy

My *String Quartet No. 6 in E*, composed in 1950, was the first work based on the twelve-tone technique. After a performance at the annual convention of the American Musicological Society, Paul Henry Lang wrote in the *New York Times* ("Twelve Tone Music," January 9, 1955) that it was "one of the most convincing examples of such independent and non-conformist dodecaphonic music" he had heard. He continued:

> "This composer evidently believes — as do some of the other distinguished composers who avail themselves of the tone-row technique — that it is not necessary altogether to sanctify the past in order to advance into the future. Mr. Finney's quartet is entirely based on row technique, yet it seems less constructed than felt and heard, heard melodically and harmonically. In spite of the complicated procedure, the texture of the music is light and transparent, and the work is easily grasped. The listener, not aware of the "system" feels that he is the recipient of an effective communication. The title says "Quartet No 6 in E." This is a quiet and undemonstrative profession of faith and it is good to see it come from an American composer. The work deserves to be widely known. It is true chamber music and thoroughly enjoyable, not as an experiment but as the expression of a mature, thoughtful and independent musical mind."

All of the works that I wrote during this decade, except for *Chamber Music*, used a serial rather than a triadic technique. All are tonal, which means that the spaces and the musical functions that construct spatial form within the time-span are the result of pitch polarity. I admit that I was greatly influenced by Niels Bohr's Theory of

Complementarity, which convinced me that the large form of a musical work could be determined by the relationship of pitch points (usually in the bass) while the melodic and harmonic details could be determined by some other method, either modal or triadic or twelve-tone.

My use of the term "complementarity" is often confused by critics with various contrasts that are so evident in music: loud and soft, slow and fast, high and low, long and short, etc. My meaning comes more directly from Bohr's effort to make compatible the "classical" (wave) system in physics with the quantum (particle) system.* My reasoning came from three sources: (1) When Alban Berg suggested I study and analyze Schoenberg's *Quintet,* Op. 26, he showed me how to set up the row in its four different forms and on the twelve levels of the chromatic scale. (2) I had long talks after the war with my brother Nat, who, as a journalist, was aware of the experiments at Los Alamos and knew Niels Bohr. (3) In the mid-fifties when I lectured at the California Institute of Technology, I talked with Robert Bacher about Bohr's Theory of Complementarity. It seemed to me to have meaning in my efforts to make my concept of tonality compatible with the chromatic integration of the twelve-tone system. Tonality (pitch integration) had to do with the functions that control large (macrocosmic) form, while serialization (twelve-tone technique) dealt with the small (microcosmic) organization of pitch.

A musical work has always come to my mind as a complete entity possessing an overall shape but lacking the durational factor of time, which is implied in the pitches that generate the idea. This idea or theme, if you wish, is like a projectile shot at a certain angle and with a certain force which determines the time-span of the work. As a young composer I would play the first measures of a Beethoven piano sonata such as the "Waldstein" and ask myself the question, "Is this to be a long work or a short work?" My musical ideas (which often stay in my mind for years, waiting to be used) always seem to have a central motive or core made up of a few notes.

I had no intention of turning to the twelve-tone technique in 1950 and no commitment whatsoever to the academic interpretation of the system. What happened was that the motivic idea that formed the musical concept in my mind contained all the twelve pitches of the scale. I hadn't consciously willed that situation. The composition I was working on started as a sonata for violin and piano and then changed into the slow movement of my *Sixth String Quartet.* When I turned to composing the first movement, I consciously tried to find a similar

---

* See: Gerald Holton, "The Roots of Complementarity," *Daedalus, Journal of the American Academy of Arts and Sciences,* Summer 1988, pp. 151-59

twelve-tone motif. The first few measures of the "Allegro appassionata" resulted. For the scherzo movement I wanted a humorous statement, and the result was a row that uses the white keys of the piano first and then the black. After I'd finished the work, using these three rows, I decided there should be an introduction and a conclusion that used all three together.

The *Violin Sonata No. 2* that followed resulted from single rows and systematic permutations of those rows. ("1-2-3-4-5-6-7-8-9-10-11-12" could be changed to "1-3-5-7-9-11-12-10-8-6-4-2".) Working with permutations, I became aware of hexachords and trichords — *i.e.*, subdivisions of the row — and I found that these smaller segments tended to generate in my mind more interesting musical ideas. A twelve-tone aggregate destroys harmonic rhythm whereas a six-tone aggregate does not.

For some time I had been interested in Josef Hauer's "Tropes" which I found in Karl Eschmann's book *Changing Forms in Modern Music* (1945). This table, in which the "tropes" are organized as hexachords, led me to be interested in symmetrical hexachords, *i.e.*, two identical hexachords that together result in a twelve-tone row. I found that musical themes that resulted from such hexachords brought about a much more cohesive musical structure, partly because of motivic association and partly because of the clearer harmonic rhythm.

I had never accepted the idea that "all pitches were equal." In my works that use tone rows, I tried to escape a rigid order by using permutations. I tried to make my melodies sing and reflect my personal feelings.

The *Fantasy in Two Movements for Solo Violin* that I wrote for Yehudi Menuhin typifies my thinking in the mid-fifties. It is based on a row that is made up not only of symmetrical hexachords, but those hexachords are in turn made up of symmetrical trichords. The first movement uses the row quite strictly, but the second movement uses permutations of the row that result in a much lusher sound for the violin.

The four works that I composed during the rest of the decade, with the exception of a short "Fantasy" for organ, were completely dominated by a single row made up of symmetrical hexachords. (See Example 1 on the next page.)

This row with its strong melodic feeling, sweeping from A down to the upper leading tone on B-flat, released my imagination and gave the temporal design for the *String Quintet* composed in 1958.

When I chose E as the "horizon tone" and gave numbers to the pitches of the row, the resulting pattern led immediately to the design

Example 1: String Quintet (1958)

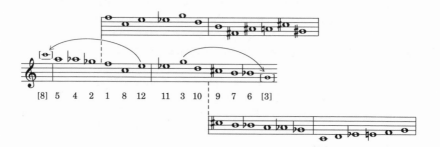

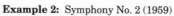

[8] 5 4 2 1 8 12 11 3 10 9 7 6 [3]

Example 2: Symphony No. 2 (1959)

Example 3: Edge of Shadow (1960)

of my *Second Symphony*. These numbers determine duration, sometimes pitches in melodies but more often harmonic rhythms. While the
symphony was written rapidly, I found it exhausting because it often
challenged a more natural and simple phrase structure. (Example 2)
The symmetrical hexachordal structure that resulted from combining
the two central trichords of the row gave a strong triadic implication. I
decided to use this row for the cantata *Edge of Shadow* that Grinnell
College commissioned for their festival of contemporary music. Example 3 is the simple love song in the middle of the work.

During the decade I had moved from the acceptance of twelve-
tone technique as a device for composing my music to an examination
and a transformation of that system to fit what I considered my own
style. I was committed by the end of the decade to symmetrical
hexachordal structure to such an extent that the term "twelve-tone" was
no longer completely valid — at least not in its academically accepted
sense.

Although I faced a dichotomy, I found both branches interesting. I
could use serialization for the musical aspects other than pitches, as I
had in my *Second Symphony*, or I could compose music largely based
on the sound of the hexachord as a cluster. As usual, I let my decision
depend on what came to my ear as I was composing.

Gretchen gave up teaching and was very busy not only with the
demands of our household and a very active social life, but also with
working on her book *Musical Backgrounds for English Literature,*
which was to be published by the Rutgers University Press in 1962. Our
oldest son Ross, after receiving his diploma from Exeter, enrolled in the
University of Michigan. His early interest in chemistry finally gave way
to a profound interest in mathematics. He continued right through to
his Ph.D., spending a year in Paris on a Fulbright Fellowship, and when
his thesis advisor moved to Harvard, transferring to Cambridge in order
to finish his thesis. Our younger son Henry went to the University High
School. He didn't seem happy there, and we felt that the Ann Arbor
environment wasn't good for him. He was accepted at Exeter and did
very well, getting his diploma in two years. He claims that he didn't like
Exeter and found the social environment disturbing. I think he gained a
great deal from the experience, and without that background, his
university study at Michigan would have been jeopardized. He got both
his B.A. and M.A. degrees in sociology, and then got his Ph.D. at the
University of California in Berkeley on an NEA grant.

We spent the time between commencement and summer school
and the start of the fall semester at our little house on Chappaquiddick.
During one summer the boys built an addition to our house from the

materials they were able to buy when the lighthouse-keeper's house was torn down. The new addition was connected by ramps to the old house and included a toilet, a garage and workbench, and a studio for me. The porch of the old house had been entirely enclosed with storm doors with windows replacing screens when needed. We lived through hurricanes, gathered clams and crabs, fished and rescued boats.

I always arrived exhausted after the school year or the summer school, which became increasingly frustrating. My Midwestern background had not prepared me for the sea. I loved to sit on our porch and look out over the sand dunes to the ocean. It made me very sad that after the boys had worked so hard to build me a studio, I was never able to compose in it. I tried. I took down an electric piano that ran on a storage battery, but the wind erased all musical ideas from my mind. Probably the fact that I forgot music and all the university problems was a blessing.

The boys had modernized the kitchen with metal cabinets that kept out the mice, a gas stove that had an oven, and a gas refrigerator which gave us ice for cocktails. I would gather a couple of buckets of quohog clams, making chowder out of the big ones and eating the others on the halfshell. Once when there was a "Nor'wester" our beach was six inches deep with scollops, and we collected as many as we could before the sea gulls got them. Then we had a feast.

Opening our place for the summer was always an ordeal because of the blowing sand and the field mice. Our improvements made closing in the fall easier. We all loved the place so much that we didn't mind the work.

In 1953 I was invited to lecture for two weeks as a part of a year-long symposium on creativity at Caltech. We lived in the Atheneum during the month of January and made many friends in Pasadena. Gretchen worked every day at the Huntington Library and I tried, not very successfully, to compose. January was an easy month for me to be away from Michigan since it was given over to a study period and examinations and a break between semesters. I advised students not to try to compose but to concentrate on their other courses.

We drove to California several times, selling our car and flying back afterwards. The collection of the Huntington Library in Gretchen's field was very strong, and she was given a grant to work there. In 1959 Scripps College offered us an apartment and a studio in a beautiful house the school owned in the mountains above Glendora. It was an avocado farm and kept us supplied with all kinds of fruit during our stay. French Fogle, an English scholar who had been a student of Marjorie Nicolson at Columbia University, lived in the house with his charming wife. In the late afternoons we would join the Fogels for a swim in the pool before cocktails and dinner. I composed a great deal of my *Second Symphony* in the lovely studio that Scripps College made available.

In 1954 Ralph and Ursula Vaughan Williams visited the University and came to dinner. Gretchen decided to serve a large red roast of beef with Yorkshire pudding, and I thought Scotch whiskey would provide a pleasant introduction. The evening was a great success and marked the beginning of a warm friendship.

My sabbatical leave came up in 1956, and the Rockefeller Foundation gave me a grant to study the growing relationship between conservatories and universities in Europe. The State Department asked me to give folksong concerts throughout Germany, Austria and Greece. We decided that it would be valuable for Henry to study German at the Goethe Institute in Bad Reichenhall and French during the summer at the University of Grenoble.

We sailed on the "Andrea Doria" before Christmas, but Henry had to finish his examinations and sail at the end of January. It was my first trip to Europe since the War. We left the ship at Algeciras and visited Tangiers, Seville and Cordova. When Henry arrived, we rented a car and drove to Grenada. We caught a boat from Algeciras to Venice. From there Henry went to Bad Reichenhall and we to Munich to pick up a Volkswagen we had purchased.

I soon realized that I had bit off more than I could chew. Giving concerts in Germany and Austria was interesting but often frustrating, and sometimes unpleasant.

While there were stimulating conservatory-university relationships in such cities as Freiburg, Berlin and Cologne, the relationship with the radio stations was much more important. In Cologne I met Stockhausen, who invited me to spend the afternoon at the radio station (WDR) with him, listening to his tapes, looking over his studio and talking generally about music. I didn't find him a very likeable person, but I did find his work very interesting. He had just finished composing *Gesang der Jünglinge*, which still seems to me one of the best electronic musical scores ever written. He was very interested in mathematics and acoustics and was studying at the University of Bonn.

Darmstadt was a pain in the neck, mostly because of the American military presence, but also because of the arrogance that I encountered at the musical establishments. We were glad to leave for Berlin, where I gave several concerts at the America House and felt a little as I had at the WPA Composers' Forum in New York City in the thirties. People came from East Berlin just to have some warm place to go. A relationship between the Hochschule für Musik and the Freie Universität existed, but there was no real integration.

When we arrived in France, I was glad to be done with concerts and eager to have a little relaxation for a change. We drove to Grenoble to visit the family with whom Henry would live during the summer, and then through Switzerland to Interlaken, where we learned that Henry had had a skiing accident. Without stopping, we drove through the Arlberg Pass and arrived to find that Henry's accident had not been as serious as we had feared.

Henry's experience in studying German had been a good one, but it was obvious that he was lonely. He persuaded us to buy him a Vespa motor scooter and permit him to make the trip to Rome with us after he had finished his term.

I gave several concerts in Austria, but only at the Academy of Music in Vienna was I reminded that I was a professional composer and had studied with Alban Berg in Vienna almost three decades before. Ernst Krenek was teaching at the Academy that year, and he organized a concert where I played tapes of my music and talked with a group of young composers.

We met Henry in Florence, much to our relief, and together visited the lovely towns en route to Rome. Henry had to live in a pensione, since Gretchen and I were guests of the American Academy. It was only a few days before he had to leave to start summer school in Grenoble. We followed him to Civitavecchia where he took a boat to Corsica. He rode his scooter across the island and embarked for France, arriving in Grenoble so dirty that the Grolle family, with whom he was to live, made him take a bath before they fed him. I guess it was all very exciting for him and probably safer than going by scooter through Italy to France, but Gretchen and I often wished we had not given in to the purchase of that motor scooter. I don't believe that his study at the University of Grenoble was as successful as the Goethe Institute had been. We hoped that the language would help him in his graduate studies.

After Rome we drove to Paris, stopping in Menton in the hope of recapturing some of the pleasures we had felt in 1937. After a week or so in Paris we picked up Henry in Grenoble en route to Genoa and sailed on the "Christoforo Columbo" for New York.

Ross met us in New York and drove us to "Chappy" for a few weeks before we returned to Ann Arbor. I returned with scores and such recordings as existed of music by Messiaen, Stockhausen, Nono, Boulez, Berio, and Dallapiccola, ready to study them during the next year in my seminar.

Our next trip to Europe was in 1958 to hear the premiere of my *Fantasy in Two Movements* performed by Yehudi Menuhin at the Brussels Exposition on June 1. It was a much more enjoyable and rewarding trip. We flew to Ireland and toured the country for two weeks and then continued to Brussels where we were immediately involved in all the social activities of the occasion. The Menuhins were genuinely friendly and helped us to do the right things when we were invited to the palace to meet Queen Elizabeth, a patron of chamber music and herself a violinist. Menuhin performed my work beautifully and it was telecast all over Europe.

With a Volkswagen that we bought in Hamburg, we toured Denmark and Norway, returning finally to Oxford where we had rented F. P. Wilson's home on Cumnor Hill for the summer. The Wilson house was very pleasant with a lovely view of the Cotswold Hills and a big garden carefully tended by a gardener. Dr. Wilson's research library was exactly in Gretchen's field, and a small morning room made a nice studio once I rented a piano. Every morning I drove Gretchen to the Bodleian Library and returned to work in my studio. At four o'clock I picked her up and we drove into the Cotswolds for dinner at one of the many small town inns.

It was in Oxford that the symmetrical hexachord that formed the basis of my next three works came to my mind. (Example 1, p.166) I was working on the *String Quintet* and had a very clear idea of the work in my head. Every morning I would begin to look for the theme that would give temporal form to my idea. The next morning I would throw it all away and start over again. I kept this up for about two weeks until suddenly, while I was improvising at the piano, the row came to my mind — not as a system, but as a very energetic thrust, having both melody and harmony. It was like a floodgate bursting. I composed in white heat, the work unfolding almost by itself, and finished it before we left for Ann Arbor.

We traveled to the West Coast in 1959 where I finished my *Second Symphony* and then, during the fall, to the East Coast for performances that Eugene Ormandy and the Philadelphia Orchestra gave not only in Philadelphia but also in New York City, Baltimore and Washington, D.C. The premiere had its amusing moment when the legs of the grand piano fell off and a piano concerto had to be performed after intermission and my symphony before. The only trouble was that the harpists weren't properly dressed and couldn't appear. Despite his excellent performance Ormandy was furious afterwards. When I took my bow with him, he was in a rage. I told him that it was probably the only time that I would really hear the celesta in a performance.

171

The reviews were generally very good, and since this was the first major performance of an orchestral work that I had ever had, I was very pleased. Howard Taubman wrote in the *New York Times* (Nov. 26, 1959), "It was pleasant to encounter a work so sure of itself." Paul Henry Lang wrote in the *Herald Tribune*, "It was only a day ago that I heard a distinguished American work in which the twelve-tone technique, so feared by audiences, was put to imaginative use, so free of the grimness that so often companions it...Ross Lee Finney received applause amounting to an ovation." Menuhin performed my *Fantasy in Two Movements* at the Metropolitan Museum in December. It was an even better performance than the premiere in Brussels.

My *String Quintet* was premiered on October 30, 1959, at the Founder's Day Concert at The Library of Congress. Irving Lowens wrote in the *Washington Star*: "The quintet is a difficult work to assess on first hearing, but it strikes me as having a good chance to go down in the annals as a major achievement. In many respects, it is reminiscent of the intense music by Alban Berg, who is spiritually as well as actually Mr. Finney's mentor." Lowens later wrote an extended analysis of the work for the *Musical Quarterly*.

Getting to know Menuhin was one of the most important events of this decade for me. The other was meeting the music publisher Walter Hinrichsen at a party at Virgil Thomson's the following year. I mentioned the performance Menuhin had given of my *Fantasy* in Brussels, and Mr. Hinrichsen immediately suggested that C. F. Peters publish the work with Menuhin's fingerings and editing. Thus began the many years of pleasant relationships with the firm of Peters.

CHAPTER XV

1959 - 1961

Daryl DAYTON, the Cultural Affairs Officer of the United States Embassy in Greece, wanted me to give concerts there in the spring of 1960. The American Academy in Rome wanted me to be composer-in-residence during that academic year. I didn't feel that I could be away for the entire year, but I persuaded the Dean to give me leave without pay for the second semester and to use my salary to bring an important composer to the campus to do my teaching.

I wrote to Roberto Gerhard in Cambridge, England, offering him the position and our house for the semester if he and Poldi would consent to come over. Roberto had never taught composition, nor had he ever visited the United States. The student group was talented, mature and a little rebellious. I felt that Roberto would be an excellent experience for them. He would give a seminar in twelve-tone technique and teach a small group of graduate students. Leslie Bassett had been appointed to the composition faculty and would have the responsibility of helping Roberto.

It was the first time that a distinguished European composer was brought to the University of Michigan to teach. The students were devoted to

Roberto. He, in turn, was genuinely interested in all of their activities. He gave himself completely to the community, making many friends and presented a thoughtful seminar in serial techniques that influenced musicologists as well as composers.

In January, before the Gerhards arrived, Gretchen and I embarked for Naples, so tired that we went to sleep before the ship pulled out of the harbor. We spent several days in Naples, making trips to Amalfi and Paestum. When we got to the Academy in Rome, we found that we had been assigned to the largest apartment in the Villa Aurelio, with a large terrace that looked out over the city. All our needs had been anticipated: a grand piano, a maid to keep the apartment clean, and netting to protect us from mosquitoes.

George Wilson was spending his second year at the Academy and did everything in his power to make our life pleasant and to introduce us to the other fellows. He had become very knowledgeable and interested in art, and we came to know friends of his such as the sculptor Dimitri Hadzi, the painter Jack Massey, and the art historian Henry Millen.

They and the other composer, John Eaton, frequently joined us for cocktails on the terrace. Wallace Stegner and his wife lived next door. One day I permitted a young composer to bring Ezra Pound to my studio so that he could hear some settings of his poems. I tactfully left, but Stegner listened from his apartment to what happened: Suddenly the poet pounded the piano keys and drove the young composer from the house. When we returned, Ezra Pound was wandering around the garden muttering, "I am undone!"

While I composed, Gretchen worked at the Vatican library. I finished my *Third Symphony* rapidly, composing it immediately in full orchestral score. This is the only orchestral work I have been able to compose in that way, and that was due, I think, to the fact that everything was so clear in my mind before I started. The work was a reaction against the demands I had faced in composing my *Second Symphony* the year before. While it is based on a tone row made up of symmetrical hexachords, there is no attempt to apply the row to anything other than pitches. I also finished my *Eighth String Quartet*, which the University of Alabama had commissioned.

At the end of the day we would drive to the lovely towns of the Campagna di Roma or some place in Rome which we had not yet seen. We would eat at the Academy, which was always very pleasant, or in some restaurant that had been recommended to us. Later in the evening we would drive down the hill to Trastevere and sit at a cafe watching the gaiety of young Romans riding scooters across the square. The whole atmosphere of Rome was relaxed and friendly.

I got to know Petrassi, Dallapiccola and Nono that spring and heard some fine performances of their works. In Florence I visited Dallapiccola, who listened to tapes of my music. No composer I have ever met listened so intensely with his whole body. He almost danced while he listened. His critical comments were perceptive and influenced me a great deal. Without my realizing he was doing so, he pushed me in the direction of serialized rhythm.

We had trouble meeting Nono in Venice, due largely to my ignorance of the city. When I telephoned Nono's wife Nuria (who was Schoenberg's daughter) and invited them to dinner, I suggested that we meet at Harry's bar, which was located at one of the stops on the canal. They didn't want to be seen at an American tourist trap, so we met at a restaurant they suggested across the canal and had a very special Venetian dinner, talking long into the night. I found them both lovely people. He held forth on the idea that orchestration should be thought of not in terms of instrumental sections but rather of rhythmic and melodic potentials.

In February of 1960 I was scheduled to give folksong concerts all over Greece. Daryl and Peggy Dayton accompanied us on the tour. Daryl would perform and talk about my music and then I would sing folksongs. We drove as far north as Salonika, stopping at many cities along the way and making detours to visit Delphi and other monuments. I sang in several towns in Crete, sometimes making stops that were not scheduled. At one such stop they had a regular banquet for us and the local bard improvised a long poem greeting us and setting forth the beauty and the importance of the town.

In Rhodes I sang in the opera house. The audiences were always very large, and the priests always sat in the front row. A free concert was so rare in many towns that people would come just to be going someplace. Wherever we went, everybody was very curious. If we stopped to photograph something, children would gather until finally there was a crowd. If we photographed one person, we ended up having to photograph everybody. The cheerful crowd always laughed.

We were given an official welcome at Lesbos, where the mayor treated us to a banquet of local seafood and told us of the island's wartime activities. In Athens I gave a concert for the Women's Club, which was held in the royal palace and attended by the two princesses.

The most rewarding part of our visit to Athens was the performance of my music at the Hellenic-American center and meeting young Greek composers. John Papaiannou was largely responsible for both. He was a professor of city planning at the University and also a brilliant pianist and a friend to all Greek composers. He gave a party for me at his home so I could meet young composers and listen to tapes of their music. I was particularly impressed by the works of Theodore Antoniou and Jani Christou. There was an interesting conflict between those composers who felt that serial technique was incompatible with Greek folk music and those who were more international in their views.

The spring at the Academy in Rome culminated with a big exhibition at which, in the garden of the Villa Aurelio, the RIA Orchestra performed works by the academy fellows and also my *Variations for Orchestra.*

We left Rome in June, driving directly to Paris, where we had rented Donald Harris's apartment on Montmartre. This was a new part of Paris for us, and we enjoyed our month-long stay, especially seeing the fireworks on Bastille Day over the city. From Paris we drove to Oxford where we had a lovely old house in Elsfield from which we could see all the towers of the universities.

Elsfield is a small village on the hill north of Oxford and was the home of John Buchan. The Queen Anne house we rented had beautiful gardens, attractive rooms and the worst beds I have ever slept in. The kitchen was very old-fashioned, but we inherited the Italian maid who did all the cleaning and cooking.

Gretchen worked, as before, at the Bodleian Library and I composed in the dark living room that had a decrepit, out-of-tune piano. My brother Theodore and his wife Mollie visited us and admitted that a bathtub would be a better place to sleep than our beds. Rosemond Tuve was working in Oxford and came to dinner. We had gotten to know her at the Connecticut College for Women in New London, and Gretchen very much admired her writing.

I began thinking of two commissions I had accepted. One was my *Second Piano Quintet,* which was to be premiered at a festival of contemporary music at the University of Southern California in 1961. The other was my *Sonata quasi una fantasia* for piano, which had been commissioned by a group in Quincy, Illinois, for William Doppmann to perform at a festival there and, later, on his recital in New York City.

I decided that the piano work would start with the movement I had abandoned when composing the solo violin work for Yehudi Menuhin. The piano quintet was a very different matter. It was generated by my interest in rhythmic serialization that had been stimulated by my talks with Luigi Dallapiccola. I dreaded being involved in such a demanding process again.

When I returned to the University in the fall, I felt that Leslie Bassett badly needed an opportunity to expand and flourish as a composer. He had finished his graduate work and had handled the problems of the department admirably during my absence. I urged him to apply for a Rome Prize and everyone was delighted when he received it. George Wilson had finished his two years in Rome and joined the composition department when Homer Keller left to teach at the University of Hawaii.

During the summer of 1960, while we were still in Europe, there was a special conference of avant-garde composers in Stratford, Ontario, which Robert Ashley, Roger Reynolds, George Cacioppo and Gordon Mumma decided to attend. On returning from the conference, they thought they could do a better job than had been done at Stratford, and forthwith organized what they called the ONCE Group, which would present annual festivals not only of their own music but also of avant-garde composers such as Cage and Berio, whom they would bring to Ann Arbor.

It was an ambitious plan, and that autumn was filled with activities and rehearsals which added to the ever-increasing burden of teaching. George Crumb had returned from his Fulbright year in Berlin, and had finished his doctoral thesis. Although he was not active with the ONCE Group, he was interested in all their activities.

The first concert of the ONCE Group, sponsored by the Dramatic Arts Center (which had developed from the Inter-Arts Union), took place on February 24, 1961 at the Unitarian Church. For me the highlight of that concert was Berio's *Circles* performed by Cathy Berberian. The second concert (February 28) included works by Mumma, Scavarda, Reynolds, and Ashley, some of whose works had been performed on the Composers' Forum. *Bottleman*, a theater piece with an electronic score by Ashley, indicated the unconventional direction that his work would take. The third concert (March 3) was given over to classic modern works performed by pianist Paul Jacobs, and the last concert (March 4) was a chamber orchestra concert conducted by Wayne Dunlap and including works by Sherman van Solkema, Bruce Wise, Roger Reynolds, George Cacioppo, Gordon Mumma and Donald Scavarda. My contribution to the festival was to persuade William Revelli to allow the use of percussion instruments belonging to the University Band. You can imagine my consternation when the percussionist used metal hammers on the marimba, damaging the instrument. But the festival was a great success and continued for several years thereafter. Though I had varying reactions to the works performed, I had only admiration for the group's willingness to experiment with all kinds of sound production and acoustical effects.

Robert Ashley was very eager to establish a new kind of theater at the University, so I organized a conference where the views of the

ONCE Group could be expressed. I suppose I should have anticipated the conservative viewpoint of the theater department which quickly turned its back completely on the idea of an experimental theater. The Dean of the School of Music was receptive to an electronic-music studio but not to the experimental studio that Ashley suggested.

Students were affected in different ways by the ideas and the concerts of the ONCE Group. Even the element of shock, which often angered people, opened their minds to new musical possibilities. Gordon Mumma, who had not thrived academically as a composer, revealed a remarkable gift for electronics and theater. George Cacioppo, whose music had been gentle and lyric and only slightly influenced by Bartók, found new vistas in free improvisation. Roger Reynolds, who always brought a greater intellectual control to what he wrote, suddenly began to produce highly individualistic scores. Ashley moved more and more into the theatrical concept of performance.

These students had all been influenced by Roberto Gerhard, but Gerhard had also been influenced by them. They were less interested in the serial techniques and ideas of Boulez and Stockhausen than in the freer experimentation of Cage. In fact, during these early years, there was more concern for neglected American composers such as Ives than for contemporary European composers. Popular American music was certainly a part of their aesthetics, but new technology and theatrical fads were more important.

To some degree these young students faced the same dichotomy I faced as a composer, though my age and experience protected me from the popular fads that younger composers found difficult to escape. They were, perhaps, at the right age to deal with conflict.

CHAPTER XVI

1961 - 1966

FACING the deadline of a premiere, I worked hard on my *Second Piano Quintet*. This work was completely dominated by the serialization of rhythmic spaces, and is, I think, crabbed and over-intellectual. It is certainly not easy to perform. John Crown took over the premiere in Los Angeles but refused to invite me to a rehearsal, perhaps fearing I would make last-minute changes. But the performance was excellent, and the work was well received. I joked that it was a little bit like waffles: one should eat the waffle, not the waffle iron.

The School of Music at Michigan moved into its new building on the North Campus. In many ways it was a lovely building and my studio was no longer under the bombardment of bells, which I appreciated. However, I could never seem to achieve in the new building the same informality in my seminar that I had felt in Burton Tower. Though I left the subject matter open-ended, the seminar had to be changed to a credit course with required attendance. Academia had crept up on me.

I spent the summer of 1962 in New York City working at the Columbia-Princeton Electronic Music Center under the guidance of Mario Davidovsky, who had recently arrived from Argentina. He was

179

a wonderful teacher, tolerant and very helpful. As soon as he discovered that I had listened to a lot of electronic music and had brought along a score of *Three Pieces* for strings, winds, percussion and electronic tape (all finished except for the tape part), he got to work and showed me how to get the electronically-generated sounds I wanted. In this work everything was to be serialized, even the electronic pitches. Looking back on the work now, I feel that while this serialization was perfectly possible, it wasn't a very rewarding way to compose music. Actually, there was considerable doubt at that time whether one should combine tape with traditional instruments. It was my conviction that electronic tape was another instrument in its early stages of development and could be utilized as a solo, in a chamber ensemble, or as a part of the orchestra. Mario didn't completely agree with me, but he helped me make the tape part as I heard it in my mind and was responsible for the first performance the next year. During that summer Milton Babbitt and Mario Davidovsky advised me on what kind of electronic-music studio we should start at Michigan.

Around this time the University Musical Society of the University of Michigan commissioned me to write a large work for chorus and orchestra to celebrate the Fiftieth Anniversary of the construction of Hill Auditorium. Thor Johnson was to conduct the premiere with the University Choral Union and the Philadelphia Orchestra at the Seventieth Annual May Festival. *Still Are New Worlds*, the work I composed, is the first of a trilogy of works concerned with man's relationship to the universe. It uses texts from the seventeenth century and Albert Camus which reflect man's consternation when faced with the concept of an infinite universe. It ends explosively with a passage from Milton's *Paradise Lost*, where Satan is thrown into the "dark abyss," reflecting in my mind the horror of the atomic bomb and leading me to change Milton's line "And justify the ways of God to man" to, "Justify the ways of men to God."

(*The Martyr's Elegy*, the second work in the trilogy, is based on fragments from Shelley's "Adonais." The third work, *Earthrise*, which gives the name to the whole trilogy, combines passages from Lewis Thomas' *The Lives of a Cell* and Pierre Teilhard de Chardin's *The Mass on the World* to reveal man's fear when he first saw the fragile, living cell of the earth rising into view from the moon, bringing into question all of our beliefs of nature and divinity.)

Still Are New Worlds, the largest work I had yet composed, requires a large orchestra and chorus and a speaking voice. While the work can be performed without the electronic tape I had produced in New York City, the tape does add night sounds in the setting of the fragment from

Camus' *The Myth of Sisyphus* and gives a sense of chaos to the setting of Milton's words.

My music was being performed more widely during 1962 and 1963, not only in the U. S., but also in Europe and South America. I was able to attend only a few of these performances. I heard my *Symphony No. 2* beautifully performed by the Pittsburgh Symphony Orchestra under William Steinberg. The work was recorded by the Louisville Orchestra under Robert Whitney. My *First Piano Quintet* had been recorded for Columbia Records by Beveridge Webster and the Stanley String Quartet. As a part of an award from the National Institute of Arts and Letters, my *Sixth String Quartet* was recorded by Composers Recordings, Inc.

In 1962 I was made a member of the National Institute of Arts and Letters. Gretchen and I found that we enjoyed their dinners, and I was soon serving on several of their committees. Having joined ASCAP, I began to have some small income from performances and publications. In Rome I had discovered in Valentino Callegarin an excellent music copyist who freed me from the miserable job of preparing scores and parts.

C. F. Peters Corporation committed itself to printing all of my music or making it available through rental. Obviously they couldn't publish all my earlier music or guarantee quick publication of everything I wrote, but it was nevertheless a great comfort to have a reputable music publisher taking care of the distribution of my scores and the collection of fees. In the years that followed Gretchen and I became close friends with Walter and Evelyn Hinrichsen.

My *Sixth String Quartet* and *First Piano Quintet* had been published by the University of Michigan Press, but the press eventually lost heart in facing the problems of distribution and brought all the unsold copies to my house for storage. When Walter Hinrichsen agreed to take the copies into the Peters catalogue, I packed them all up and shipped them to New York. Peters published the scores of my three symphonies and also my *Spherical Madrigals,* which found very good sales. I began to receive regular royalty checks.

With registration in the composition program increasing, a new group of gifted students was soon enrolled. When Barry Vercoe wrote me from New Zealand, I was so impressed that I immediately offered him a teaching fellowship. David Maves came from Oregon, Richard Toensing from Minnesota, and Terrence Kincaid from the University of Washington. Kincaid was one of the most talented students I had known, but he refused to work in a traditional way and moved more and more into the development of electronic equipment, as did Barry Vercoe.

Phi Beta Kappa made me an honorary member and asked me to be one of their Visiting Scholars during 1962. For four weeks I travelled to eight universities and colleges, meeting students and lecturing. I was on the Fulbright Committee in Washington and on several important university committees. Though I blamed myself for my overloaded schedule, I began to feel that the administration had completely forgotten the terms of my appointment. I decided that after my sabbatical in 1963 my schedule would have to be adjusted so that I could spend half of my time composing.

When I received a Fulbright grant for France, Virgil Thomson let us have his Paris apartment on the Quai Voltaire from Christmas to June of 1963-64. Once again we left for Europe more dead than alive. Donald Harris who was studying in Paris, met us at the Gare St.-Lazare and helped us get settled into Virgil's apartment. It was extremely cold for December, and Gretchen came down with a virus. Donald invited us to the New Year's festivities at Raynouard, a Jesuit establishment in a beautiful old building outside of the city. It was a wonderful experience, but the frigid weather and inadequate heating brought on a relapse of Gretchen's illness, making our January miserable.

We loved Virgil's apartment. It was on an inside court and the noise of the heavy traffic along the Seine was barely audible. There was a lovely old fireplace with a large, ornate mirror above. The large living room was filled to the ceiling with paintings, some very lovely, some bizarre. French windows looked out on the court both from the living room and from the small kitchen which was beautifully equipped with every modern necessity. A balcony at the back of the living room was constructed over an alcove with two comfortable beds. In back of the alcove were closets and a modern bathroom.

I had a small piano moved in and got to work. Gretchen spent her day at the Bibliothèque Nationale doing research for her next book, which was to be about music and medicine. We went to London for two weeks while I lectured at Cambridge, Oxford and the University of Nottingham. When we returned to Paris, there were signs of spring.

Donald Harris, who directed the musical activities of the United States Embassy, arranged performances of my music at rue du Dragon and the French Radio and introduced me to many of his friends in Paris. I finally visited Max Deutsch and attended his studio class. Eugene Kurtz, who had composed a work for the University of Michigan's radio station, introduced me to Madame Jobert, the music publisher.

I was asked to serve as the United States representative on the UNESCO International Rostrum of Composers. It gave me the chance to meet many composers from all over Europe and to listen to tapes of their music. I had a long visit with Madame Olga Koussevitsky, while driving her back to her hotel in a typical Parisian traffic jam.

During 1963 Roger Reynolds was in Paris with his wife Karen, who was studying flute on a Fulbright Scholarship. We took them out to dinner at the "Restaurant des Beaux Arts," our favorite in Paris. Roger showed me his new orchestral work, *Graffiti*, and I introduced him to the American Music Center on the Boulevard Raspail. After our day's work Gretchen and I would drive out of Paris and have dinner at one of the nice restaurants along the Seine or the Marne.

I composed my *Divertissement* for piano, clarinet, violin and cello, commissioned by Bowdoin College to celebrate the opening of a new Senior Student Center in the fall of 1965. I enjoyed composing this work, for though it had an intricate structure (the last movement is a crab of the first), it was deeply rooted in memory and often seemed almost an improvisation. I found myself remembering youthful nights spent in Paris as a student in the twenties. There was humor in the work and also starry-eyed nostalgia. I used the instruments more freely than I had previously done, asking the pianist to play inside the piano and the clarinettist to use his highest register. The work might be called "A Night on the Town." It was the beginning of a new concern for memory which came to be more and more important in my music.

Our spring was made complicated by trips back to the United States. The Philadelphia Orchestra under Eugene Ormandy premiered my *Symphony No. 3* on March 6, 1963, and took it on tour that month to Washington D. C., New York City (Lincoln Center) and Baltimore. My son was teaching at Princeton, and we stayed in his apartment during that period.

We had hardly returned to Paris when Gretchen was called back to Alexandria, Minnesota because of her mother's very serious illness. She was able to join me, however, for my tour through Greece singing folk songs. We spent Easter there and found the celebrations of the Greek Orthodox Church deeply moving, especially in the small towns outside of Athens. On our way back to Paris, we stayed two weeks at the Academy in Rome and celebrated Easter again at St. Peter's.

Spring was at its most beautiful when we returned to Paris, and we spent the last month in Virgil's apartment wondering how we could bear to leave for Oxford, as we planned, for July and August. We had rented Fred Sternfeld's lovely thatched cottage in Eynsham, not far from "The Trout," a deservedly famous pub just across the river from the town. Sternfeld was a music professor and had a lovely studio with a grand piano, so I was able not only to finish my *Divertissement* but to start on a new work *The Nun's Priest's Tale*, scheduled to be premiered in 1965. As usual we visited all the little inns in the Cotswolds.

It became obvious to me during this year that being a composer was a full-time job. While my income from composing had increased, and my "sock" had become a bank account, it was still inadequate to support a family. I had to continue teaching, but I began to resent the burden of my heavy schedule at the University and became determined to do something about it on my return to Michigan. Teaching two courses, giving some twelve hours of private lessons, and fulfilling the administrative and committee demands, required more time than I had. The more I lectured throughout the country, the more talented young composers applied for admission as graduate students. It was a great relief when Leslie Bassett returned from his two years in Rome, but with the establishment of an electronic music studio a faculty of three was inadequate.

The Rackham Graduate School furnished funds to equip an electronic music studio. Duane Mrose, who handled all the electronic equipment for concerts and listening rooms in the School of Music, purchased the machines and housed them in a room in Hill Auditorium which had been made available to us. I appointed George Wilson to head the studio but also persuaded the dean to appoint Mario Davidovsky as a visiting professor for a semester to teach the faculty.

Mario made a great contribution, overcoming much of the faculty opposition and giving great encouragement to both Wilson and Bassett. We established what is known as a "classical" analog studio: a technique of working entirely with electronically generated sound recorded on tape, which is then spliced and combined to make an electronic composition. (This system is obsolete today, though still of value pedagogically.) It was our conviction that emphasis should first be put on the student's being a composer, treating the electronic medium as one of many devices he could use in producing music. That policy remained for some time the focus of the department, though *musique concrète* (the modification of natural sounds) has sometimes been combined with electronically generated sounds.

The impact of the studio on the faculty and students was felt immediately. I realized that a composer nearing sixty (like myself) had to make electronic tape conform to his sense of musical style and taste, while a young composer whose style was evolving could absorb that medium much more easily. I had neither the time nor the energy to become an "electronic composer," but the impact on my orchestration, on instrumental articulation, and even on the importance of pitch was considerable. Some students became so interested in the equipment and so adept at electronic construction and engineering that they stopped being composers. Only a few students, such as Gerald Plain and David Bates, developed individuality in their electronic music.

Except for the addition of the electronic studio, the events of the academic year of 1964-65 were unexceptional. The ONCE concerts had reached a point where they were less controversial. Perhaps the group was already looking for a more national audience. Student rebellion was no longer focussed on the arts but rather on the social problems arising from the Vietnam War.

Gretchen and I went to the premiere of the *Divertissement,* which was performed twice by a group that included William and Camilla Doppmann, Ling Tung and Richard Waller. The concert was in the great hall of the new Senior Center at Bowdoin College, and the performance was very good indeed. We spent a few days in Maine, eating lobsters and visiting with the local music faculty. I encouraged them to start a little music press and offered to let them have the *Divertissement* as the first issue, even paying for the printing, if I could have a certain number of copies. Thus, the Bowdoin Music Press was born. Their young composer, Elliott Schwartz, took it in hand and developed an interesting series of publications.

On December 9 and 10, the Louisville Orchestra under Robert Whitney performed and recorded my *Symphony No. 1 ("Communiqué 1943")*. Bill Woolsey, the local critic, described it as "an essay in a popular harmonic idiom," and continued: "It remains viable today, to judge by the unrestrained applause that brought the visiting composer back to the stage of the Brown Theatre for three curtain calls after his composition was finished." It was also performed on three concerts of the National Symphony Orchestra in Washington, D. C.

I was invited to be guest composer at the Symposium of Contemporary Music at the University of Kansas where my *Edge of Shadow, Seventh String Quartet* and *Spherical Madrigals* were performed. The critic Sandor Kallai of the *Kansas City Times* wrote these nice words: "Coupled with those of his works I had already heard, these were more than sufficient to convince me that Finney is one of the towering musical creative forces of this generation." (May 5, 1965)

I faced deadlines on three commissions during 1965. The United States Department of Commerce asked me to organize music for the International Fair at Poznan, Poland, beginning June 13, and to write a work for the Poznan Percussion Ensemble, one of the oldest in Europe, headed by Jerzy Zgodzinski. I had also accepted a commission from Carleton College to compose an orchestral work celebrating their centennial, to be premiered by the Minneapolis Symphony Orchestra under Stanislaw Skrowaczewski. Mario di Bonaventura planned to devote two weeks to my music in August at the Dartmouth College Congregation of the Arts' new Hopkins Center, and invited me, as guest composer, to write an orchestral work for that occasion.

While in Oxford I had started a humorous setting of Chaucer's The *Nun's Priest's Tale* which Bonaventura wanted to premiere. For Poznan I decided to write *Three Studies in Fours* for percussion, and since my mind was so much on that medium, I decided to compose for Carleton College a *Concerto for Percussion and Orchestra*. All very well, but when would I find the time to compose them?

That autumn I finished *The Nun's Priest's Tale* for a Narrator (tenor, dressed in priest's robes and singing from a lectern), Chanticleer (baritone), Pertelote (soprano), the Fox (bass), a women's chorus of chickens, a men's chorus (dressed, like the fox, in tails), a folk-song singer guitarist who would start and end the show singing "Fox went out on a stormy night," and a small orchestra with lots of percussion. It turned out to be a secular miracle play which could be staged in various ways. I was amused by the different viewpoints of Chaucer's tale and the old folksong, which is told from the fox's viewpoint. The perform- ance was funny and got laughs from the audience.

The *Concerto for Percussion and Orchestra* was not to be per- formed until 1966, so I could work more leisurely on that. *Three Studies in Fours* was soon composed and copied.

We left for Paris late in May and spent two weeks there waiting for our baggage that had gone astray, forcing us to buy new outfits before going on to Poznan in mid-June. I received a Certificate of Merit for my work at the Fair, which I find very funny. It is true that I sang folk songs all over Poland and enjoyed myself a lot, but at the Fair my job was to organize a rock group and a jazz band to play on the terrace outside the American Pavilion!

The orchestra was made up of young Polish kids who played on beautiful instruments manufactured in the United States. Each per- former was given an imitation leather jacket. Of course, they had never had such instruments to play on before and they loved every minute of it. They were really nice kids, and I had to guard the guitar strings, because they were almost unobtainable in Poland and our supply had a tendency to disappear quickly. But we had anticipated that and had plenty in reserve. The boys' pleasure in playing was contagious, and we always had crowds gathered to listen. Poland was a little grim, so it was a joy to see young people having such a wonderful time and feeling so proud of their accomplishment.

Three Studies in Fours received a very professional performance, but the hall in which it was performed was so resonant that the instruments were blurred. No matter! It was a great event, and I was loaded with flowers after the performance.

In Warsaw I saw many of the important Polish composers and heard their music. Several had studied with Nadia Boulanger. Some were interested in electronic music and showed me through their national electronic studio. I was amazed to find that composers gave their sketches to technicians who produced the tapes. There is something to be said for this process, but it was not the way I would handle the problem. I visited the Polish music-publishing establishment in Cracow and found interesting their technique of copying by a kind of assembly line. I couldn't imagine sitting all day and making one kind of spot or one kind of line, but I did realize why the fad of omitting the staff when an instrument was not playing had come into vogue.

The young composers I met made me a little sad. Unless they had gained enough reputation to have their music performed in the West, the state bureaucracy became a serious obstacle for them. Young composers were frustrated. They were given enough paper to compose the score, which was then sent to Warsaw for the parts to be copied. The wait could be very long, sometimes many years. It must be said, however, that no composer was starving and all were respected as a part of the musical community.

We flew from Warsaw to Budapest, where I was able to meet young composers whose music I had heard in Paris at UNESCO in 1964. When we flew to Holland, it was like coming out from under a cloud. The rest of the summer was spent in Stockholm, Copenhagen and Scotland. In Scotland we rented a car and drove through the Highlands to the Isle of Skye.

When we arrived back in Ann Arbor, we found a letter saying that my *Divertissement* would be performed at Tanglewood on August 4. So we packed up the car and left almost immediately for the Berkshires. After the performance we drove to Northampton where we spent the intervening days before the two weeks at the Congregation of the Arts in Hanover, New Hampshire.

Except perhaps for the part of the Fox, the premiere of *The Nun's Priest's Tale* was just as I hoped it would be. James W. Symington sang the folksong with perfect diction. The soloists, especially Michael Best who sang the difficult Narrator's part, were all first rate, and the orchestra and chorus were excellent and well rehearsed. The performance had a real gusto.

We got back to Ann Arbor just in time for the opening of the school year. Faced with the heavy teaching load, the burden of having all the composition students in our home immediately, and the long list of house guests and other social demands, I realized that I could not continue as I had the last sixteen years.

In February, when I was offered a very attractive position at the University of California in San Diego, I went to talk with Roger Heynes, the Vice President for Faculty Affairs at the University of Michigan. We had a frank discussion about the failure of the University to live up to the contract wherein I had accepted the position in 1949. (The letter from Dean Moore, which I had of course kept, spelled out clearly that understanding.) Heynes pointed out that if I were on campus, it would be difficult for me to protect my time. He advised me to spend one semester on campus and the rest of the year away and unavailable.

I had no desire to start out on a new and demanding job, so we went to New York City to look around for an apartment that we could rent from January to August. Our friends, Matthew and Hannah Josephson, whom we had met at the Academy/Institute, planned to leave for Europe after Christmas and offered to rent us their apartment in Greenwich Village. With this delightful prospect in mind, we struggled through the fall knowing that we would spend the winter, spring and summer in New York City.

The highlight of the fall of 1965 was the Music Department's first festival of electronic music. The concerts included important works by Milton Babbitt and Mario Davidovsky, who were special guests, as well as compositions by Leslie Bassett, George Wilson, and my own *Three Pieces*. Wilson, as director of our studio, did a superb job of organizing the festival and the concerts of electronic music.

In 1966 we started employing student composers to house-sit for us when we were away. George Wilson was the first, and he repaired the screen on our porch. Our first real "house boy" was Richard Toensing. He helped with the yard, zipped through the house with the vacuum cleaner, drove us to and from the airport, forwarded our mail, and telephoned us whenever there was a problem. We payed these students, of course, but I think they enjoyed the greater contact and the criticism I could give them as composers and the chance to use my music studio when I was away.

During the fall the copying of the *Concerto for Percussion and Orchestra* was finished and everything was ready for the premiere, scheduled for November of 1966. On December 30, Russell Stanger conducted the Minneapolis Symphony Orchestra in my *Variations for Orchestra*, and I flew out to hear the performance of that work composed a decade earlier. When I returned, we flew to New York City and settled in at 23 Bank Street, an address which has since become a very important part of our lives.

CHAPTER XVII

1967 - 1970

As a member of the National Academy/Institute of Arts and Letters I belonged for the first time to an organization that was an established part of the artistic life of New York City. While I had often visited the city during my twenty years at Smith College, I had never been a member of any group. The Academy/Institute was not just an honorary institution that held social gatherings in its impressive building on 155th Street. It was also dedicated to giving awards to young or neglected artists. The members were friendly to us when we attended dinners, and I enjoyed serving on committees, especially those that rewarded young composers. I felt that I could make a special contribution by speaking for artists from the Middle and Far West.

A young American composer dreams of going to New York City and becoming known as a freelance composer. Of course, it doesn't usually work out that way, which is perhaps just as well. When I studied with Boulanger, most of my friends were from New York City, and they had every intention of returning there. Certainly the older composers that I looked up to — men like Copland, Sessions, and Harris, all members of the Academy/Institute — were New York oriented.

I had been very lucky to find a job at Smith College which was a stimulating cultural center and located in the peaceful New England countryside. I realized I was not really the aggressive urban type who could deal with the professional demands of a large city and that I enjoyed living in a small college town. So, I made an immediate compromise, which all through my life, and for valid reasons, has led to more compromises. Nevertheless, the attractions of New York City to me, as a composer, remained.

Just as we were settled into the new apartment in January we had to fly down to Miami for a performance of my *First Symphony*. When we returned, I immediately went up to Gimbel's and bought an electric piano. Though I hated the sound of the thing, for some mysterious reason I composed better when I had a piano around, even if I never used it. It was portable, so I could easily carry it up to our apartment on the top floor of the old house.

In March we flew back to Ann Arbor and then on to Kansas City where Hans Schwieger was performing my *Second Symphony*. We made a second trip to Kansas in late April where I was to be guest of Wichita State University's Fine Arts Festival at which my *Third Symphony* was performed. Then we returned to New York for the annual ceremony of the Academy/Institute in May.

Just as we had loved getting back to our home for the spring, we found it wonderful to return to the little apartment on Bank Street, and to the feeling of anonymity of the big city.

During the spring Catherine Anthony, the owner of the Bank Street house, died. She had willed the property to her niece, but with the provision that the tenants of the apartments could not be put out. That led to the formation of a cooperative with the tenants buying the house. The Josephsons were to move to Miss Anthony's apartment on the second floor, and a lady was going to buy the top-floor apartment. Just as we were packing to leave for Ann Arbor, Matty Josephson called me from the country and said that the lady had decided not to buy the top floor apartment. Would I like to buy it? Without hesitating, I said, "Yes." It was, I must say, the best business investment I ever made.

When we left for Ann Arbor, we realized that we would have to spend the fall furnishing the apartment. The co-op planned to hire a contractor to make some basic changes and repairs, such as adding air conditioning to our apartment. We decided to move furniture that we had stored in our attic in Ann Arbor and to buy there other things that we would need, trucking everything east at one time. I would at last have the studio in New York City that I had long dreamed of.

July and August were filled with commitments on the West Coast, all very pleasant but interrupting our stay in New York. I was guest at the Summer Academy of Contemporary Arts at the University of Oregon in Eugene, lecturing and listening to programs of my music. I remember most the beautiful countryside and the chance to get acquainted with Vincent and Dorothea Persichetti, who were also there. I taught for a period of time at the University of Washington in Seattle, living in Jack Verrall's house with its enormous boysenberry garden.

The fall term at the University of Michigan was heavier than usual. I felt I should lighten Leslie Bassett's load as much as possible since he would have a very full schedule when I would be away during the second semester. Leslie had just won the Pulitzer Prize for his *Variations for Orchestra* and needed time to finish commissions that were coming his way. He had developed into an important composer, and each new work seemed to me better than the last. Since I would be sixty in December, I began to see retirement ahead and felt that the stature of the composition department would depend on Bassett and Wilson.

A new, talented group of young composers had come to the university, and represented, I thought, the next generation. They were hard to teach, and only slightly concerned with the Vietnam situation. They loved to bombard me at their lessons with four-letter words. But to my amazement OSS had schooled me in a vigorous vocabulary and I could return as good as I received. My seminar was lively. I had decided to devote it to the study of Debussy, but the students rebelled, demanding the right to teach themselves whatever they wanted to study. Robert Morris took over and brilliantly introduced the class to Hindu musical practices.

William Albright, Robert Morris and Russell Peck had transferred from Eastman to Michigan. Sydney Hodkinson had left his job in Ohio to do his doctoral studies at Michigan. Kurt Carpenter was an undergraduate with considerable talent. Jack Fortner, David Maves and David Bates were still enrolled. Gerald Plain, one of the most interesting students, was extremely talented but unable or unwilling to cope with the requirements for the doctoral degree. He was lined up to take care of our house while we were away in the spring, and when we returned we found things in better shape than when we left. We are still devoted to Gerald, who is now a very original composer. He has had trouble adapting to any academic environment and has turned instead to cabinet work which is unusually creative and beautiful. His lovely wife is a distinguished librarian at the Eastman library.

Like many other students, Gerald was very much involved in working with electronic tape. I delighted particularly in the way that he and David Bates reflected their personalities in their tapes. Bates achieved a lyricism that was quite unusual. Gerald reflected his Tennessee roots in such works as *The Chattanooga Choo* and *Golden Wedding*, in which he used the family music box as the source of sound. He was able to fix anything that needed fixing in our house and could whiz through with the vacuum cleaner like a Tennessee tornado.

During the spring of 1967, Marjorie Nicolson helped me again to find a text for a choral work which the University of Michigan had commissioned for the centennial celebrations of the University Musical Society and for performance in the May Festival. We wandered through the Princeton Library talking about what kind of text should follow *Still Are New Worlds* in the trilogy. Suddenly, Marjorie thought of Shelley's "Adonais," which is concerned with Man's inhumanity to Man. When I went over the poem, I found ways to shape the text to give the emphasis I wanted. Thus, I spent the fall working on the score of *The Martyr's Elegy*, which is the work that resulted.

The School of Music devoted the Festival of Contemporary Music in November to a celebration of my sixtieth birthday. They repeated *Still Are New Worlds,* giving me a tape of the work, and included two works of mine on each program, concluding the Festival with *The Nun's Priest's Tale.* I gave a lecture in which I argued with a tape that I had made in advance. It seemed to me a lively way to give a lecture, since the questions came from speakers around the auditorium. The title of the lecture was "Does Music Have Form?" and I discussed the circular form of my *Variations for Orchestra.* We were kept very busy with house guests and gatherings of composition students. Zoltan Kodály and his wife visited us in the fall and we had a party, inviting all the composers in town.

In November I made several trips to New York City to serve on committees, and during one of these trips our furniture finally arrived at 23 Bank Street. I was able to have things put in more or less the right places so that when we came down for the winter it wouldn't be too difficult to get the apartment in shape. French Fogle, our Claremont friend who was now teaching at New York University, came over and helped me get things in shape.

I flew from New York to Minneapolis and met Gretchen at the airport where we rented a car and drove to Carleton College. My *Concerto for Percussion and Orchestra* was premiered at the college on November 17, and performed the next evening in Minneapolis. After the concerts we flew to New York City and Gretchen settled the apartment while I went down to Baltimore to hear my *Fantasy in Two Movements* performed by Gabriel Banat, who was then playing it all over the country. We were in New York only a few days, enough time to get the apartment operating and to visit Grant Beglarian in New Jersey.

Activities in Ann Arbor proceeded at a hectic pace during December with concerts of the ONCE Festival very much on the students' minds. Morton Feldman and Theodore Antoniou were guests during the fall and there were endless social gatherings. I began to long for the quiet life of New York! Still, we had a pleasant Christmas holiday with Ross and Becky and on December 30, George Wilson drove us to the airport for our first real escape to Bank Street.

On New Year's Eve we went to a party at the Josephsons where we met Jerry Piel, the editor of *Scientific American*, and many other writers. We started off the New Year watching the Rose Bowl game on television and trying to get our apartment warm. The house had an old furnace that gave us lots of trouble for a decade, and our north windows let in blasts of cold air. By putting strips of newspaper in the window cracks and having a fire in our fireplace, we could get the temperature up to the mid-sixties.

We were invited to a big party for Elizabeth Lutyens, the English composer, at the Sonnenberg residence on Gramercy Park. As Virgil Thomson put it, "You are going into society." I had to buy a tuxedo for the occasion. We set out in great style to our one and only venture into that sort of thing — and were bored to death. Little by little during January we settled into a more relaxed routine. When the Kansas City Symphony Orchestra telephoned to commission a symphonic work, I settled into my studio and started the sketches for the score that became my *Symphonie Concertante.*

We had many friends to lunch or dinner — Jean and Bob Bacher from Caltec, Wallace and Maxine Berry and Leslie and Anita Bassett from Ann Arbor. I served on several committees, among them The American Society of University Composers (which was then being organized) and The American Academy in Rome. I even went to a few concerts of contemporary music. But I was able to compose and was stimulated rather than depressed by the activity.

In late February we flew back to Ann Arbor where Gerald Plain met us at the airport. We had been worried about leaving our house for too long, but we found everything in good shape. I went to rehearsals of *The Martyr's Elegy*, and to a performance of my *Concerto for Percussion and Orchestra* which the Minneapolis Symphony Orchestra was playing on its tour. Finally, I had to spend a week in the hospital having a minor operation.

Neither Gretchen nor I were in very good health during the sixties.

I was fighting hypertension, and the medication I took had physical side-effects of dizziness that frightened Gretchen. Her arthritic condition was worsening, which made walking and sleeping difficult for her. We lacked our usual energy and we would get depressed when our activities left us exhausted, but we could find no way to cut down on routine demands. Our sons were both doing well and were involved with their own professional lives and their growing families. We certainly had no reason to worry about them. But we did, of course.

Returning to New York in late March, we stopped for lectures and concerts in Rochester before finally arriving for activities at the Academy/Institute. I had to fly to St. Louis for meetings of the American Society of University Composers. Arriving back at Bank Street, I found that our roof leaked and our skylights had to be repaired. That spring I received the Gold Medal from Brandeis University for my lifetime contribution as a composer, and for this ceremony my two brothers and their wives came to the city to visit us. Nat had given us two large pictures painted by the Mexican artist Jeime Oates who also visited us at that time.

We had to go back to Ann Arbor at the end of April for the premiere of *The Martyr's Elegy* at the May Festival. In spite of all the social activities, I was able to finish my *Symphonie Concertante* before we set off on the long car trip which eventually led us back to New York City.

We drove to Urbana to visit Ross and Becky and on to Millikin University for a festival devoted to my music. From Illinois we drove to Maryland where the Baltimore Symphony Orchestra performed my early work *Hymn, Fuguing and Holiday.* Back at Bank Street, we found the repairs had been done and our air conditioner installed. We went to the Ceremony of the Academy/Institute of Arts and Letters with the Josephsons and entertained Daryl and Peggy Dayton who had driven up from Washington. Finally, on the first of June, we drove to Martha's Vineyard to open up our place on Chappaquiddick for the summer.

Even though the job of opening our house on "Chappy" was an ordeal, we loved the little place so much that it always seemed worth the effort. I had promised to give the commencement address for the New England Conservatory, so we drove to Boston for that and back to "Chappy" before leaving for New York City.

That summer we combined teaching at Tanglewood with going to New York to see the Hamburg Opera perform Hindemith's *Mathis der Maler,* Berg's *Lulu* and Gunther Schuller's *The Visitation.* We drove back to Ann Arbor so that I could be on hand for concerts of my music at Oberlin, performances that were badly prepared and that I might better have missed.

After we got back to Bank Street in late July, I began to work on the libretto for *Weep Torn Land*, an opera I had originally called "Bent's Sons." Gunther Schuller conducted my *Concerto for Percussion and Orchestra* at Tanglewood, and we enjoyed visiting Madame Koussevitsky again at Saranac.

We flew back to Ann Arbor for the start of the academic year and the dinner which we always had for the composition faculty and students soon after Labor Day. Eugene Kurtz had arrived to teach and talked to the group about being a composer in Paris. Niccolò Castiglioni had spent the spring at Michigan and to judge from the looks of my studio, had practically lived in it.

The big events of the fall were the concerts celebrating the sesquicentennial of the University. Roger Sessions had been commissioned to write a symphony for the celebration (his *Symphony No. 7*) and Luigi Dallapiccola was invited as a special guest. Roger and Lisl were our house guests and Luigi spent most of his time with us. He and Roger were close friends and spent hours talking about their respective operas: *Ulysses* and *Montezuma*. They were both very strong, self-centered individuals, and though I enjoyed every minute of their visit, we were completely exhausted when it was over.

Once again, when we got to New York we felt a release from the tensions of our life in Ann Arbor but dreaded the commitments that had accumulated for the spring. We had to fly back in February for lectures and concerts at Kent State University, then almost immediately we drove to Santa Fe and Bent's Fort, and from there on to Kansas City for the premiere of my *Symphonie Concertante* which Hans Schwieger conducted beautifully. My piece was written to give exposure to his best orchestral performers and proved to be brilliant but demanding.

Nat, who was president of the Gridiron Club in Washington, D. C., wanted us to be on hand for the annual Gridiron Banquet. Gretchen bought a spiffy new dress and I found a homburg hat which failed to give me the appearance of a professional business man. But we enjoyed very much meeting Nat's distinguished friends and were very proud of the way he handled the festivities.

Even when we got to New York, I was trapped into doing things that I should have refused: sitting on a panel at Yale University to advise the president on the faculty of the school of music, meeting with Norman Lloyd of the Rockefeller Foundation to discuss a future recording project, and attending meetings of the National Music Council at the Academy/Institute of Arts and Letters.

We loved having our friends come to dinner and especially enjoyed having Ross and Becky stop with us on their way to Africa. We enjoyed going to many of the concerts, though it was becoming harder for us to work the next day when we went out in the evening. I was working on *2 Acts for 3 Players* and Gretchen was writing an article for the *Dictionary of the History of Ideas* which Scribner's was publishing. There was never enough time, and certainly no time to just sit and think.

I was now entering into a very productive period. My music was moving more and more into the area of memory, and I had become deeply committed to my concept of form based on symmetrical hexachords. Commissions could be accepted only if I could make the work fit somehow into these dominating ideas. When G. Leblanc, Inc. called and asked me to compose a sonata for clarinet and piano, I gasped and said "I don't think I can compose a sonata." "That doesn't matter," they replied. "Can I make it for clarinet, percussion and piano?" "That, too, would be all right." The result was *2 Acts for 3 Players,* the work that drew on my memory of the "flicks" I had seen as a child.

Memory has a curious impact on time and since music is so much a temporal art, memory has a great impact on a composer's work. Memory makes the past into the present. A temporal art is of necessity involved only with the present and can only seem to move backwards in time. Even in science fiction, the future, by imagination, becomes the present. It was this impact of memory on time that interested me.

I realized that a system of symmetrical hexachords could easily negate the whole idea of twelve-tone music, and I was intrigued with the fact that a technique that seemed so revolutionary was actually rooted in the oldest traditions of Western music. Consider the following symmetrical hexachords that result from the traditional circle of fifths starting on F:

Example 4:

Each hexachord fits the pentatonic scale on which are based many folk tunes that I sang as a child.

I needed time to think out where I was in my musical career — at the end of something or at the beginning. I had moved so gradually to this position and was so flooded with musical ideas that I could not think that I was at the end. And if I had indeed reached that point, it hardly mattered to me. There seemed to me to be such an enormous potential in the theoretical basis I had evolved (a basis so related to the modal, triadic and serial techniques of the past), that my creative path was perfectly clear.

I spoke to the dean about the possibility of retiring in 1973 when I would be sixty-six years old. I pointed out the need for a junior appointment in the composition department and suggested William Albright, who seemed to me the student most likely to develop into a national composer and who would bring ideas that would complement both Bassett and Wilson. I felt that the teaching staff of the department could handle the increased registration.

We left for New York on January 2, and spent the most relaxed winter there that we had ever had. When Yale University telephoned to ask whether I would be interested in heading their School of Music, I had no trouble at all refusing. My only commitment was to attend concerts of my music and to lecture at Baylor University in late February. We decided to spend two weeks in Mexico visiting Nat and Flora in Taxco. We returned to Ann Arbor in April and drove to Indiana State University in Terre Haute to hear Thomas Briccetti and the Indianapolis Symphony Orchestra perform my *Symphonie Concertante.*

July of 1969 was important to me because of the remarkable pictures from space of the "earthrise" seen from the moon. It was then that I realized that the final work of my choral trilogy would be called *Earthrise.* That July also brought tragic news. I was shocked and saddened by the death of Walter Hinrichsen who had meant so much to me in my relations with C. F. Peters. I was feeling no enthusiasm for the semester ahead.

I had accepted too many invitations to be guest composer at festivals devoted to my music. There was one in Urbana, with the chance to see my new granddaughter; one in Cincinnati, with a gratifying visit with Paul and Christa Cooper; one in Columbia, Missouri, which we did en route to New York City. These trips broke up the semester, but they took more energy than I should have given.

I don't think I was doing a very good job of teaching. I lost my temper too easily. I found it hard to tolerate dull students, especially those who set out to convert me to some idea that had been a part of the avant-garde ideology two decades earlier. Some students were deeply concerned over the Vietnam War and I could certainly sympathize with them. The times were hard for both students and teachers. I simply didn't have enough energy to give the students the technique to deal with any musical situations that might develop in the future.

We decided to fly to Portugal in February just to break up the winter and relax a little. Charles and Betty Odegaard joined us, but on returning to New York, they had to fly to Seattle immediately when Charles learned there had been riots at the University of Washington where he was president. Gretchen and I settled back into our usual Bank Street routine.

CHAPTER XVIII

1970 - 1973

FROM our large south windows on Bank Street
we look out on lower Manhattan over the chimney
pots to a beautiful view of the World Trade Center
and southeast to the tower of the Jefferson Market.
I have always found that I compose best when I
am above the street sounds. Musicians often walk
down the center of Bank Street, singing Italian
opera arias or playing on the accordion or the
trumpet, periodically picking up the coins that
people throw from windows. At Christmas small
groups sing carols. In the winter the southern sun
beats in, so warm that I strip to my waist while
working at my desk. In summer, when the sun is
high, little heat comes from the windows and
there is usually a soft breeze from the ocean.

Our apartment is a "walk through," which
means we get breezes from both the big windows
facing south in the living room and studio and the
windows at the other end of the apartment facing
north. The dressing room is really a part of the
living room and has built-in closets and cabinets
and a skylight. A door separates these rooms from
the dining room with its very large, north-facing
skylight, and next to that, separated only by a
folding screen, is our bedroom with big windows

that look out onto the gardens below. One of our neighbors has two handsome geese that she brings in from her farm. From the dining room a door leads to the entrance and the kitchen and bathroom.

The old house was built in 1850 and has fine marble fireplaces, even on our floor, and beautiful brass hinges and knobs on all the doors. Although we have to walk up three flights of stairs, we prefer our apartment to all the others because of the sunlight, the sea breeze and the view of the city. We hear bird songs most of the year: finches and song sparrows, mockingbirds, jays, cardinals, and a mourning dove that builds her nest on the fire escape.

Over the years there have been many changes. The house needed a new furnace, roofing, painting and new brownstone steps leading to the front door. I put storm windows on the north where they would not be seen from the street and new windows on the south. (Bank Street is in an historic area, and we are not allowed to make any changes to the exterior.) Our bathroom has an old-fashioned tub that is actually built into the partitions and is too big to be removed through the door, but we like it because it is deep and easy to get into. Our kitchen is small but very adequate. The furniture that we brought down from Ann Arbor is also adequate and includes a few antiques that we bought cheap during the Depression and refinished.

I often speak of the "miracle of Bank Street," because when we get there, the problems of the University disappear and I can give my mind over to my own music. It usually takes only a few days before Gretchen is working on her book at her desk in the bedroom and I am composing in my studio at the other end of the apartment.

I was becoming bored with teaching; I was weary. I hope my students didn't suffer too much from my lack of energy. I have always taught on the basis of what I hear in a student's work and not on the basis of a predetermined theory that I wish to impose. It is not an easy way to teach, because it demands an open-minded concentration on what the composer is trying to accomplish and a ruthless attempt to develop a student's self-criticism, without belittling his effort. I have never been able to accomplish very much with a student in a short period of time, since I have to wait until the student solves his problems for himself. Still, young composers do often come up to play their scores for me. I try to be frank, but kind, in my criticism.

Being able to use one semester to teach at the University and the other to compose in New York City proved to be a blessing for me as a composer but a handicap as a teacher. I always went away in January feeling that I had failed — that I had left for my colleagues a job unfinished.

My classroom teaching was another matter. I felt no such guilt. It was inevitable that over nearly fifty years of teaching I should repeat myself, and it sometimes seemed to me that I could hear myself echo. The important thing was to make the students articulate and critical in their aural analysis of music. I suspect I talked less, which was probably all for the good. But I always posed the question: "What's happening in the music?"

Because I spent so much time in New York, it was often possible for me to help students receive financial grants or jobs, and on one occasion I was able to get a grant for the electronic studio to buy badly needed equipment. So that I might be more aware of what students were thinking, I made a point of going to concerts where I could hear the compositions that younger composers were writing. For commissioned works, I gained the time to compose in a more leisurely and thoughtful way, and perhaps for this reason was able to get my blood pressure under control.

We became very attached to the talented composition students who looked after our house for us and drove us to the airport. During the seventies Thomas Jansen, Stephen Chatman, Jerrod Beynon, Craig Urquhart, Peter Farmer, John Lennon, Ted Dollarhide, William Neil and Skip Stahley took care of us. During the eighties Richard Lavenda, Michael Kurak, Geoff Stanton, Richard Campanelli, Frank Ticheli, John Kennedy, David Asplin and Evan Chambers took over. They were a wonderful group of young men, and talented composers, too. I think they all felt they learned something from working in my studio, and since I got to know them and their music so well, I gladly helped them in any way I could to forward their careers. Several received Charles Ives Scholarships from the Academy/Institute of Arts and Letters; several received Rome Fellowships; many hold important academic positions. We are profoundly grateful to all of them.

We had an entirely different group of friends in New York City, contacts at 23 Bank Street, at the Academy/Institute and at C. F. Peters Corporation. Roger Sessions was teaching at Juilliard, and he and Lisl would come up for dinner at the end of a busy day, as did Mario and Elaine Davidovsky.

I served on various committees, which in time became burdensome, but during this period, I enjoyed giving awards to other composers. Harmony Ives had just given the entire income from her late husband's music to establish the Ives Scholarships to be awarded by the Academy/Institute to young, talented student composers, and to forward for a limited period the recognition of Ives' music. We were eager to give the first scholarship in 1970, to get it started, even though the awards committee had already met in January. Elliott Carter and I served on the Rome Prize committee that year, and after the meeting we stopped at his home on Twelfth Street, a few blocks from Bank Street, to see whether one of the names passed over might not be given the first Ives Scholarship. We decided on Joseph Schwantner. John Kirkpatrick received an award for his editing of Ives' music. As time went on, the royalties increased substantially, partly because of the grants that were given to forward the editing and publication of Ives' music. Later we found that we could legally give an award to an experimental composer who was no longer a student, and thus honor Ives' unusual place as an American composer. These committees were very conscientious, listening to hundreds of scores over a period of three days. There were prejudices, of course, such as my eagerness to include composers from the Middle and Far West, but the winners often became important composers.

Speaking of prejudice, I think there is no doubt that women and Black composers should have received more awards. That has changed over the past two decades, as the membership of the Academy/Institute has changed. The problem that committees face today is how to judge music that is improvised immediately onto tape but not notated so that others can repeat the performance.

During these years I had more performances than I can hope to recall. The Bucharest Quartet performed my *Divertissement* on their world tour, and I was able to hear them in Baltimore. I was most impressed by their young clarinetist, Aurelian Octav Popa. My *Concerto for Percussion and Orchestra* was not only performed by the Blackearth Percussion Group with orchestras in the Midwest, but also in Poland by the Poznan Percussion Group. My chamber music was performed in Athens and Paris. The Royal Christchurch Musical Society in New Zealand performed my *Edge of Shadow*.

All of the works that I composed in the early 1970s were premiered: *Landscapes Remembered* by the Contemporary Music Festival at Cornell University under Karel Husa (November 5, 1972), *Spaces* for large orchestra by the Fargo-Moorhead Orchestra under Sigvald Thompson (March 26, 1972). When we were in Fargo to hear the premiere of *Spaces*, we drove to Valley City, for sentimental reasons, only to get caught in a very bad blizzard. *Summer in Valley City* was premiered under William Revelli in Ann Arbor by the University of Michigan Band on April 1, 1971, and then taken on tour to Europe and finally performed at Carnegie Hall on May 28. That excellent performance was recorded. The School of Music had a party to celebrate my sixty-fifth birthday. William Doppmann performed my *Second Piano Concerto* with the University Orchestra under Theo Alcantara, and Thomas Hilbish conducted my cantata *The Remorseless Rush of Time* (November 1, 1972). The most exciting event for me was Sergiu Comissiona's performance of my *Symphony No. 4* on May 9, 1973, with the Baltimore Symphony Orchestra, which had commissioned the work. Since it was broadcast, I was able to get a good tape of the performance. There were many social occasions thanks to the board of the orchestra, and to Robert Hall Lewis, who has done so much to promote my music in Baltimore. We saw Otto Kraushaar, the president of Goucher College and an old colleague of mine from Smith College days. We stuffed on oysters and crab cakes and thoroughly enjoyed ourselves. The work was generally well received with a few hisses mixed in with the cheers. The critics liked the work, and Comissiona performed it several times in Europe.

I have always been very close to my two brothers. Theodore M. Finney, whose *A History of Music* had become very popular, was head of the Music Department of the University of Pittsburgh. He had a lovely farm near Bedford where he grew roses. About this time a telephone pole, eaten by termites, fell on him and damaged his back, and he suffered terrible pain for years before his death in 1978.

Nat S. Finney, after serving as head of the Washington Bureau of the *Buffalo Evening News*, retired, just at the moment when his wife died. He did free-lance writing for a while, and then decided to sell his home and move to Taxco, Mexico, hoping to write the novel he had long had in his mind. It was, of course, a very foolish move, especially selling his house and moving all of his belongings to Mexico. He fell in the early summer of 1971 and broke his hip. When he first telephoned me, he minimized the seriousness of his fall, and we continued our plans to drive to Chappaquiddick. When we got there, we received a call that he was in very serious condition and needed to be moved to a hospital where he could receive better care. I called my son Ross and asked him to fly to Mexico and bring Nat to Ann Arbor. Then I called the bone surgeon at the University Hospital and made arrangements for Nat to enter as soon as he arrived. We packed up the car and drove back to Ann Arbor.

When Nat arrived at the airport, we rushed him to the hospital where he was immediately operated on. There had been so much infection that he was never again able to walk easily. After a few days in the hospital and a few more in a nursing home, he was able to fly back to Washington and move into an apartment in Leisure World where he was comfortable and could see his old friends. But his spirit was broken, and he never recovered full mobility.

My colleagues asked me to devote my last seminar to my own music. I have tapes of most of my works and could play them as I wished, since I felt no pressure to cover any special ground. Because I have a vivid memory of the experience of composing each work, it is no burden for me to talk about my scores. I had always avoided discussing my own music with students, largely because I wanted to keep my professions as a composer and a teacher separate.

Our sons both had jobs in the East, Ross in the Boston area and Henry at the University of Vermont in Burlington. We thought of selling our house in Ann Arbor and buying a place in New England near New York City, but the more we looked at property, the more we realized how much we loved our home in Ann Arbor and valued our friends there. Our house was too large for us, but I loved my studio and Gretchen her study. It was expensive to fly back and forth to New York, though it took less time than it would to drive into the city from New England. We were worried about inflation, but during my final year when I wouldn't be involved in teaching, I would receive full salary and also income from the Teachers Insurance and Annuity Association (TIAA) and from Social Security.

Retirement for my brothers and for many of my friends had been a catastrophe, and I left for Bank Street with some fears. In a sense I wasn't retiring at all, since I had commissions to work on. A composer doesn't retire. I knew that the Composition Department would continue to grow with Leslie Bassett as the new head and with William Bolcom recently appointed to the faculty. The student enrollment in composition was healthy, even if a little excessive, and certainly very talented. It took a little longer for us to relax and start working when we arrived at our apartment, but once again the miracle of Bank Street happened.

CHAPTER XIX

1973 - 1976

EVEN though I did not intend to "retire" as a composer, I could find many reasons both for and against an early retirement from the University at the age of sixty-seven. Because of the rapid inflation of the time, I felt some fear of no longer having an annual salary, and the administration urged me to wait until I was seventy. For my last year of teaching, I would be on double salary, but after that my only income from the University would be the annuity I had built up over fifty-three years. Income from my compositions had increased substantially, and it seemed to me that we could live without the burden of academia. I needed more time to compose some of the large works that were in my mind.

At the University, departmental organization had changed fundamentally in the three decades since I had been hired to "organize and head a department of composition." Now the head of a department was elected by its members. This "democratic" procedure may have helped large departments, but it did little for small ones. I had always felt a School of Music should be made up of four divisions: History and Theory, which emphasized scholarhip; Music Education, which was concerned with teaching; Performance, which dealt with skills; and Musical Organizations, which were the school's laboratories. But where did composition belong in all this? I felt that it belonged essentially with Performance rather than Theory, because, however valuable theory is to the composer, he evolves a skill that creates its own theory, and scholarly method is foreign to that evolution. Quite rightly, most deans take it slow and play it safe.

I must admit that teaching had become oppressive. The attitudes of students had changed rapidly since the 1950s and while I had not been influenced very much by the fads in composition which followed one on the heels of the other, the students definitely had. They were very talented, but I found them harder to teach and lost my temper too often, which was bad for my blood pressure. They were more concerned with their own economic futures than with social problems and more willing to become involved in public-relations gimmickry, an attitude that led to conformity and a resistance to dealing with purely musical problems. They lacked the dedication to traditional theories and practice characteristic of the students of the early fifties, or the rebellious enthusiasm for experimentation of the early sixties, or the technological expertise in dealing with electronic machines of the early seventies. They looked instead for ways to promote their reputations. Their attitude was perfectly understandable in a scene that denied them performances and professional income and put such emphasis on popular music, but I sometimes felt that my teaching had become an echo rather than an involvement. My age, my hypertension and my diminished energy all made it harder for me to respond to the new situation.

I knew that in retirement Gretchen and I would be forced to establish a new work routine, and that our lives would be complicated by living in two places, both requiring all the materials we needed for our work. We had already made that adjustment and were eager to accept the new challenge. For all my energy and optimism, I sometimes became embittered and felt that my music was being neglected. There were many times when I would walk down the stairs to my studio, only to turn away, not bearing to face the ordeal of composing. But the great need to hear the completed work would force me back to my desk. My only defence against depression and inactivity has been routine. It has been said that persistence as much as talent characterizes the artist. Talent without persistence adds up to little. Routine is a product of persistence. I realized that the problem I faced in retirement was a serious matter.

And so I made the decision to terminate my connection with the

School of Music of the University of Michigan at the end of the academic year of 1972-1973.

The Rockefeller Foundation had invited us to be in residence at their Villa Serbelloni in Bellagio, Italy, during the fall of '73. In September we flew to Milan and on Lake Como spent several of the most pleasant weeks I can remember. From my studio up the mountain and above the town, I could hear the church bells and children's voices from the schoolyard below. It was a joy to work, and the scores I planned to finish were not problematical. I completed my *Concerto No. 2 for Violin and Orchestra,* which had been commissioned (thanks to Paul Cooper) to be performed by Robert Gerle and the Dallas Symphony Orchestra at the Music Teachers National Association's centenary celebration in 1976. I also worked on *Two Ballades for Flutes and Piano,* commissioned by Keith Bryan and Karen Keys for a premiere at Dumbarton Oaks in 1974.

Climbing down the long stone steps to the town of Bellagio gave us plenty of exercise and the capacity to deal with the wonderful meals that the Villa served. We took long trips on the ferry that runs on the lake, often stopping for a picnic or a meal in some country restaurant. Once we took the bus into Switzerland and viewed the route celebrated in Hemingway's *A Farewell to Arms.* But the view from the Villa was the most beautiful of all, and we passed much of our time talking with the other guests in the lovely gardens.

When we returned to New York City, I found it difficult to get started on a new composition, partly because I had council meetings at the Academy/Institute and also because I had to fly out to Duluth, where I was to lecture and listen to programs of my music at four colleges in the area.

I had expected to be completely free of teaching activities, but I was now obliged to write a stream of letters of recommendation. I didn't have sense enough either to refuse judging contests from all over the country, for which I was rarely paid and which meant receiving big boxes of scores that had to be returned — after struggles with the U. S. Post Office. I found these jobs burdensome, especially in New York City where I had no secretarial help. It was around this time that search and tenure committees were dreamed up, and I seemed to be a perfect target. To be frank, much of my correspondence gave me little pleasure and was very time-consuming.

The new work I was composing, commissioned by David Fetter, the first trombonist of the Baltimore Symphony Orchestra, was to be a collection of pieces for everything from one trombone to five trombones. It contains duets, trios, quartets, and the entire suite can be performed by a quintet. I call it *Tubes I*. It's a light work that I thought trombonists would find useful, but so far as I know it has never been performed since its premiere.

The year passed very quickly with few of the tensions that we had feared. I had not yet found the routine of work that I needed, but I felt sure I soon would. After writing four big works between 1970 and 1973, it was only natural that I should feel "burned out."

The next year we got off on the wrong foot, and for two seasons could never quite get into a comfortable stride. We made unwise decisions that over-taxed our energies and interfered with our work routine. We were productive and enjoyed our activities, but we took on too much.

My schedule shows that in early September of 1974 we drove to Indianapolis where I lectured at the Jordan College of Fine Arts. At the end of the month we visited Ross and Becky and their young family in Urbana, and then flew to New York where I became immediately involved in the affairs of the Academy/Institute. Every day was filled with meetings, concerts and social engagements. Joel Thome and the American Symphony Orchestra da Camera performed my *Landscapes Remembered* on November 3, and then we left without delay for Ann Arbor where the Bryan and Keys Duo performed my *Two Ballades for Flutes and Piano* on the Contemporary Directions concert. After that, it was back to New York for the Academy Luncheon on December 6, with an opera performance squeezed in, and finally home to Ann Arbor for the Christmas holidays. And this was called my "retirement"!

I went down to Baltimore for the premiere of *Tubes I*, and then Gretchen and I flew to Las Vegas to hear Ed London and the University of Nevada Orchestra perform my *Symphony No. 4* on January 26. With all this activity it was no surprise that both of us came down with bad colds. We rented a car and drove to Death Valley, hoping for warmer weather, but the temperature plunged to the freezing point and our colds got worse. Driving on to San Diego, where I was to lecture at the University of California, we enjoyed our stay with my very talented former student, Roger Reynolds, who was also our frequent guest in Greenwich Village. We were both miserably sick during our visit. We flew back to New York just in time to hear Harvey Sollberger and Bennett Lerner give a remarkable performance of my *Two Ballades* at a concert given by the Group for Contemporary Music. I was so ill that I had to stay in bed for a week until we flew back to Ann Arbor. My doctor said I had stomach ulcers, put me on a medical regimen and told me to slow down.

Easier said than done! I had consented to serve on the Editorial

Committee of the Rockefeller Foundation's Recorded Anthology of American Music, then in its formative stages. We met daily from 9:30 to 5:30, establishing the ground rules of the Project.

I don't believe there ever was a time in the history of the country when making such a series of records was so difficult. The project had to be completed in time for the American Bicentennial year. The production staff was eager to establish an on-going recording company to be called "New World Records," and a Board of Trustees, chaired by Michael V. Forrestal, set the guidelines that the Editorial Committee had to follow.

We soon discovered all the prejudices that could easily doom the project before it got off the ground. The committee, at the time it was formed, was chaired by music librarian Don Roberts, and included Milton Babbitt, David Baker, Neely Bruce, H. Wiley Hitchcock, Cynthia Hoover, Gunther Schuller, Mike Seeger, Michael Steinberg, and myself. Herman Krawitz, President of New World Records, and Elizabeth Ostrow, its Director of Research, often sat in on the meetings. It was a diverse group.

As one of its first guidelines the Board of Trustees established that fifty percent of the recordings had to be popular music and fifty percent classic. Nobody questioned the importance of producing recordings of popular music, especially those germinal performances in jazz and rock, which had long been unavailable from the commercial recording companies. However, anyone who has ever taught a course in American Music realizes that the most serious neglect in recordings has been in the areas of classical music and ethnic folk music and that this music spans more time and demands more space. One can cover a great deal of popular music on one side of an LP record which is hardly large enough to contain a symphony. Thus, from the very beginning, an unrealistic limitation on classical and ethnic music was established.

Even the excellent Editorial Committee had very valid differences of viewpoint, based on the experiences — and the prejudices — of the individuals. Perhaps it was inevitable that critical decisions were often made merely on the basis of "I like" or "I don't like." It was thanks to the knowledge and skill of Gunther Schuller that John Knowles Paine's *Mass in D*, reflecting our Civil War, was performed and recorded. Certainly Neely Bruce contributed greatly to our understanding of nineteenth-century American music and agreed with me that more attention should be paid to such figures as Anthony Philip Heinrich and Arthur Farwell, as well as other neglected figures of the last century. The prejudice that only the experimental and popular composers contributed something new to our musical culture leaves the anthology out of balance. There were some important contributions to the music of ethnic groups, thanks often to the leadership of David Baker, the Director of the Institute of Jazz Studies at Indiana University. Looking back, it seems such a pity that the Anthology was made before videotape was easily available, for this media would have been ideal for opera or ballet.

I came away from meetings somewhat depressed because I was made to feel that most of the classic composers in our history were viewed as unimportant. It took more assertiveness than I possessed to ignore the prevailing attitude. Still, the final Anthology seems to me an important contribution, whatever its faults, and I am glad I had a part in putting it together.

Even as a child, I was very sensitive and easily put upon, although very accommodating and very stubborn. Perhaps these qualities came from the fact that I was the youngest and always had to work hard to win praise and attention from my brothers. My father constantly warned I could be easily hurt and imposed upon. Matty Josephson called me "the Happy Composer," perhaps because I whistled a lot. Vincent Persichetti wrote about me on my seventy-fifth birthday: "One of the reasons I like Ross Lee Finney is because he is a Midwesterner. I think that is partly responsible for his being an independent man and an independent composer. No one ever told him what to do and got away with it for long." Though I never lacked confidence in the value of my music, I had no ability to promote its performance. I owed a debt to both Aaron Copland and Virgil Thomson for sponsoring my music with conductors and at festivals. Colleagues such as Gilbert Ross and John Kirkpatrick had eagerly performed my chamber music through the years.

We returned to Ann Arbor in the spring to hear Donald Sinta and the University of Michigan Band under George Cavender premiere my *Concerto for Alto Saxophone and Wind Orchestra* (April 17, 1975). We soon found ourselves very near to complete physical exhaustion, but wouldn't admit it because of the many social events planned. My brother Theodore had a heart attack and I went to Pittsburgh to visit him in intensive care. I refused offers to teach at the University of Texas and the University of Illinois, and to be in residence at the American Academy in Rome. When we returned to New York in May, I was able to finish composing *Variations on a Memory* for the Chamber Music Society of Baltimore's concert celebrating the Bicentennial. I was asked to serve on the board of the Composers Forum, and there were more meetings of NWR's Editorial Committee.

In October of 1975 *Variations on a Memory* was premiered in

Baltimore with Sergiu Comissiona conducting. Elliott Galkin praised the work in his column in the *Baltimore Sun* (October 20, 1975):

> In general, the language, while highly chromatic, is unproblematic. Like much of Finney's music during the last quarter of a century or so, it is imbued with that mysterious quality of emotional intensity that is immediately communicative and unmistakable for the vibrancy of its impact upon the listener.
>
> It is also a work of exquisite craftsmanship, confirming the fact that great music is always an amalgam of exalted substance and inspired construction. . .

These kind words helped me face the many committee meetings necessary to complete the Recorded Anthology of American Music on schedule.

Robert Gerle premiered my *Second Violin Concerto* on March 31, 1976, with the Dallas Symphony Orchestra, Louis Lane conducting. It was well received, and Olin Chism wrote in the *Dallas Times Herald*: "The concerto was a fresh and vigorous piece, and I would have been perfectly happy to have heard a repetition of it right on the spot. Come to think of it, I can think of quite a few works in the standard repertoire that I would less prefer to hear."

Between the two premieres we spent two weeks in Florida, attending a festival of my music in Gainesville and driving south for a short vacation on Sanibel Island. I had promised to attend some concerts of my music in Canyon, Texas. We flew to Denver en route, rented a car, and made the long trip to see Bent's Fort, which was to be the setting for the new opera I had in mind. After the Texas performances, we drove to Santa Fe, on to Monument Valley, and finally back to Denver via Durango and Gunnison, the town I had enjoyed so much as a child. We got back to Detroit just in time to hear Lukas Foss and the Detroit Symphony Orchestra give an excellent performance of my *Variations for Orchestra* on May 6. Then it was back to 23 Bank Street for the spring festivities — and the ordeal of painting our apartment.

I was less exhausted by the year than I had expected to be, partly because I was in better health, but mostly because the Editorial Committee for the Rockefeller Foundation had finally completed its task.

I had reached, I think, a new understanding about my retirement and realized that we would have to travel less and conserve our energy for our work.

CHAPTER XX

1976 - 1980

NEW YORK has never lost its charm for us. Every time we fly into the city and see Manhattan Island spread out before us, we feel as though we are entering a foreign country. The skyline of the towers as we drive in from La Guardia makes me remember how excited I was as a young person entering the city. We can hardly wait to get to 23 Bank Street, which in a very real sense has become our home. We love our Ann Arbor home, buried as it is among beautiful trees, but Greenwich Village symbolizes a chance to think differently and to live at a different tempo.

Much has been done to make Bank Street an oasis in the city. There is a neighborliness that one finds only in a very small town. "Mom and Pop" stores, though they are disappearing, were very common when we first moved in. Even now I will be welcomed by name when I go into a store, or meet Charles Kuralt, who lives across the street from us. Trees, donated by some lady on Bank Street, struggle valiantly for a little light. The front patios are filled with spring bulbs and flowering shrubs that blossom unusually early each year. The purple finches and mourning doves start singing in February.

212

By the end of the seventies things had changed at 23 Bank Street. Isa Brandon died, and Glen Oxten, a marine lawyer, bought her first-floor apartment. He was a very nice person with thoughts of marriage and many ideas about improving the house. A new furnace was installed which gives us very adequate heat.

We were delighted when Bill and Eileen Bowser bought the garden apartment of the building. Bill has a thing with plants and is a personal symbol of Greenwich Village. He knows everybody, is constantly concerned with community affairs, and is always happy and friendly. Eileen is curator of films at the Museum of Modern Art and an authority on the history of cinema. She got us in to the Picasso Show when it visited New York City in 1980.

Later, when Glen Oxten married Debbie, they bought the Josephson apartment on the second floor and turned their two apartments into one, connecting them with a spiral staircase. Pictures of it were published in *House Beautiful.* Barbara Michael, just below us, lives the busy life of an advertising executive. We and she have resisted modernizing our apartments until very recently, perhaps because we are both away so much.

We are on the top floor, which has advantages and disadvantages. Three large windows look south over lower Manhattan giving us winter sunshine and ocean breezes. Three big windows at the back give us views of the gardens, and wonderful cross ventilation. Two big skylights make our dining room a perfect painter's studio with northern light. But we have to walk up three flights of stairs, which becomes more difficult as we grow older.

Getting into my studio at nine o'clock in the morning with the whole day ahead of me without interruption is what I value most. It is hard for people to realize that we use our apartment for work and not as a base for going to shows and concerts. The city gives us a feeling of anonymity which we value. When I hear Gretchen banging away on her typewriter, and she hears me thumping the piano now and then, all is well.

It is very restful to live on one floor; there are so fewer steps to be taken. There is always the hazard, of course, that we will start working and forget the stew cooking in the kitchen, but usually we catch it before it has ruined the pot. The apartment is too small to accommodate overnight guests, though our sons visit us now and then and sleep in the living room. They like our place as much as we do, and we enjoy their visits.

Our windows are ideal for growing plants and flowers, and Bill Bowser kindly waters them when we are away. They thrive on the carbon dioxide from my pipe smoke, and Bill insists that they like music. I love red geraniums and they do well in our front windows. The begonias, however, thrive under our skylights. The kitchen window is fine for basil and parsley. Every week Evelyn Hinrichsen sends us flowers.

I do all the shopping and have my favorite stores in Greenwich Village. For cheese, Italian pork products and bread, I walk along Bleecker Street to where it crosses Sixth Avenue. Seafoods and meats I buy at the Jefferson Market. Vegetables seem best at a nearby chain store, though in the spring and summer there is the farmers' market. I used to shop at a semi-wholesale store on Fourteenth Street and Eighth Avenue, but those places are disappearing as that area of the city changes. The Village is always interesting and reminds me of shopping in Paris.

I like to hear sounds from the street below me: children playing, someone singing with an accordion, workmen talking in foreign languages. The sounds of ambulances going to St. Vincent's Hospital or of fire engines and police cars with sirens blaring don't seem to bother me. They are a part of the city's sound. Only in the summer do we hear voices in the gardens in back of us. The birds sing in the Village with more determination than they do in Michigan, perhaps because the chimneypots keep them warm. Finches and song sparrows are my favorites. The mourning dove always tries to build her nest on the fire escape outside our back window, but only once was she successful in raising a brood. Sometimes we hear a mockingbird.

After many years of fighting the weather, we can now keep the apartment warm in the winter and fairly cool in the early summer. Being on the top floor, we hear the winter winds and the spring showers on our skylight. It reminds us of our little place on Chappaquiddick. We are very aware of the ocean breeze, so unlike anything we experience in Ann Arbor.

The academic year of 1976-77 was full of activities. We attended the premiere of *Narrative for Cello and Small Orchestra* at the meetings of the American Society of University Composers in Urbana, Illinois. I felt that the *Narrative* needed another, more brilliant movement, a revision that I later made. I served on the Board of the American Composers Orchestra which was struggling to get started, and gave them permission to premiere my *Concerto for Strings* without fee payment.

When Brooklyn College asked me to compose a work for their concert band, I accepted the commission because I had developed very strong ideas about the band as a symphonic organization. I first decided on the largest volume of sound available (the *tutti*) and made a musical form that took shape from the dynamic and tonal points of the work. In between these points were soloistic sections that exploited the wonderful color of the wind instruments. My first work for band had been *Summer in Valley City*, and this new work also drew on my childhood experience in North Dakota. I have always felt that humor is an important and often neglected quality in music. I remembered the fun we used to have ice skating, and I decided to call my piece *Skating on the Sheyenne*. The first movement, "Figure Eights," is filled with all kinds of musical circles, rightside up and upside down, like one skates a figure eight. The second movement, "Northern Lights," tries to capture that awesome experience. "Crack the Whip," which ends the work, is funny. I think the work succeeds in using the band symphonically, and while bands find it demanding, they enjoy performing it.

The Dean of the School of Music asked me to write a work for chorus, soloists and orchestra, celebrating their Centennial (1880-1980). They promised me a fine performance but no fee. I didn't feel obligated to do the work, but since it gave me an opportunity to complete the *Earthrise* trilogy that was so clearly in my mind, I accepted their offer.

Still Are New Worlds and *The Martyr's Elegy* had been previously commissioned by the University Musical Society for performances on their May Festival. The new work, to be performed by the combined forces of the School of Music, was to complete the questions asked by the seventeenth century's discovery of infinity and the human fears expressed in *The Martyr's Elegy*. My request that the entire trilogy be performed and taped in lieu of a fee, was promised but never carried out.

The premiere of *Earthrise* in December of 1979 gained from the meticulous conducting of Gustav Meier and the careful choral coaching of Thomas Hilbish. The speaker, H. D. Cameron, whose voice was taped, projected a love of the words which came from his being a poet. Of the two soloists, the tenor was adequate but the contralto was not. The engineers who produced the tape of the performance did an excellent job. My only regret is that I do not have a tape of the entire trilogy, which will probably never be performed in its totality in my lifetime.

Roger Sessions started to think about composing *Montezuma* when he lived near Northampton in the thirties. Giuseppe Antonio Borgese held the Neilson Chair at Smith College at that time and was working on the libretto based on the diary of one of Hernando Cortez's soldiers. Over the years Roger had talked a lot with me about the problems he faced in setting the libretto. It was much too long, and he found that he was using about one word out of ten. He felt guilty about performing such surgery on the text, fearing that it might jeopardize both the plot and the social thesis (the conflict of two cultures) which were so important to the opera.

At about the same time I read David Lavender's *Fort Bent,* a scholarly study of Charles and William Bent's experiences on the frontier from about 1820 to the end of the Civil War. These two sons of the distinguished Bent family in St. Louis became trappers and explorers. Charles, the older, became the first governor of New Mexico and married a Mexican girl. He was assassinated in Taos. William Bent established Bent's Fort on the Santa Fe Trail and married the daughter of a Cheyenne chief. He had five children, all raised by their mother with the tribe, and all later educated in Missouri. The two older children made the adjustment, but the three younger did not. Robert, the oldest, became an officer, with his father, in the Union army. The two younger sons, George and Charles, ran away and joined the Confederate army. Lavender tells the story of the Sand Creek Massacre of the Cheyenne tribe by the Colorado Volunteers under a bigot named Chivington. Partly because of that massacre, William Bent was alienated from his two younger sons.

This situation seemed ideal for an opera, which I view as an obsolete literary form in which the characters are bigger than life. It was located in a part of the West related to the Dakotas, allowing me to use songs that were part of my memory. It not only reflected the prejudice against the "half-breed," but also suggested the classical conclusion of patricide and fratricide. I decided that I would call the opera "Bent's Sons."

My attempts to find a librettist were both frustrating and a little funny. On one occasion a writer came to see me, and I outlined for him what I had in mind. He left, saying he would send me a libretto, which he did. It turned out to be a television script about two lovers in West Virginia! I decided to write the libretto myself.

In the late seventies I began working seriously on it. I made many drafts before I arrived at anything I wanted to use. The title "Bent's Sons" bothered me, too, and for a while I thought "William Bent and Sons" sounded better. Finally by the end of the decade I started to compose the music, hoping in that way to find the delineation of the characters. As it turned out, I hardly set a line of the script as it was written.

I came to realize how impossible it would have been had anyone else written the text. Either there were too many words, or the words would not set properly to the melody I wanted to write. It gradually dawned on me also that the orchestra was the major character in the opera. It was the music that defined the time-space, just as it did in a symphony. The work began to take its own shape, and in the process the libretto was completely rewritten.

A composer in his seventies ought not to be writing his first opera. No producer had encouraged me to do the work, nor had I sought financial aid, though I knew that before there could be a production, there would be the expense of copying the orchestral parts. Let me see if I can explain why I was so pig-headed as to embark on this project.

When an idea for a musical work has been in my mind for as long as this opera — I could hear the music except for the temporal design — it becomes a torture. I would certainly have accepted a commission if one had been offered. But to tell the truth, I didn't want to face any more deadlines; I didn't have the nervous energy to face a battle over production. I wanted the work to be a reflection of my own personality, not of the theatrical fads of the time. Perhaps it was an indulgence, but I enjoyed working on the score.

1977-78 was made more complicated when I consented to be a travelling scholar for Phi Beta Kappa. The first tour took us in October to the West Coast, where I visited the University of California in Irvine, the University of Arizona in Tucson, the University of Oregon in Eugene, and finally the University of Hawaii in Honolulu. When we got back east in November, my *Concerto for Strings* was premiered by the American Composers Orchestra in Alice Tully Hall. In February I went to Rice University in Houston, to the University of Missouri in Columbia, and to Ohio State University in Columbus. In April we went to the University of Rhode Island in Kingston where we met for the first time Kenneth Peacock and Jane Brockman, who have become such close friends. My tours for the year ended with a visit to the State University of New York at Binghamton, where I had a nice visit with Edith Borroff, who had studied at Michigan in the fifties. During the spring my *Skating on the Sheyenne* was premiered in Brooklyn.

I was determined to refuse engagements during 1978-79. The only trip that we made was to Vancouver. Wallace Berry, the distinguished composer and head of the music division of the University of British Columbia, had organized a festival of my music and wanted us to be there for a week. I was glad we hadn't refused, since it was a great pleasure to renew our friendship with Maxine and Wallace Berry. They put us up in a lovely small hotel that looked out over Stanley Park and the bay, and entertained us royally, showing us all the things of interest in that beautiful city. Our stay was a very happy one.

In early December of 1979 two works of mine were performed at the University of Michigan. Robert Reynolds conducted *Skating on the*

Sheyenne with the concert band. Stephen Fisher came out from C. F. Peters for the premiere of *Earthrise*, and we enjoyed having him as a house guest and showing him the town.

We returned to Greenwich Village for Christmas, and Evelyn Hinrichsen came up to our apartment for dinner. The city is very festive during the holiday season. From our windows we can look out on the Christmas Lights — the Jefferson Market tower and the lighted Christmas trees on terraces of the buildings — and hear groups of young people singing carols on Bank Street. It makes one glad to live in New York.

CHAPTER XXI

1980 - 1983

1980 was a very special year for us. In September we would mark our fiftieth wedding anniversary. We often wondered how we would celebrate it. We didn't want a big party and a lot of fuss. We talked of going to Europe or even Australia, but not very seriously, since sightseeing demanded too much energy and time. Our nostalgia for Chappaquiddick returned from time to time, for we were trying to sell our cottage and we knew it might be the last summer that we could go. So we picked up Henry's Ford "Bronco" in Burlington and travelled on to Martha's Vineyard, where we spent two lovely weeks.

It was during this stay that I caught the biggest sea bass of my life. I had gone for a swim when I saw a huge fish in the shallows, thrashing around. I got an iron rod from the garage and pushed it through the gills and mouth of the fish which was well over a yard long and must have weighed over twenty pounds. It had broken the line while being towed by a fishing boat and would not have survived an attack from the gulls. We had no camera to verify my "fishing story" to my sons, but we did have many wonderful meals from that fish!

On the third of September we drove to Edgartown to eat a fried-clam lunch and fetch lobsters for our celebration dinner. On the return ferry we happened to see our names on two boxes of yellow roses. Sent by Paul and Christa Cooper, the beautiful flowers had been peacefully riding back and forth across the inlet until we discovered them, quite fortuitously. Later in the day we had a call that flowers from Evelyn Hinrichsen were being delivered by boat, so we drove over to the dock to pick them up. We could see the boat crossing the pond with the wind blowing the green paper around enormous bouquets of red roses. We put the flowers on our porch and watched the humming-birds trying to get through the screens to them.

After leaving the Bronco in Burlington, we returned to New York City for the remainder of the fall. David Gregory, a young composer who had taken care of us in Ann Arbor and was now in New York working for a dance group, assisted us in getting settled. We felt much better and had a productive stay.

Living in New York City has been a broadening experience for both of us. Most of our friends there were young people, and behavior that once might have shocked us, no longer did. When we asked them to dinner, we didn't suggest they bring wives or husbands (unless we knew they existed), but "companions." Young composers came up to play tapes of their music and talk about their scores. Their talk was never vulgar, but neither was it guarded.

We discovered that when they suggested we go out to a restaurant for dinner, we were expected to pay for what we ordered. That seemed only fair and reminded me of how we handled things when I was a student in Paris. These young New Yorkers often knew of wonderful little Italian restaurants that we would never have discovered. Amusing things would sometimes happen. Once the restaurant would not accept credit cards, and Gretchen had to go to the ladies' room to get out cash to cover the bill!

We had become very fond of Cole Gagne and Tracy Caras after they came to interview me. When we first knew them, they were students at Fordham University, broadcasting interviews with American composers over the university's radio station. They decided to make a book of these interviews and found a publisher who expressed interest if they would include some new interviews of composers. After graduation Cole had taken a job writing for *The Old-House Journal*, and Tracy was taking a degree in Law. They were delighted with the prospect of interviewing such people as Morton Feldman in Buffalo and Conlon Nancarrow in Mexico City. Don Gillespie at C. F. Peters did a lot to help them. When they got back from an interview they would come up, always with some unusual, gastronomic contribution, like half a watermelon, and gleefully talk over their experiences. *Soundpieces: Interviews with American Composers* was finally published in 1982 by Scarecrow Press. Cole and Tracy came by one day, proud as punch, with a copy for us, which, with a great flourish, they signed.

The meals we made were a combination of Midwestern and French cooking often using recipes suggested by Julia Child. When young people came to dinner, they often loved to have a big roast to feast on. We could never have a roast by ourselves, because it made so many leftovers to use up. It gave us pleasure to have it all eaten. I especially liked a beef tongue, because the stock made wonderful onion soup and we enjoyed the tongue cold as well as hot. I remember once when Don Gillespie and Yvar Mikhashoff came unexpectedly for lunch, we had tongue sandwiches, much to the bewilderment of Don, who had never eaten tongue before and wasn't sure he wanted to!

Work on my opera would sometimes reach a point where I felt the need of thinking before continuing further, and then I would do something else. One such interruption resulted in a set of short piano pieces for children that reflected my North Dakota memories. The last piece was called "Jack Rabbit." I called the set *Youth's Companion* after the magazine we had loved so much as children.

It was about this time that Erick Hawkins came up to see me. He had heard my *Concerto for Strings* and wanted to use it for a dance. The problem was that it required a large number of strings, and he had no money either for that or for the rental fee C. F. Peters would charge. He told a woeful tale about money and showed me the holes in the soles of his shoes. I found Hawkins both sad and funny at the same time, but when one ignored those qualities, there were flashes of genius.

He believed in dancing only to live music — no recordings for him — and I found something genuinely appealing in his ideas. He told me about the orchestra that he always used: flute (piccolo), clarinet (bass clarinet), trumpet, bass trombone, percussion, violin and double bass, with a conductor. Could I arrange my *Concerto for Strings* for that group? Well, of course, that would have been an impossibility, but I might write him a concerto for that group of instruments. It was not a commission, and I suppose I should not have gotten involved, but for some reason I couldn't resist. He had no money even to pay for the copying of parts.

The work, called "Chamber Concerto," was composed in the spring of 1981. The score was written for the troupe's small orchestra so that the instrumental parts could be cut out of xeroxed scores and pasted together. C. F. Peters allowed me to present Erick, without fee, a score and set of parts for his special use, a cultural contribution for which my publisher deserves special credit.

I stole the theme of "Jack Rabbit" (from *Youth's Companion*) for the first movement of the "Chamber Concerto," but aside from that, the score had no special association with the Midwest. Imagine my amazement, on seeing the dance, to find that it was called "Heyoka" and based on Indian clowns. But Hawkins' imagination, reflected in his choreography, took my breath away. On one of his visits, I must have told him about the opera I was writing, set at Bent's Fort. I learned then that Hawkins was born and brought up only a few miles from the fort and that he was deeply interested in Indian dances.

Even though I was working hard on my opera, I did accept a commission from the Baltimore Chamber Music Society to write a *Quartet for Oboe, Cello, Percussion and Piano.* It was to share a program with a piece by George Crumb and the group had those instruments available. I enjoyed writing the work and found the combination of instruments interesting, though the cello was easily overwhelmed.

The next summer we drove up to Johnson, Vermont, where I was to be in residence two weeks at the Composers Conference. Art Gottschalk, Jane Brockman, Ken Peacock and Dick Toensing were there and showed me the new music they had written. Of the younger composers Michael Gondolphi seemed to me very gifted. We visited Mario and Elaine Davidovsky in the home they had built near Johnson and then stopped in on Henry and Helen in Burlington.

Henry had become deeply committed to painting. He had shown talent in art at Exeter, but had not continued his study of painting at the University of Michigan. He did a highly original mobile when he was working on his doctorate in sociology at Berkeley. At the University of Wisconsin he was so pressured as a young teacher that he had no time for painting, but when he moved to the University of Vermont, his interest in art returned with a fervor, and he became increasingly productive. He has continued his sociological studies, recently giving a course in Art and Society both at the University of Vermont and at M.I.T. During the eighties he has gained some recognition as an artist in Vermont, and will, I feel sure, make his own individual contribution in the future.

During the winter I was invited to be the first appointment to a newly endowed chair in music at the University of Alabama in Tuscaloosa for the academic year of 1982-83. There were no specific teaching assignments. They would furnish us with a house. There would be a travel stipend, and I could be away whenever I wished. The salary was large — twice as large as any salary I ever received at the University of Michigan. I had visited Tuscaloosa several times in the past, as visiting scholar for Phi Beta Kappa, as visiting composer at the Symposium of the Southeastern Composers League, and as a guest to hear the premiere of my *Eighth String Quartet,* which the University had commissioned.

Almost immediately after I wrote accepting the appointment, I received a telephone call from Dr. Frederic Goossen, the outstanding composer on their faculty, asking if I would compose a piano quartet for them. Nothing seems to me harder to compose than a piano trio or quartet. The lack of balance makes the group sound like a ship's orchestra. I had to refuse because I didn't feel I could write such a work, but I mentioned that I had a *Piano Quartet* that I had composed in 1948 and had never heard. (It was written for an Elizabeth Sprague Coolidge Concert at The Library of Congress in 1948, when we were in California, but I could not afford to make the trip east to hear the premiere.) I sent the score and parts to Alabama, and the work was beautifully performed during the year. An excellent videotape was made and broadcast over public television in the Southeast.

Fred Goossen also asked me for a manuscript that could be published by the University of Alabama Press. When he decided they would like to do the lectures I had delivered over the years, I gave him copies of all of them with the understanding that he would do all the editing. He probably didn't realize what a thankless job he was taking on. The lectures are not scholarly, and they range over a very wide field of interests with quotations taken from books I was reading at the time. He finally settled on the title *Thinking About Music: The Collected Essays of Ross Lee Finney.* I must admit that I have not been very helpful in this project, since I can't face going over this old material.

We enjoyed our year in Alabama, though I doubt that I contributed much to the musical environment. I had five graduate students of whom two were talented: Joel Philips composed an orchestral work, and Garry Smoke involved himself with new computer techniques. I gave my course "Making Music" to a group of students who had no plans to be composers and gave a concert of the works they produced. I was on hand for all the events when the Southeastern Composers League met in Tuscaloosa. John Lennon, who had taken care of us in Ann Arbor, made the trip from the University of Tennessee especially to see us. I was interested in the music of Gerald Kechley whose father had been at Michigan for a year in the early fifties.

My brother Nat S. Finney died on December 19, and we went to the service that was held in Washington, D.C., on January 10, 1983. Ross and Laura came down, and the evening before the service we had a party for all the Finney family that lived in the area: Martha and her family, Richard and his family, and us.

We made several trips to New York City during that fall, and each time Evelyn Hinrichsen gave a party for us at "The Old Homestead" Restaurant. Our trip to see performances of the Erick Hawkins Dance Company turned out, because of a big snowstorm, to be complicated. Our plane got almost to New York and then had to return to Atlanta where we stayed for two days. When we finally got to Bank Street, the snow was over four feet deep and we had to walk through the snow to a performance of "Heyoka."

The most rewarding thing about our stay in Alabama was our friendship with Fred and Shirley Goossen. We would have been very lonely had it not been for them. But our friendship was deeper than that and has continued ever since. Fred Goossen is a very talented composer, especially of songs and piano music. Shirley, a native of Tennessee, has a snappy wit that reminds me of Eudora Welty. Fred grew up in Minnesota and studied at the University with my old teacher, Donald Ferguson.

All through the year Gretchen and I suffered from allergies that we were never able to explain. The University's fine medical clinic did everything they could for us, but nothing seemed to help. As soon as we arrived at our New York apartment, the allergies would disappear. Perhaps the moisture and the lush vegetation in Alabama was responsible; we had never lived in a house that was constantly closed and kept at a set temperature. We often longed to open a window and breathe fresh air, but no windows would open.

In May we headed north, spent one night in our house in Ann Arbor as guests of Richard Lavenda, the young composer who had taken care of our house all year, and then flew to New York City.

I had finished the first sketch of the piano-vocal score of my opera, which I decided to call *Weep Torn Land*, a title that comes from the ending of the opera. The vocal score was really a sketch for orchestration, and I realized that as I completed the orchestral score, there would be changes in the vocal score, which then I could get into a final copy edited to fit the piano. What lay ahead was the orchestration, which for me was pure pleasure, and the final revisions.

We had sold our Chappaquiddick cottage and looked forward to spending the summer in our Ann Arbor home, a routine that we have continued to follow ever since. We always return for the last week of June in order to have strawberries and asparagus and enjoy all the locally grown summer vegetables and fruits.

CHAPTER XXII

1983 - 1986

THE orchestration of *Weep Torn Land* took almost all of my time during the next few years. It had been hard for me to follow my routine in Alabama — not because of any failure on the part of the University, but because I missed my studios. As a result I completed only one new work, *Hexachord for Harpsichord,* commissioned by the Hartt School of Music for a festival that in fact never took place. Larry Palmer, the distinguished organist helped me with the score and premiered the piece in Dallas.

It was a pleasure to get back to my studio in Ann Arbor, and to the routine of work I had followed for so many years. My desk is placed so that my back is to the French doors that look out onto a terrace, avoiding the distraction that I would experience if I looked out on the flowers and the hillside. In New York my large desk faces the wall, but I do have a wonderful view from the window. In both studios there is excellent light, and I am free from household distractions.

I orchestrate in a rather special way, pounding out a few measures at the piano until I know exactly what I want to hear, and then scoring at my desk. That means I am popping back and forth between piano and desk, but the end result is that when I have finished a page of score, it is exactly what I have heard in my head. Perhaps that is why I so often say that a work sounds exactly as I imagined it would. Too much doubling seems to me to result in a monotonous sound, especially in an opera score.

Scoring is a creative process, and frequently forces me to change my sketch. The orchestra, more perhaps than anything else, sets the temporal design of an opera, and for that reason becomes a character, almost commenting on a theatrical situation. as it does in the operas that have most influenced me: Verdi's Otello, Debussy's *Pelléas et Mélisande*, and Berg's *Wozzeck* .

Erick Hawkins came to see me again in 1983 to persuade me to do another score for his group. This time he arrived with a very definite, detailed sketch of a dance to be called "The Joshua Tree." The musical score would have no use apart from the dance and therefore would hold no interest for my publisher. I told him that I could only devote a couple of weeks — no more — to composing the music. I did the score and parts for him without a fee, but felt that this time I was being used. It is, alas, generally true that people value what you do in direct proportion to what they have paid for it. But once again, when I saw the dance, I felt Hawkins' special touch of originality.

Gretchen spent a great deal of time at uptown libraries that were often hard to reach. Her arthritis had worsened and her knee tended to buckle, causing her to fall. I feared some mishap on the street and worried all day when she went to the library. It became harder for us to go out in the evening, and if we stayed to the end of a concert, we often couldn't work the next day.

At the dinners of the Institute of Arts and Letters, we enjoyed seeing the new composers who had been elected to membership during the year. It was always a pleasure to meet Miriam Gideon and Louise Talma and, in later years, Mario Davidovsky, Chou Wen-chung and Donald Martino. The musical group at the Institute was always very congenial. Milton and Sylvia Babbitt often came, and of course Milton always had the latest gossip on everybody.

In February, 1984, the Gregg Smith Singers performed my *Spherical Madrigals*. Though I had heard the work many times (sometimes performed very well, even by quite young singers), this was a performance on a higher level of perfection. Every note was perfect, and Gregg Smith brought an understanding of words and music that was quite exceptional. I was pleased when he decided to record the work and spent an entire day with the group at the recording session.

A few days later we flew to Boston for some concerts of my music performed at Boston University, where I was especially eager to hear my *Symphonie Concertante* performed by the Boston University Symphony under Joseph Silverstein. Despite some fine performances in the past, I had no tape recording of the work. (I was making a collection of all my works on cassettes and was eager to fill in a few gaps.)

Silverstein's interpretation was excellent and the student performers were remarkably good. At last I had recordings of all my orchestral works! I was also very pleased with Karen Nectvolt's performances of my *Three 17th-Century Lyrics* and *Three Love Songs* (John Donne). Over the years my songs, except for *Poor Richard,* have been neglected. None of the voice faculty at the University of Michigan ever sang them, though they would coach bad performances by their students. I had often tried, unsuccessfully, to get a performance of my cycle of thirty-six songs to James Joyce's *Chamber Music.*

Ross and Laura came in to Boston to go to the concerts with us, and we had dinner at Durgin-Park Restaurant where the waitresses bossed everyone as is the accepted tradition there. We couldn't possibly eat everything, so following my usual custom, I took all the leftovers in a "doggie bag" to prepare a special stew for all of us next day.

During the New York Philharmonic's "Horizons '84" Concerts, many of which I attended, Mitzi Kolar arrived in New York to record my *Youth's Companion.* It was to be a pedagogical recording. First she would play each piece, then talk about its character and technical problems, and afterwards repeat the performance. I felt that I should attend all the recording sessions, which took place at the RCA Recording Studio on Sixth Avenue. About this time Martha Braden performed my *Third Piano Sonata* at Merkin Concert Hall, and began making plans to record an album of my piano music for CRI.

During the summer I composed the first of a series of piano pieces more difficult than those in *Youth's Companion,* but also deeply rooted in memory. It, too, was based on symmetrical hexachords that made inevitable a traditional association, and led to the quotation of a work that I played on my college graduation recital and for which I still have a profound love: Chopin's *Ballade in G Minor.* Commissioned by the USIA's "Artistic Ambassadors Program," the new piece was named *Narrative in Retrospect.* Supposedly it was to be premiered in South America by a young American pianist, but if that happened, I neither met the pianist, nor received a tape. Brian Connelly played it in New York City in May of 1985, and it may be that his performance was the premiere. This work is perhaps a culmination of ideas that had dominated my music for thirty years.

Gretchen and I often talked of making a trip to Europe in the fall and tentatively decided on taking Icelandic Airlines to Luxemburg and driving to Alsace. The more we thought about that trip, however, the more tired we got. Finally we decided to visit Iceland for a week. I had flown back at the end of the War via Iceland and always regretted that I hadn't been able to stop there. Also, I had known several Icelandic composers and was curious about their work.

I had written to Karólína Eiríksdótter, an Icelandic composer who had studied at the University of Michigan, and when we arrived at Reykjavik on September 11, she had arranged a meeting at the Radio Station, where I could hear tapes and meet some young Icelandic composers. We stayed at the modern, comfortable Hotel Esjo with its beautiful view over the bay and city.

Since the University in Reykjavik offered no advanced degrees in composition, the Icelandic government paid for young composers to continue their study wherever they wished, in Europe or the United States. The composers are a very active group and their music is an interesting combination of prevailing practices in Europe and America, but with roots in the very ancient Icelandic culture. Karólína Eiríksdótter gave me a collection of scores and tapes that I hoped to use in writing a report on my visit, but I gave the material to Kenneth Peacock to use in doing a paper after his visit to Reykjavik.

We made a long bus trip to see glaciers, waterfalls, geysers and primitive buildings and churches, but the most impressive site was the rift valley, where the European and American tectonic plates run together. This phenomenon symbolizes the mid-Atlantic quality of Icelandic culture. How right that it was there in Iceland where the first parliament was held in the tenth century. On our departure, the composers club, a close-knit group, gave us a very enjoyable reception in their house near the University.

Autumn in New York was busy but pleasant. The Erick Hawkins Group premiered "The Joshua Tree," which was very well received by both audience and critics. I felt that my music fit the dance better than it had in "Heyoka." Braxton Blake, the young conductor/composer, came up to see me and to show me his scores.

In October Gretchen and I went up to Albany to hear the revised version of my *Second Violin Concerto*. I had felt dissatisfied with the ending of the concerto and had added a short third movement that brought back the material of the first. The train trip up the Hudson, with the fall foliage in full brilliance, was an unanticipated pleasure. The performance of the concerto was excellent, but I am not sure even now which version I prefer. The added last movement changes the emphasis and seems emotionally better, but there is something to be said for ending the concerto with a bang.

I had a bad case of shingles all over my scalp, almost down to my eyes, and had to struggle to keep it from spreading. People came in to see us, but I had to avoid going out. We went back to Ann Arbor for Christmas only to come down with bad colds. When we returned to New York in January, we felt better but not quite up to par. Nevertheless, we made a trip in March of 1985 to Hartford, where Yvar Mikhashoff gave a concert of my piano music which he was planning to record, and the Hartt Chamber Players performed two of my small orchestra pieces. A few days later we went to New Haven to celebrate John Kirkpatrick's eightieth birthday.

During the spring in Ann Arbor the Dean of the School of Music asked me if the University could give the premiere of *Weep Torn Land.* I would be delighted, but they would have to pay the publisher's fees and the cost of copying the orchestral parts. He agreed and appointed the assistant dean, John Vander Weg, to handle the details. I supplied vocal scores so that the Opera Department could start work on the production. When the school was unable to find the money to produce the performance material, I had the parts extracted (C. F. Peters paying half of the cost) with the understanding that the rental fee would be higher. After several years of delay, they came upon the idea of giving the opera in celebration of my eightieth birthday. Finally the Opera Department informed me that they had no male soloist capable of singing the main role and that the Detroit Opera Company would not be willing to cooperate in the production.

Nobody was to blame, I suppose, except perhaps myself. The Dean should not have entered into the project without the Opera Department's being more familiar with the work, but certainly the Department could not be expected to produce such an opera without an adequate student registration or the cooperation of other local groups. It had cost me and my publisher several thousand dollars, but at least we had the large performance materials all in order. Kenneth Peacock wrote an excellent promotional sampler that Peters published, so perhaps the opera will one day be performed. It won't be the first time I've had to wait years for the premiere of a work!

In the spring of 1986 Erick Hawkins came up once again to see me. He was in a very low state of mind, feeling that his work had never received proper recognition. His depression was the result of his refusal to give in to the glitz of the theater, and of his unceasing but unrewarded efforts to leave a lasting legacy to modern dance. I suspected that he had come up for a purpose, and I was determined this time not to become involved. Finally he got around to the score he wanted me to write. The conditions were the same, with the exception that the premiere would take place during Harvard University's 350th anniversary celebrations.

The work was to be called "Ahab" (after Melville) and, as he said, it all depended on whether he could manage the problem of the wooden leg. Perhaps he could bind his leg in white. He got out his sketch of the choreography which he had mapped out down to the split second, and with great excitement drew a picture of the stage. Ishmael would only speak and Ahab would dance and speak throughout. He indicated when there would be music, what kind of music it should be, and when there must be silence. Once again I sensed the genius of the man — and was hooked.

CHAPTER XXIII

1986 - 1990

No sooner had I completed my serious opera *Weep Torn Land* than I plunged into the composition, in the late 1980s, of my comic opera: *Computer Marriage*. From the start I did the libretto myself, knowing from recent experience that my way of working demanded complete freedom with the text. I had reached the point where, if I composed at all, it had to be at my own tempo and for my own pleasure. Composing had become a self-indulgence.

I was eighty, and while the creative urge had not lessened, I had no wish to compete with young composers for commissions or performances. For this reason, perhaps, I embarked once again on the impractical project of composing an opera, knowing that I might never see it. I felt no self-pity, but only the pleasure of getting down on paper the ideas that had been forming in my head over the years.

I did decide to be more realistic about the production demands of the new opera. The cast would be small and evenly divided between male and female voices; the smaller orchestra would include flutes and clarinets, trumpets, trombones and tuba, piano and percussion, and strings; the stage designs would be less demanding. In *Weep Torn Land* I had thought of the large opera house, but *Computer Marriage* would be designed for smaller community or college productions.

I got the idea for a comic opera when I read that the astronomer Johannes Kepler used astrology to compute the qualities he wanted in a second wife. I know very little about Kepler's life, but I understand that the computing process did not turn out as he had expected. I think of Kepler as a zany kind of guy and imagined him in a Rube Goldberg setting. From the very beginning, the plot was a combination of fantasy and nonsense. Three comic operas that I love have influenced me most: Mozart's *The Marriage of Figaro*, Sullivan's *Trial by Jury*, and Gershwin's *Of Thee I Sing*.

The next step happened in 1986, when the University of Michigan made it possible for us to purchase at a discount a computer and the software to run it. The administration also set up classes and an office to give advice whenever trouble arose. My decision to "move into the twentieth century" led me into computer stores with new technical jargon and situations I found very funny. Why shouldn't the Kepler of my opera consult a modern computer shop to find the qualities he wanted in a future wife?

But that presented some difficulties in historical perspective. If one were going to combine the sixteenth and twentieth centuries, why not bring in a touch of the seventeenth? So, I added Sir Isaac Newton to the cast. The crazier the whole set-up became, the better I liked it, because it made some kind of comment on our modern worship of the machine.

And then I thought of the characters Aurora, Bore, and Alis and the Software Man who would try to sell Kepler on his special line of software. But these ladies felt they were being used as sex symbols, and that the whole business was turning into a lonely-hearts racket. They decided to put a "computer virus" in the program to squelch the Software Man's plans. A way still had to be found to bring the opera to a satisfactory conclusion.

I started composing the opera, knowing from experience that as the characters developed I would get new ideas, and that's exactly what happened. Kepler's housekeeper opened the first scene. At first I had visualized her as a frumpish, elderly lady. Why couldn't she be instead a very attractive wench whose heart was set on capturing Kepler for herself? She could even be a coloratura soprano and add sparkle to the play. It would mean rewriting the libretto as I went along — by now normal procedure for me. So the opera got off the ground in a very different way than I had expected.

Now I am more determined than ever to find the proper ending for

Computer Marriage. I have finished the libretto for the final scene and can now get to work on composing and orchestrating it.

We saw the New York premiere of "Ahab" at the Joyce Theater in September of 1986. The production seemed a little slow, but with each performance it became tighter. Later, when I saw another production, it had developed a very convincing tempo. Because of the speaking parts, "Ahab" reminded me of radio drama. The dance — part pantomime and part lyric movement — was suggestive of Japanese drama. One of the dancers made us a videotape of the first performance, and I bought a VCR and had the opportunity to enjoy the dance many times.

I learned at this time that videotapes had also been made of "Heyoka" and "The Joshua Tree" for the Jerome Robbins Collection at Lincoln Center Library of the Performing Arts. I was delighted, of course, but annoyed that they had not asked my permission beforehand to record the music. I approached Jean Bowen, who had been Gretchen's student at Smith College and was now Chief of the Music Division. Since I was giving the New York Public Library all my letters and manuscripts, and Jean and I were good friends, she suggested that I donate to the Dance Division all my letters and sketches from Erick Hawkins in return for copies of the videotapes. And so I ended up with a nice collection of all three collaborations.

In March we made another memorable trip to Houston as guests of the Shepherd School of Music. They put us up in a suite at the Wyndham Hotel, near the campus. It was always a joy for us to visit Houston and spend time with Paul and Christa Cooper, Ellsworth Milburn, and all our other good friends there. Several of my works were performed: *2 Acts for 3 Players, Narrative in Retrospect* and *Three Love Songs.* The songs were part of a program of opera duets, very showy, with the ladies dressed in elegant attire. It was hard to imagine what Jeanette Lombard and Mary Norris would do with the settings of John Donne's love poems that I had composed in 1948 and dedicated to Gretchen. But I needn't have worried. The performance was beautiful and held the audience's attention.

I have come to feel that Paul Cooper is one of America's most distinguished composers. His music has a deep emotional motivation and at the same time a simplicity and clarity that comes from his mastery of craft. The inner fabric is so subtle and the melodic flow so natural that on each hearing I find relationships I had not previously noted. Perhaps I like his music so much because his roots are much like my own.

A chamber orchestra was to perform Cooper's *Love Songs and Dances,* "dedicated with affection to Gretchen and Ross Lee Finney on the occasion of the latter's 80th birthday" and using material from my *Edge of Shadow*. When the musicians suddenly went on strike, an orchestra made up of students and friends gave a special reading just for me. That was, of course the high point of the festival.

In November of 1987 Gretchen fell and fractured her spine. She was in great pain and finally had to spend most of her time in bed. Naturally, she was very depressed, and that was as bad as the pain. We had no household help and no desire to give up our privacy and routine. It was no great hardship for me to take over the shopping and the cooking. Geoff Stanton, the talented young composer who had taken care of us for a year, cleaned our house. He and his lovely wife, Sue, stayed with Gretchen when I travelled to Cleveland for the premiere of the revised version of my *Narrative in Two Movements* for Cello and Small Orchestra.

The University of California Press had expressed interest in Gretchen's book, and the editor asked that certain editorial revisions be made. Gretchen agreed and was eager to make the changes, but she was unable to get into her study. I had the bright idea of buying a little portable computer that she could use in bed and that we could take to New York. It was a great success. I taught her the word-processing program I used, and in a very short time she was busily at work again.

Becky, who was then installing computers for a Detroit bank, came to see us frequently in Ann Arbor and made our Christmas festive. I had sent off to C. F. Peters the box of "Finney Cookies" that had become an annual event, but otherwise we did very little to celebrate. Gretchen could come downstairs for the "happy hour" in front of the fireplace and was able more and more to get into the comfortable chair in her study. I had bought a printer and a monitor that made it a little easier for her to read what she had typed. But we weren't able to make the trip to New York City until February of 1988.

Gregg and Rosalind Smith came up to dinner to discuss a two-week summer residency at Lake Saranac. Ross and Laura came down to visit us and they took Gretchen's place at the ceremony of the Academy/ Institute of Arts and Letters. Gretchen worked on her revisions with her little computer, and I composed the first two scenes of *Computer Marriage*.

Our days were very pleasant, thanks to the friends who frequently came up for dinner. The most pleasant visit we had was that of Paul and Christa Cooper who had just returned from premieres of Paul's works in Europe. They were both very tired and Christa suffered severe back pains. During their visit, Paul saw my recently published Joyce song-cycle *Chamber Music* and was determined to have it performed. I had composed it in 1951, but had refused to allow performances of single songs, because my concept of the work was of a long monody that must be heard in its entirety .

In early June Martha Braden completed her CD recording for CRI of four of my piano works: *Fantasy* (1939), *Sonata No. 3* (1942), *Sonata quasi una fantasia* (1961) and *Narrative in Retrospect* (1983). I found the sessions fascinating, since it was my first experience with digital recording. John McClure was the very able technician. An especially fine Steinway grand piano was rented for the session, and everyone was very pleased.

We flew to Ann Arbor on June 23, having arranged to have our apartment redecorated and modernized while we were away. We called in Peter Craig, an actor who lived across the street and earned his living contracting, to do the job during the summer when we would be in Ann Arbor. We added a dishwasher, a washing machine, new cabinets and sink and, in a closet, a small clothes-drier. Everything we needed could be supplied by Sears, and so as soon as we left in June, Peter got to work.

After we got home, Gretchen had congestive heart failure and had to be rushed to the hospital. We live only a few blocks from the emergency entrance and got there at about 9:00 AM, but they couldn't find a bed for her in intensive care until 2:00 AM the next morning.

The medical establishment at the University is very good indeed, and my being Professor Emeritus gives us easy access to the Faculty Diagnostic Clinic, where we are cared for by Dr. James Woolliscroft. Gretchen was delighted to learn that he had grown up in Alexandria and knew people that she had known. He had urged us to contact him at any time, and it was fortunate that he was able to call emergency immediately so that there was no delay in Gretchen's treatment.

Gretchen was in the hospital for a week and responded very well to the treatment. She lost twenty-five pounds, which was a good thing and came home with an incredible number of pills she had to take, which complicated our routine.

We were determined to keep to our schedules. The idea of moving into a retirement home was anathema to both of us. We lived for our work and the pleasures that had developed over the years related to our work. Our home in Ann Arbor and our apartment at 23 Bank Street gave us the best of two worlds. As long as we could have each other, we were happy.

Our life might have seemed boring to other people, but we were never bored. I got up at seven to cook oatmeal and make tea for our breakfast in bed, where we watched the news and Gretchen took pills.

We'd get into our studies at about nine. At half past ten we had tea and cookies, and then more work. At noon we had soup, and I had a sandwich and a banana. Then we took the telephone off the hook and had our nap. At two we had some coffee (decaffeinated) and cake and pills. Our "happy hour" at five was reduced to ginger ale and pills for Gretchen and beer for me. Then dinner in the dining room followed by decaf and dessert and pills in our bedroom while we watched our favorite television game shows "Wheel of Fortune" and "Jeopardy." Then I cleaned up the kitchen and worked for an hour in my studio, usually at the computer. We'd read until eleven, when there were more pills and hot chocolate. This routine varied, of course, when we had appointments or guests or when I went shopping, but even repeated day after day, we never got bored.

Dr. Woolliscroft told Gretchen that she could perfectly well make the trip to Lake Saranac at the end of July, so we flew to Burlington to visited Henry and his family, and then rented a car to drive to Lake Saranac. The drive was lovely and not hard for Gretchen, but the stay in a hotel for several days was exhausting. She had to walk only a block to the concerts, but that was more than she could do. We were glad to get back to Ann Arbor.

We flew to New York City at the end of September, eager to see what Peter Craig had done with our kitchen. Bill Bowser was there at the door and helped us up with our suitcases, and Gretchen climbed the stair cautiously but with no trouble.

Stephen Fisher invited us to drive up to visit Kurt and Theresa Michaelis at their lovely suburban home near Yorktown Heights. (Kurt had expertly managed the performance department of C. F. Peters for thirty years and was now semi-retired.) We had a nice visit and a gorgeous lunch. There is never any end to pleasant conversation with the two of them, talking about their travels and reminiscing with pleasure about our drive together to Dartmouth to hear a performance of my *Second Piano Concerto* in 1973. Gretchen got tired but was very encouraged with this first venture away from our apartment.

The University of Alabama asked me to be their guest and serve on a panel at the regional conference of the Society of Composers in Tuscaloosa, November 17-19, 1988. Fred Goossen met us at the Birmingham airport with a wheelchair that Gretchen could use during our visit. My *Concerto for Alto Saxophone* and *Quartet for Oboe, Cello and Percussion* were performed at the festival.

Our stay in Alabama gave us a great lift. We had a chance to see Fred and Shirley and to talk over the work they were doing on my essay collection. Someone wheeled Gretchen everywhere — to concerts and to a symposium where she was surrounded by old friends. We also enjoyed seeing Hubert Howe, who held the Endowed Chair in Composition for that year.

We thought at the time that we couldn't use a wheelchair in our house in Ann Arbor, but I bought one for our apartment in New York where everything is on one level. It proved very helpful to Gretchen; she could move herself from bedroom to living room to bathroom without any help, and she found the wheelchair more comfortable than her desk or dining-room chairs. I put a table in the living room where the light was better for her computer work.

On February 11, the Gregg Smith Singers gave the first New York performance of my *Edge of Shadow*, composed in 1959 for chorus, two pianos and a few percussion instruments. The vocal score had been published, and it was this version that Gregg used, with an added part for timpani and cymbal which I had made for his summer performance at Lake Saranac. This arrangement demands a pianist with real skill, and the timpani-cymbal part must give a suggestion of the percussion section at a few crucial places. The chorus projected the lyric and dramatic intensity of MacLeish's text with an almost flawless performance.

The highpoint of 1989 was the premiere of *Chamber Music*, the setting that I had made in 1951 of all thirty-six James Joyce poems. C. F. Peters published a beautiful edition of the cycle in 1985. Stephen Fisher, with his sensitivity to Joyce's poetry, had taken a very special interest; Bruce Taub had done a wonderful job of editing the manuscript; and Don Gillespie had solved copyright problems that seemed insurmountable. The songs were there to be performed, but nobody had yet done them.

Paul Cooper telephoned that they were hoping to perform *Chamber Music* at Rice University during the next season and asked me to send the music to Jeanette Lombard, who began in January to send me tapes of rehearsals with the pianist Mary Norris for my comments. It was very exciting to hear the songs coming to life. My comments had mostly to do with tempos and dynamics. It's a dangerous business to publish a work before it has been performed, and I was pleased that there were very few things I would change.

On February 27, SYZYGY, a new music series at Rice University, presented Jeanette Lombard, soprano, and Mary Norris, piano, in a performance of the entire song-cycle. Ms. Lombard sang from memory and without a flaw, projecting the words with amazing clarity, and Ms. Norris gave both an accurate and colorful performance. Carl Cunningham, the *Houston Post* critic, wrote: "By now, Finney's 'Chamber Music' is part of historical tradition in the evolution of 20th-century music." It was an experience that after thirty-seven years I had almost given up hoping for.

Joyce's poems are a beautiful monody on love and seemed to me like mosaics that together formed a large picture, or perhaps like a stained-glass window where small pictures made a luminous totality. It seemed unthinkable to set a few of the lyrics, since it was the total picture of love that was important. The first fifteen poems had the urgency of young love, climaxing in the fourteenth song ("My dove, my beautiful one...") in sexual fulfillment. The next fifteen are concerned with the disillusionment of love and bitter memories. The last six are utterly desolate and perhaps reflect the loneliness of Joyce's expatriation. The cycle takes more than an hour to perform, and the artists were justified in making short breaks between the three parts of the monody. The reception of the audience was very gratifying.

After the concert the Coopers had a lovely party and Paul played the tape and expressed an enthusiasm that warmed my heart. He is always so perceptive and honest in his reactions. There is now hope that the artists may record the performance. At least I have a tape of the songs and can hear them as often as I like. The event was, indeed, one of the most rewarding of my career.

I am sometimes puzzled why, at the age of eighty-five, I am composing an uncommissioned comic opera, *Computer Marriage*. It is true that the work has long been in my mind, and until now I have had no time to write it down. I get pleasure dealing humorously with matters that have become so serious in this century. I enjoy confusing time in a most unscholarly way. I like working in a small format with trivia. I even relish the thought that I will not have to be involved with the politics and problems of production. Composing music has always been a private world for me, but one that I could never resist.

We are looking forward to our sixtieth wedding anniversary on September 3, 1990, and in many ways that celebration will have a special meaning. Gretchen's book, on which she has worked for four decades, may be going to press; the University of Alabama Press's collection of my essays and lectures will be issued by that time. But the thing that will mark the event for me and our family will be the publication of Gretchen's autobiography.

For years Ross and Henry have urged their mother to write of her early experiences, and when she finished her book *Music as a Cure for Disease,* she got pleasure in setting down what she could remember about our lives together, typing away on her little computer. I can't think of a better therapy for her ailments following her heart attack.

There are many things that now give us pleasure, such as following our grandchildren as they grow to maturity — all of them individuals with their different ideas and ambitions, sometimes a little bewildering to us, but always vital and mysterious. Catherine is eyeing the world of art and business; Nathaniel is doing his doctorate at the California Institute of Technology and working endless hours at the perplexities of chemistry; Thea is an undergraduate trying to find a way to combine science and art; and Christopher is interested in the new multi-media possibilities of computers.

There are sorrows, too. Christa Cooper's death leaves an empty place in our lives. Many of our dearest friends are struggling with the indignities of old age — as are we. All the changes in medicine and technology have not made our struggle easier, but they have made the shelter of our homes and the routines of our activity more sacred. It is wonderful to reach a point in life when your loved ones say, "We love you." Often in the past there was no time for that.

INDEX OF NAMES*

* *Family members not included*

INDEX OF COMPOSITIONS OF ROSS LEE FINNEY*

246

* *Works in quotes are no longer available.*